SCREENSHOT JERUSALEM AND TEL AVIV

SCOTT SHAW

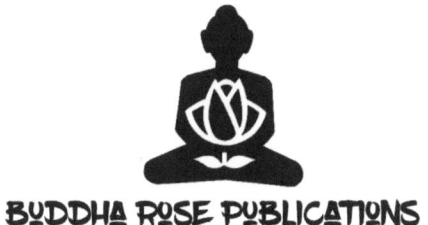

BUDDHA ROSE PUBLICATIONS

Screenshot Jerusalem & Tel Aviv
A Photographic Exploration
Copyright © 2017 by Scott Shaw
www.scottshaw.com

All Rights Reserved

No part of this publication may be duplicated
in any manner without the expressed written
permission of the publisher.

First Edition 2017

ISBN: 1-877792-96-9
ISBN: 978-1-877792-96-0

Printed in the United States of America

10 9 8 7 6 5 4 3 2 1

JERUSALEM

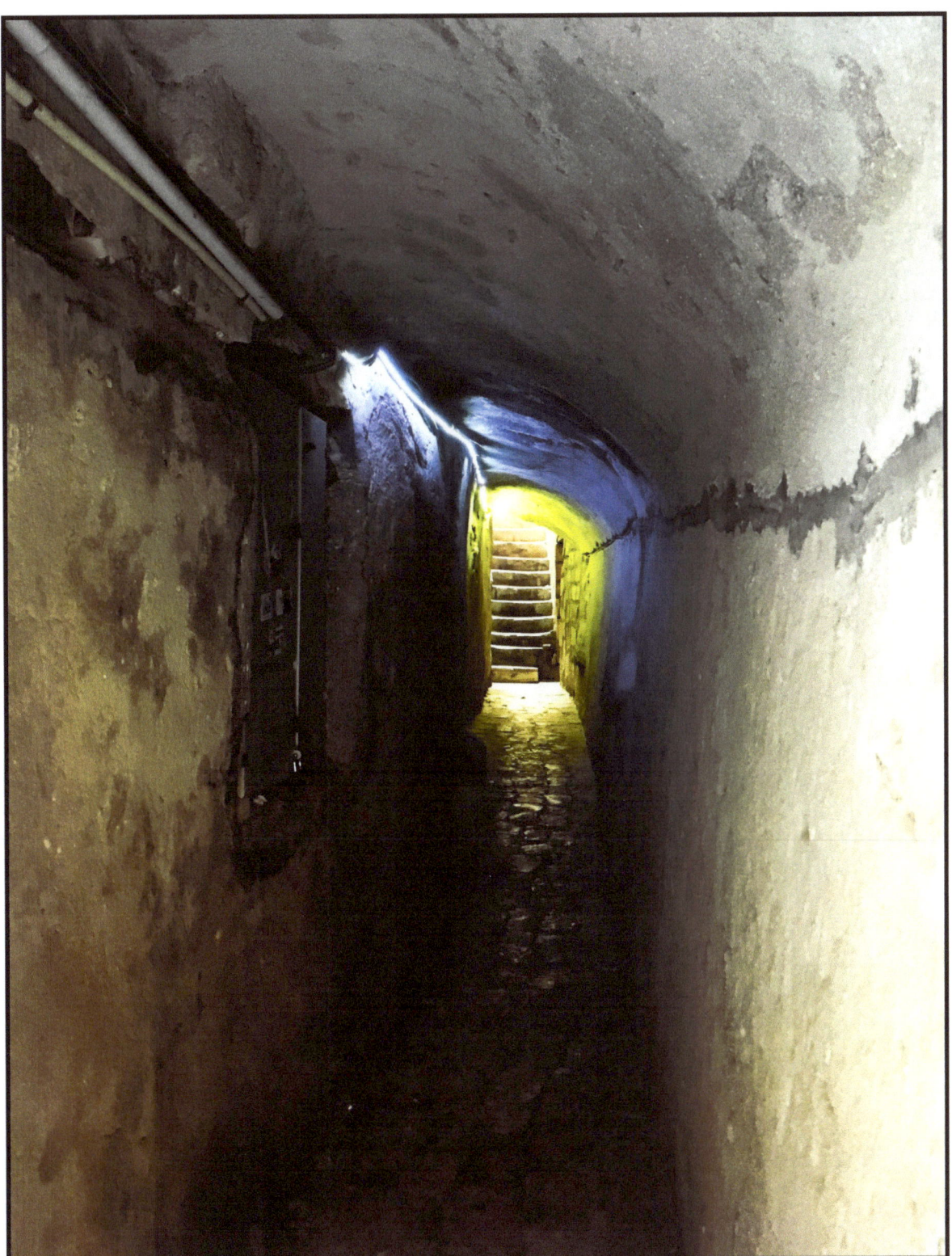

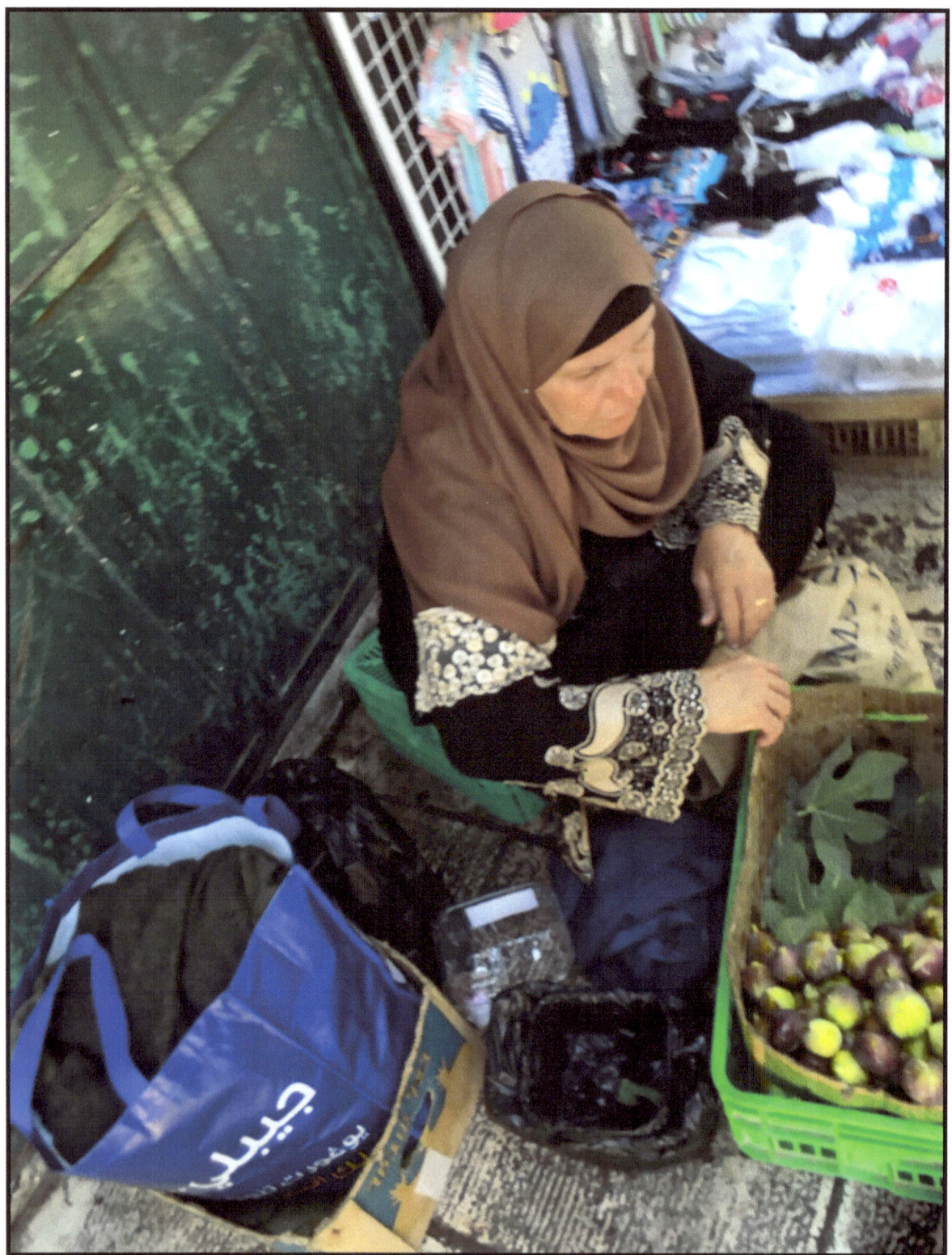

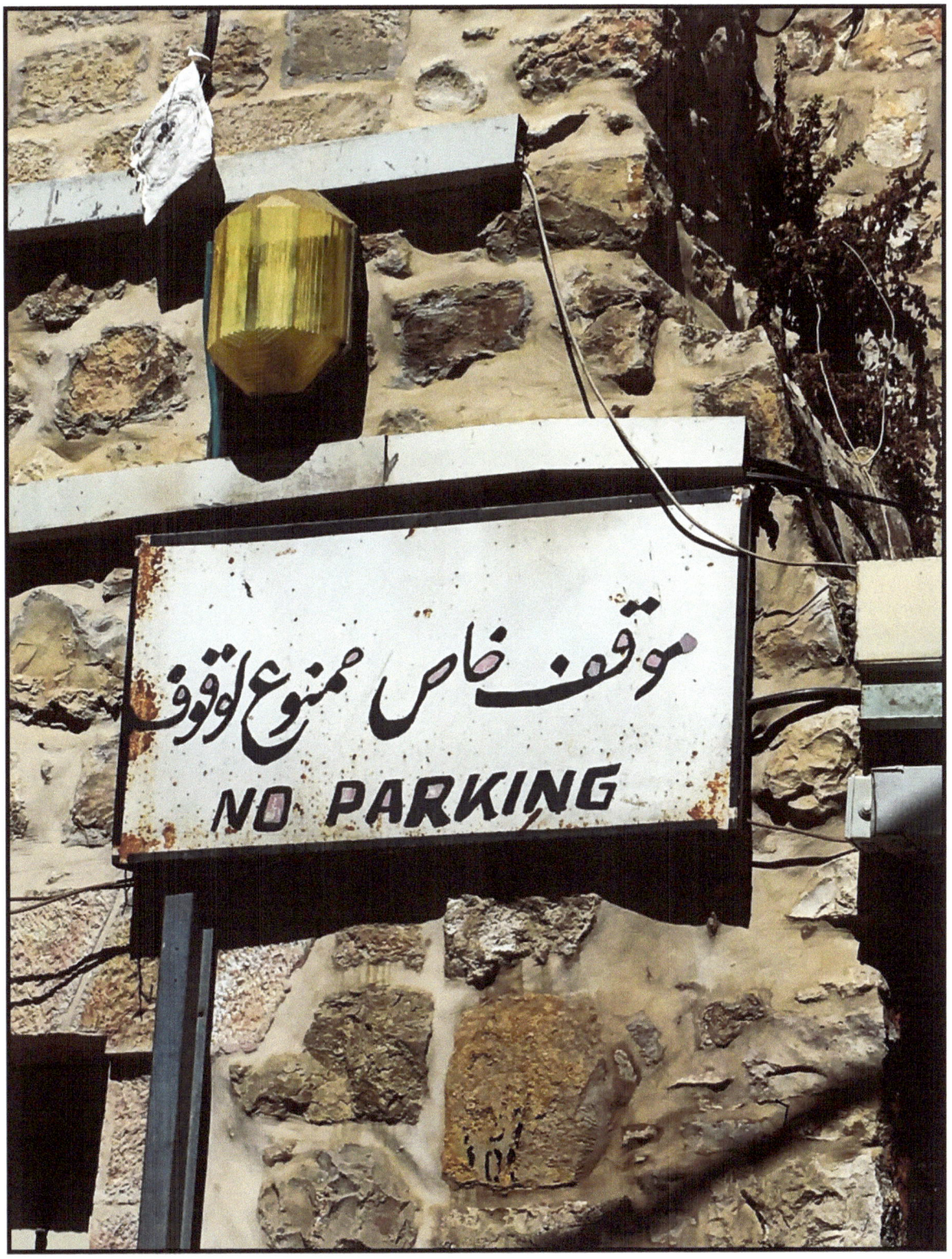

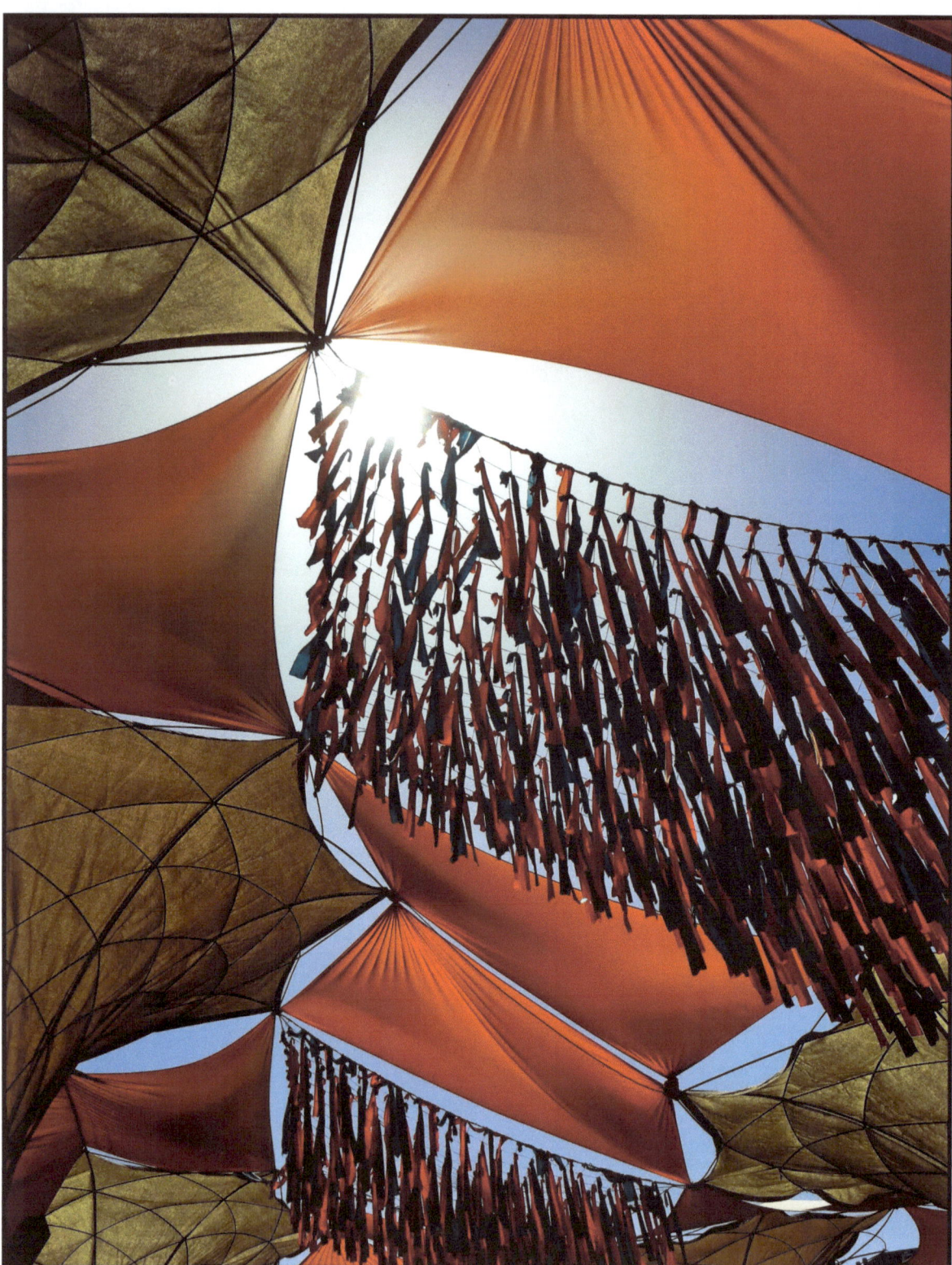

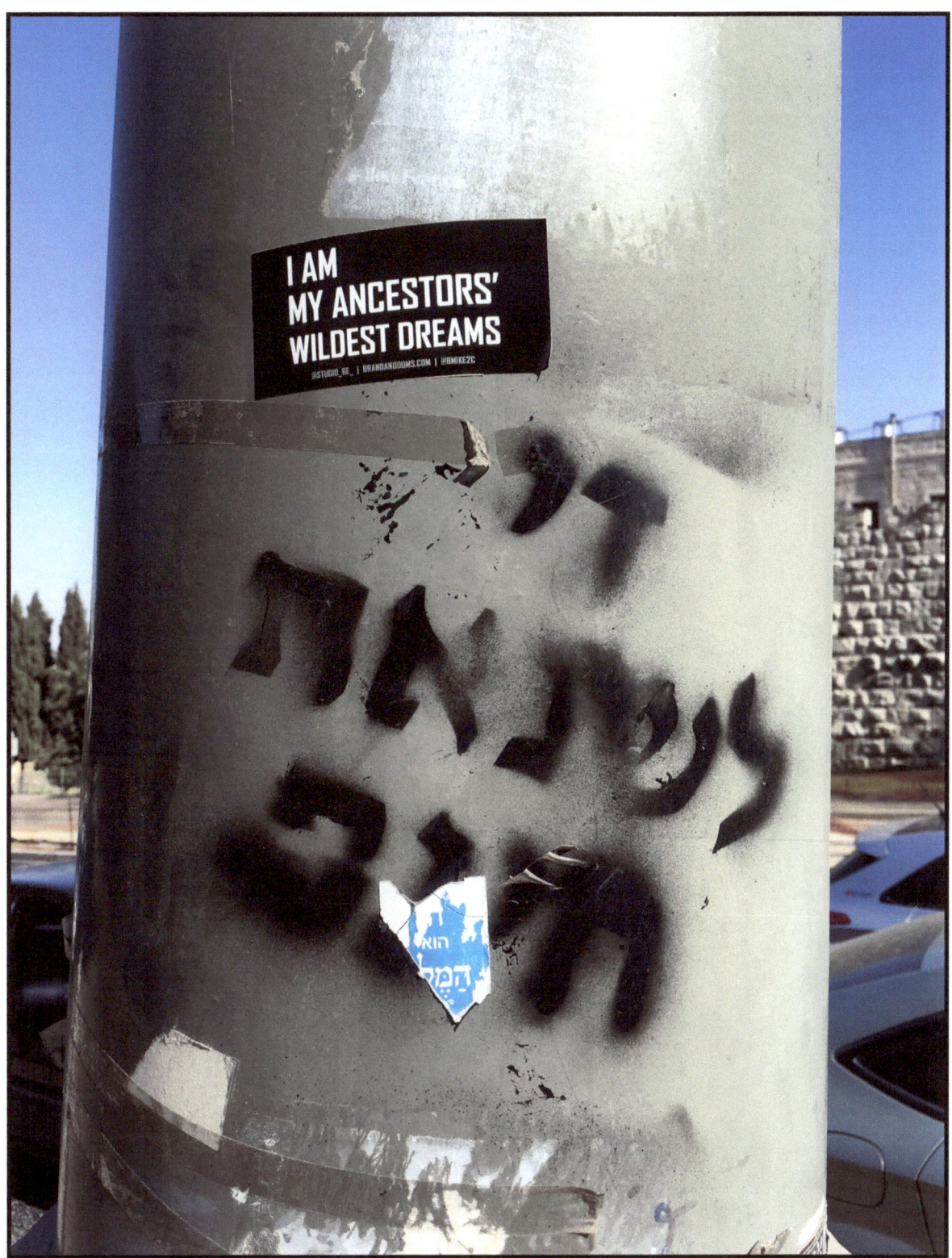

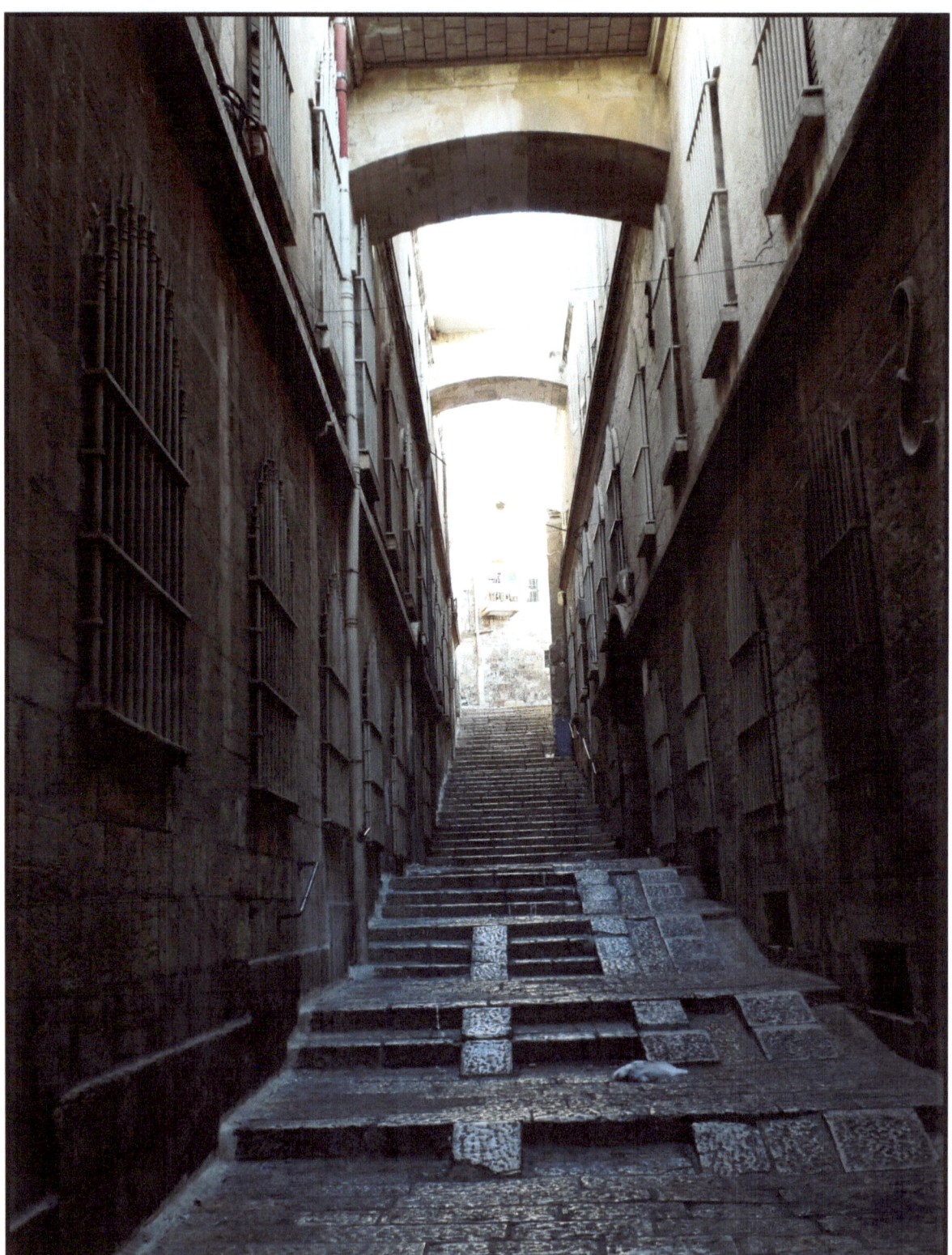

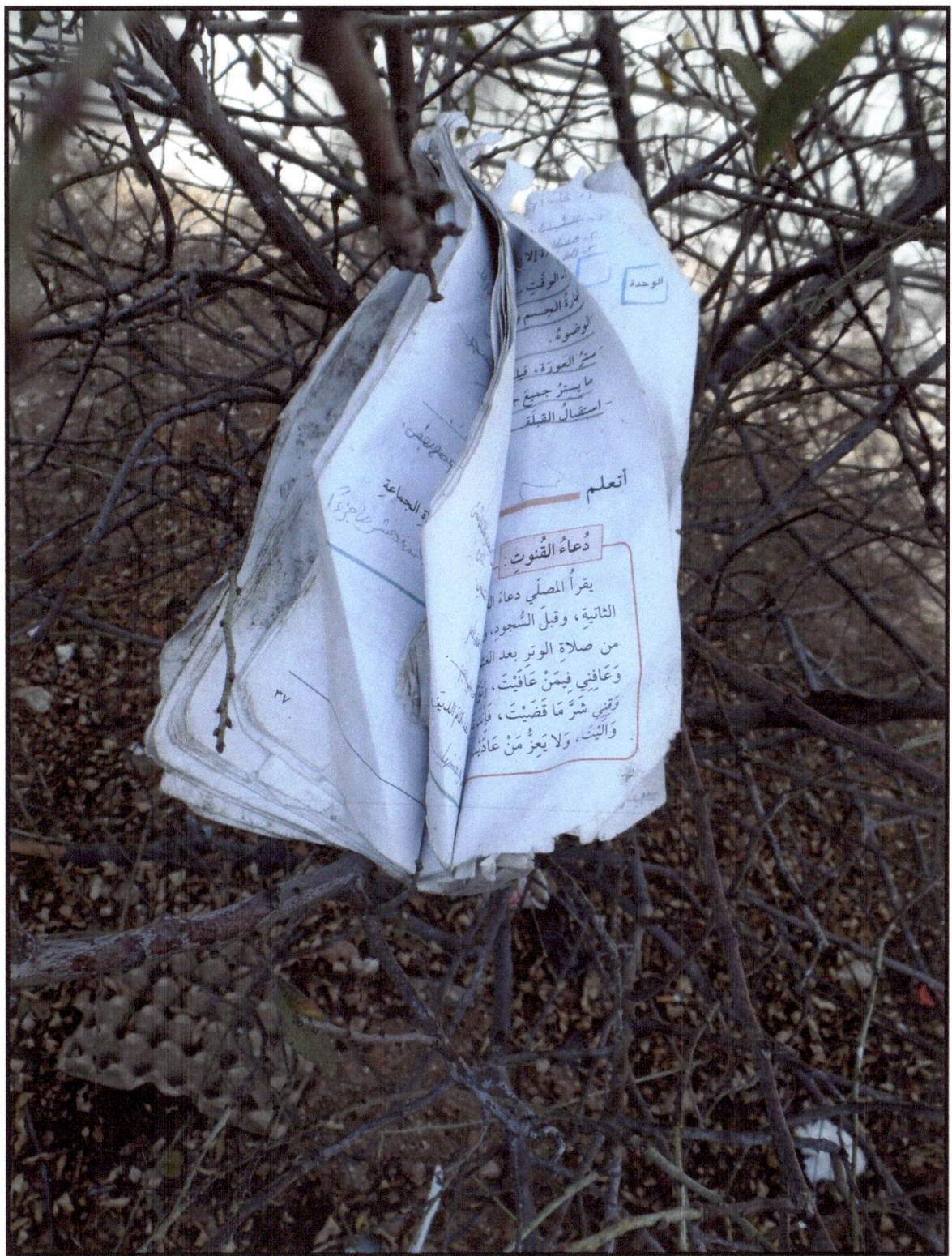

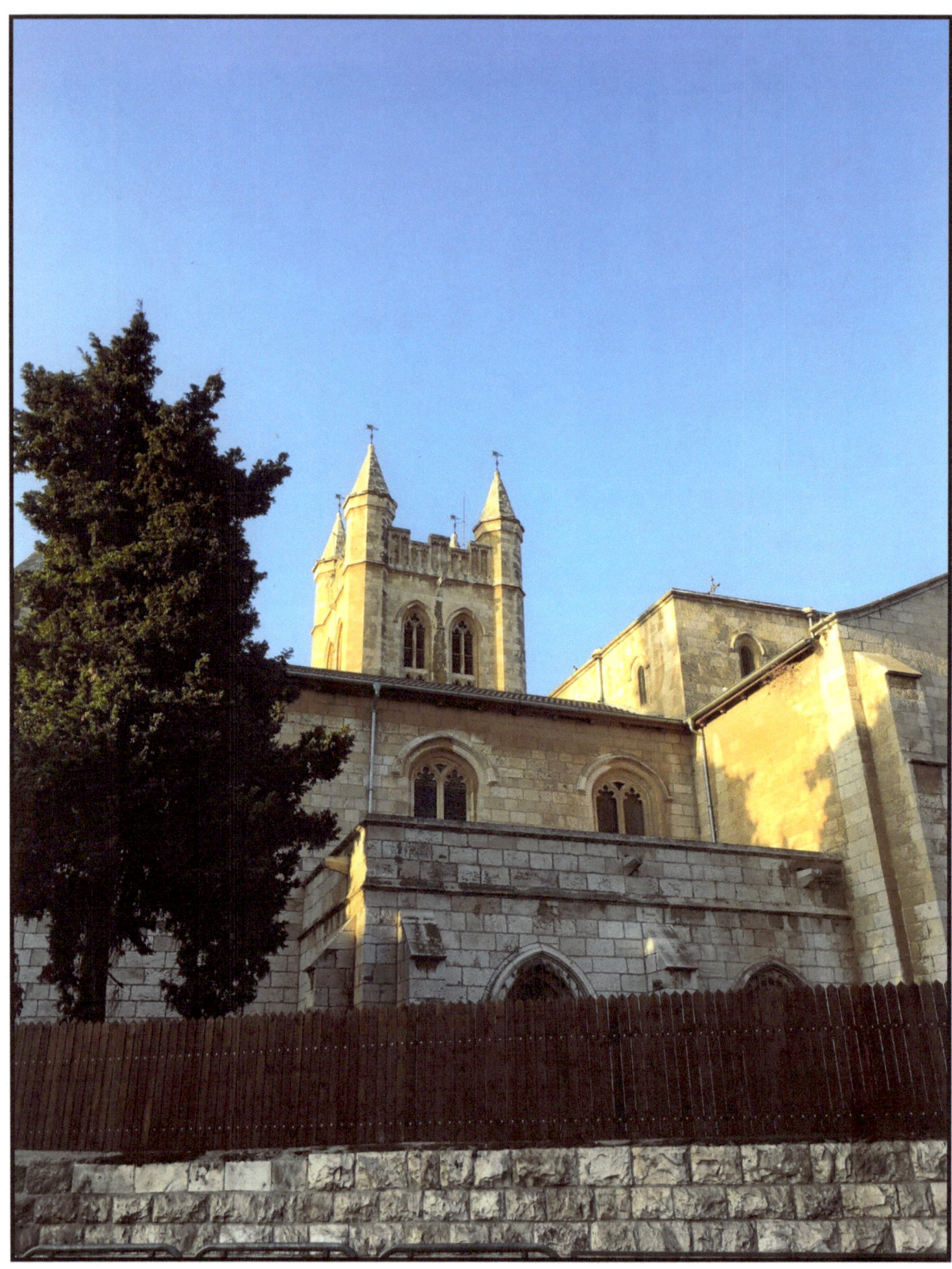

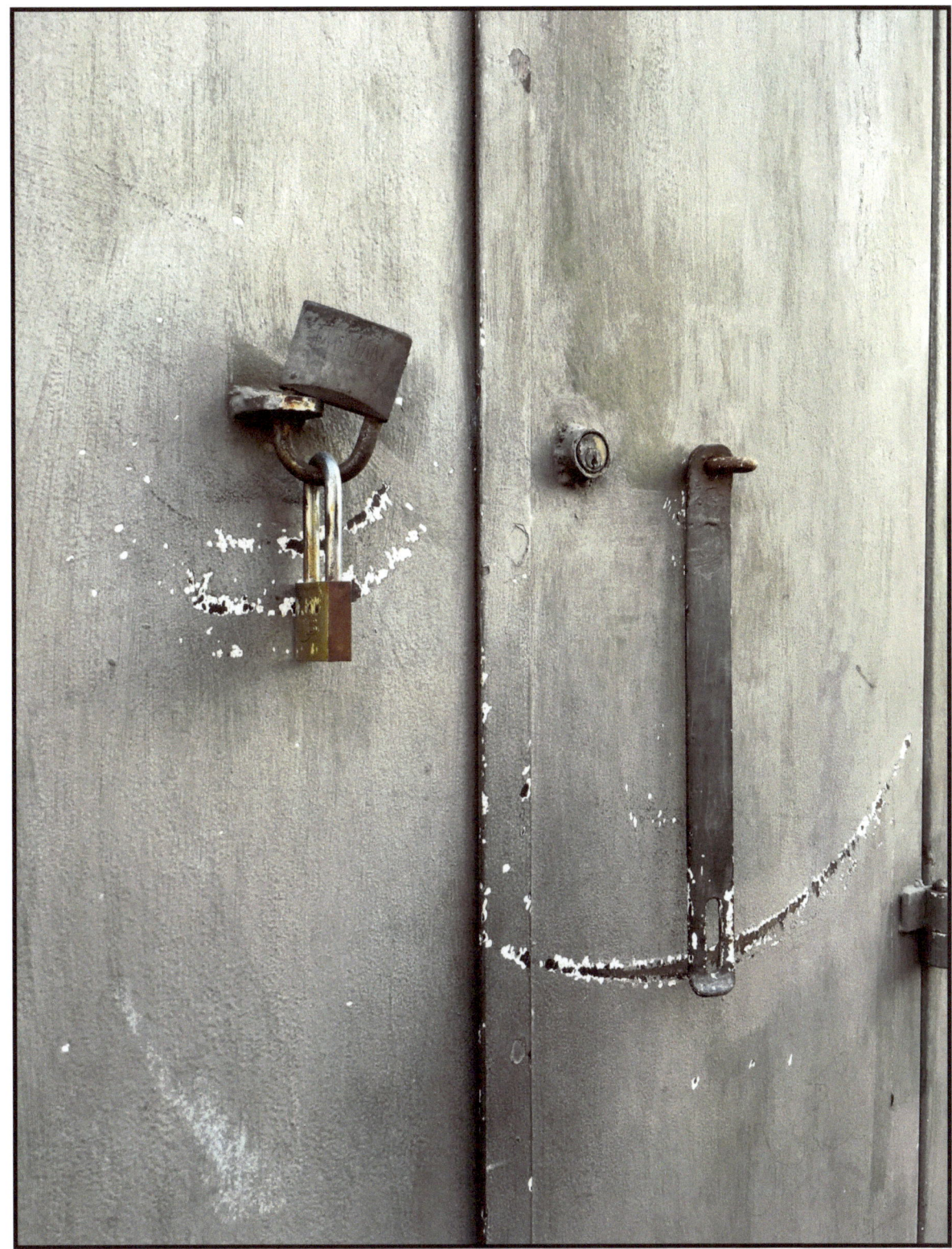

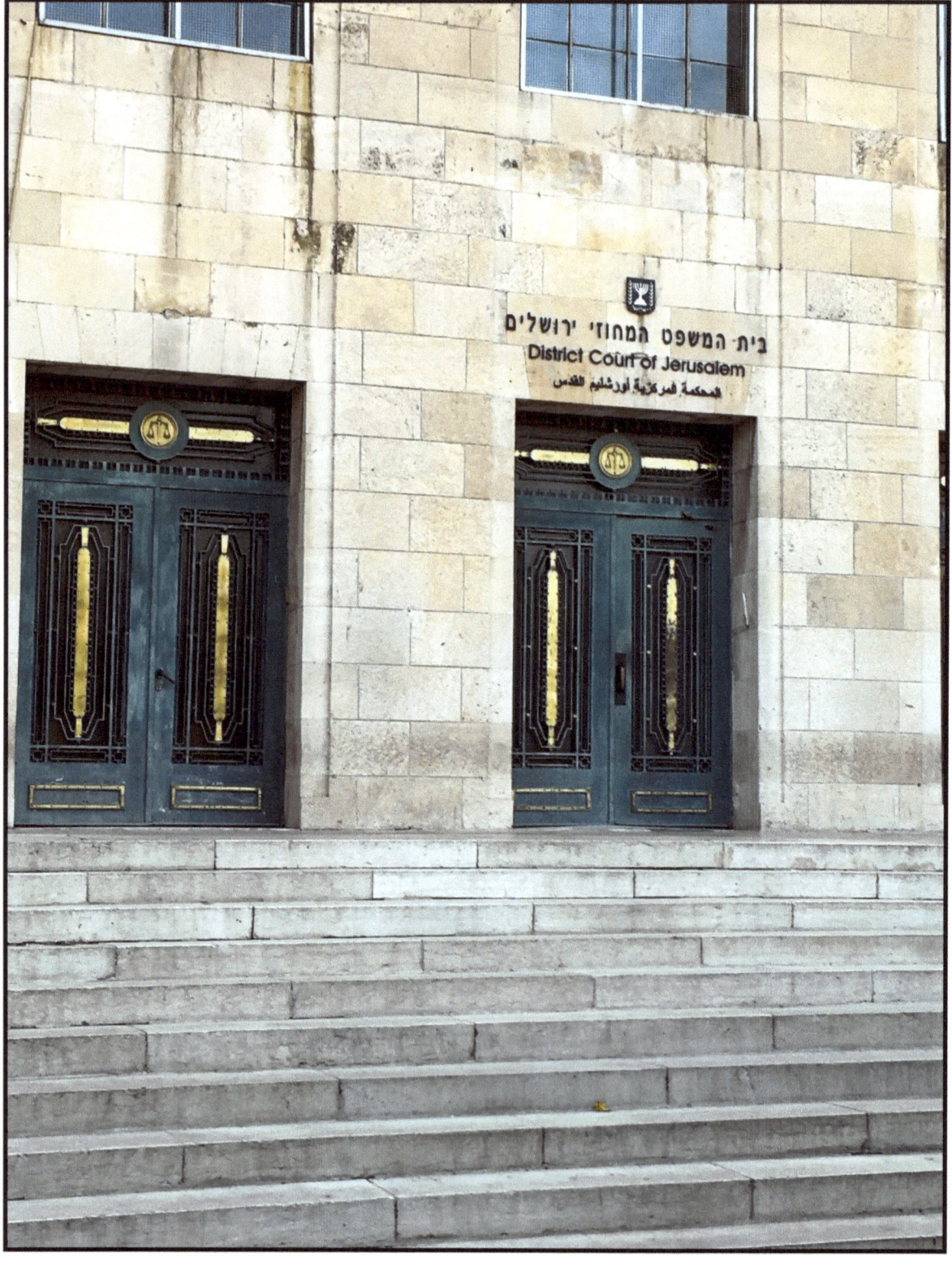

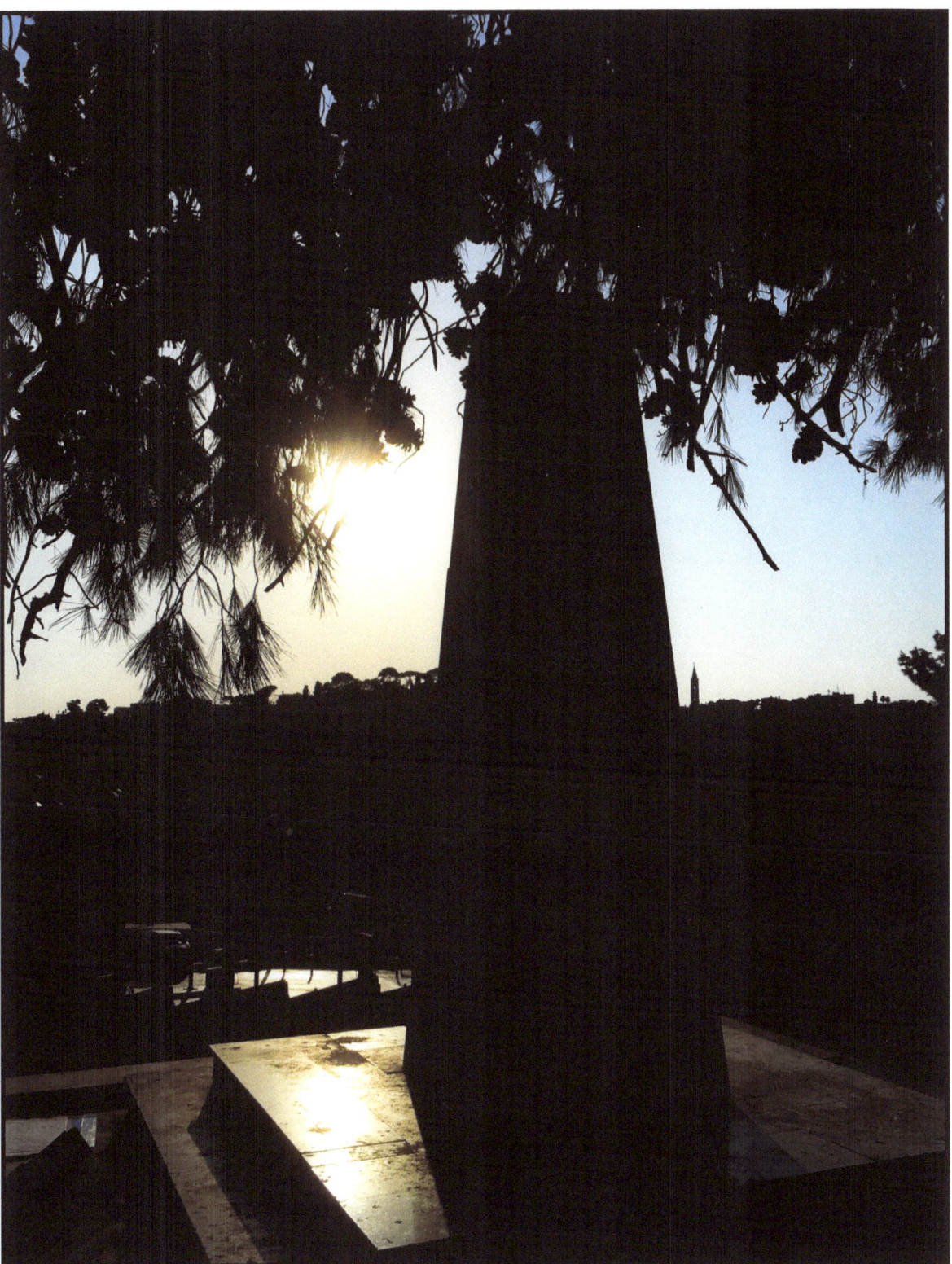

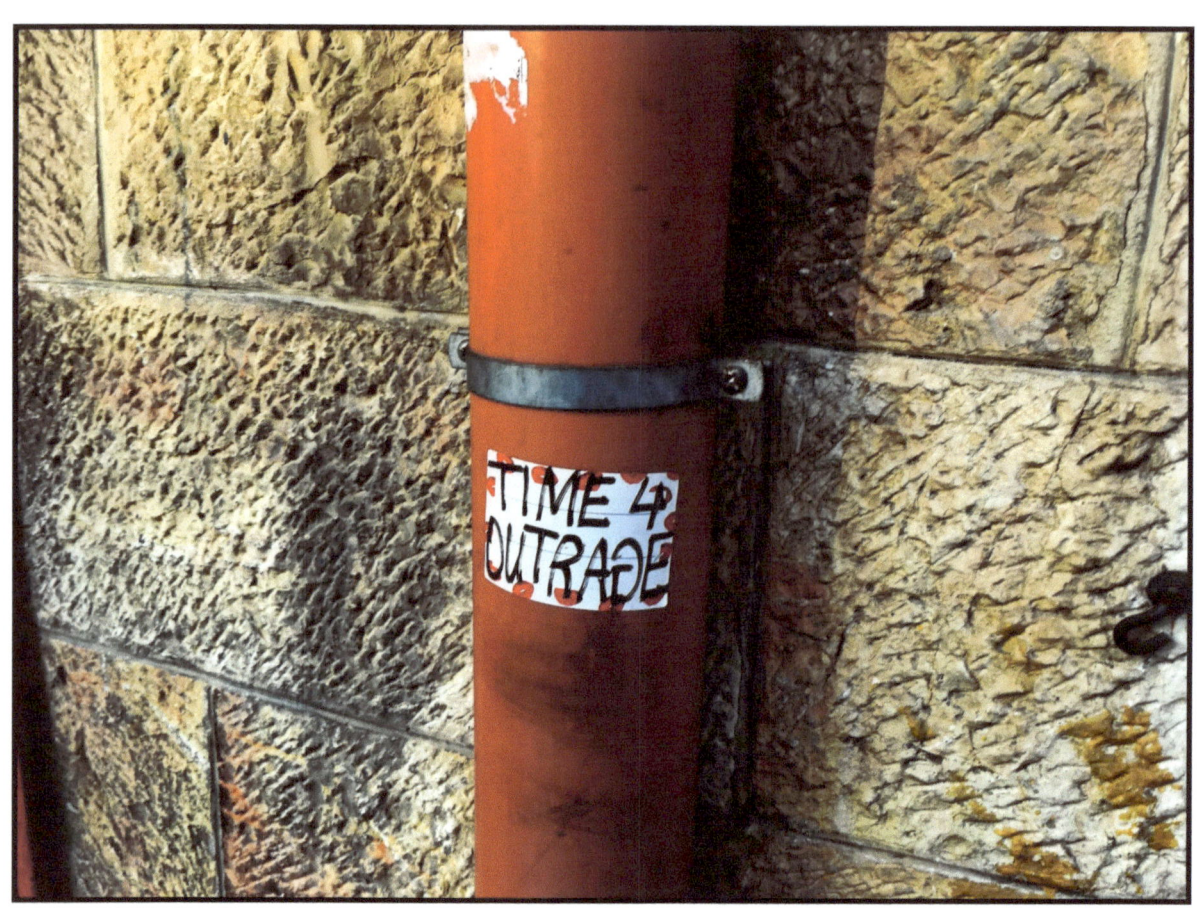

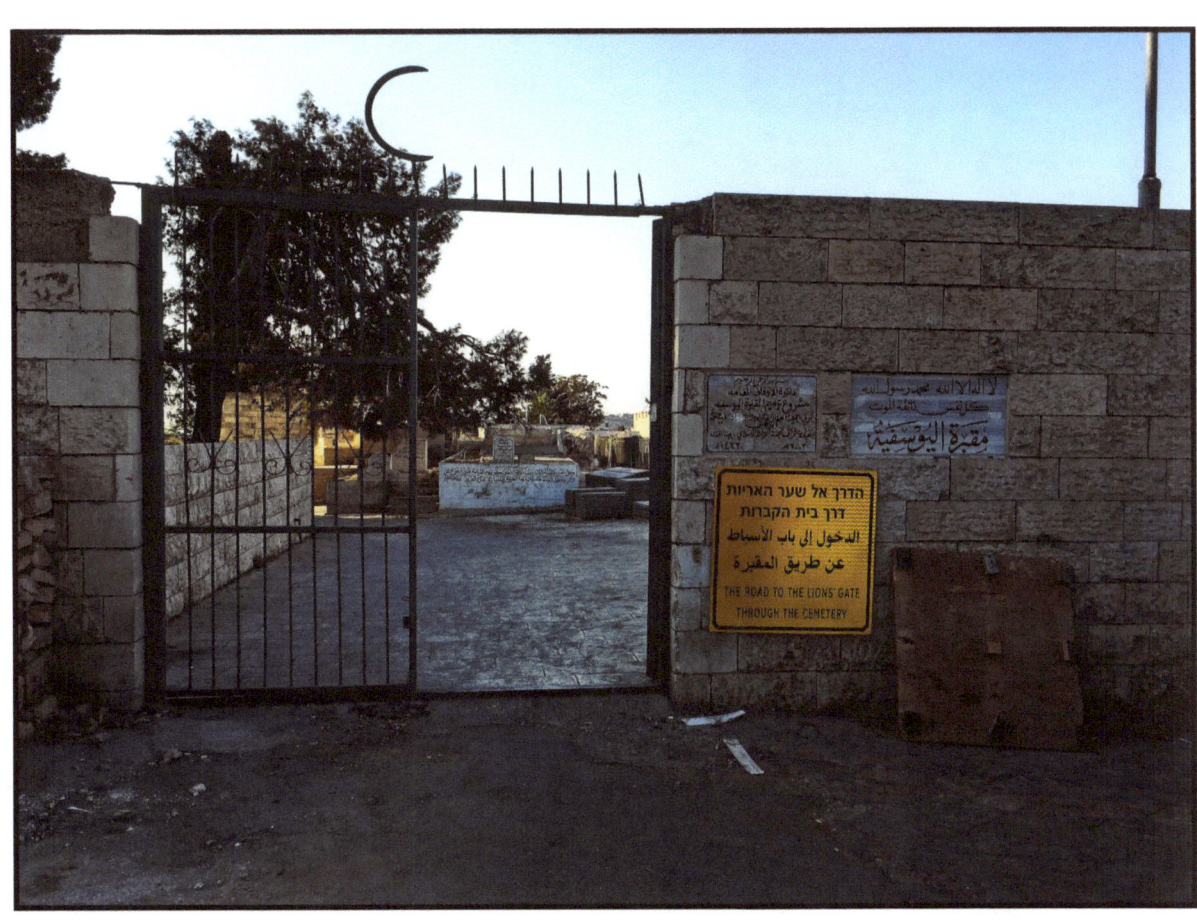

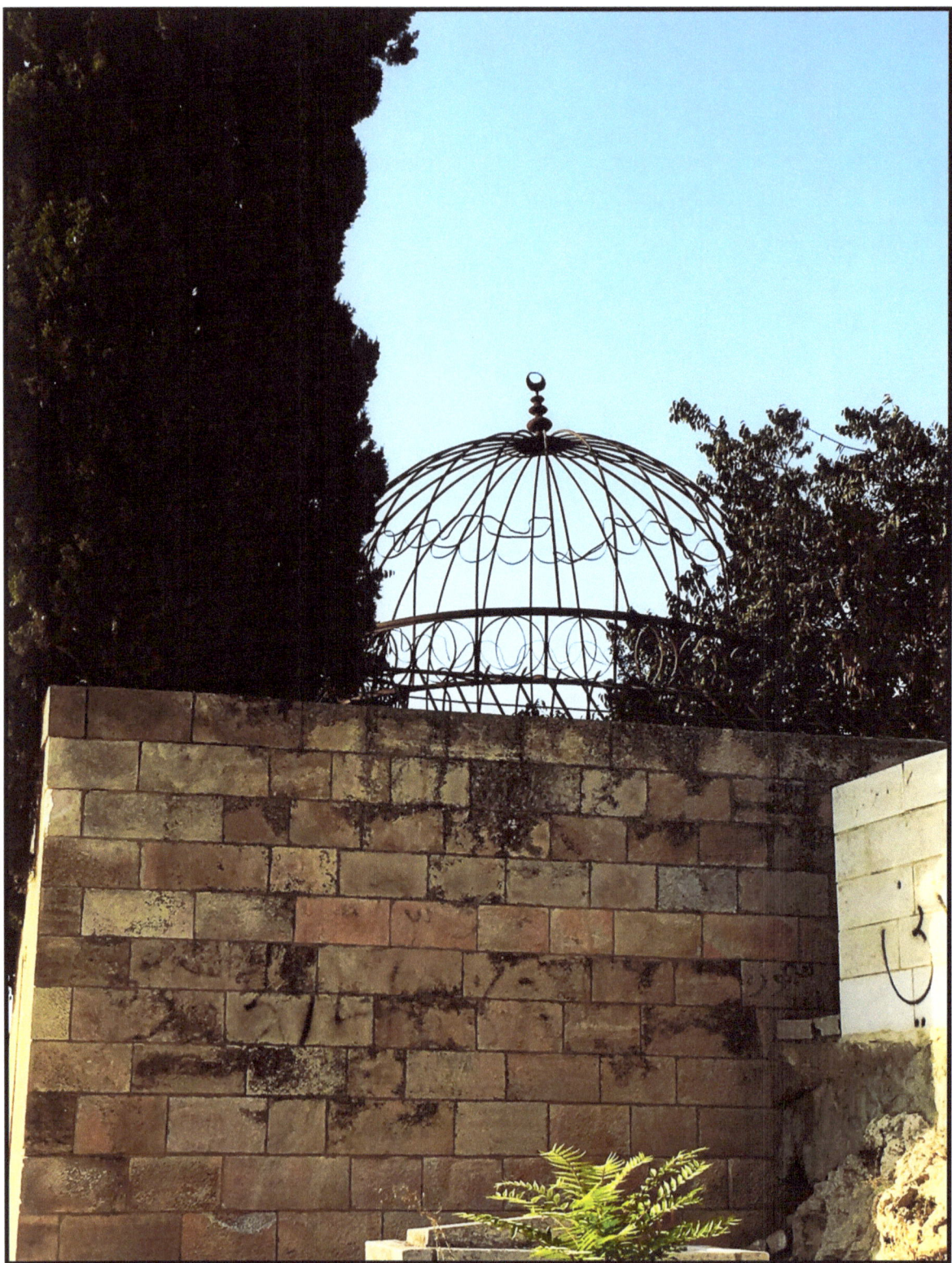

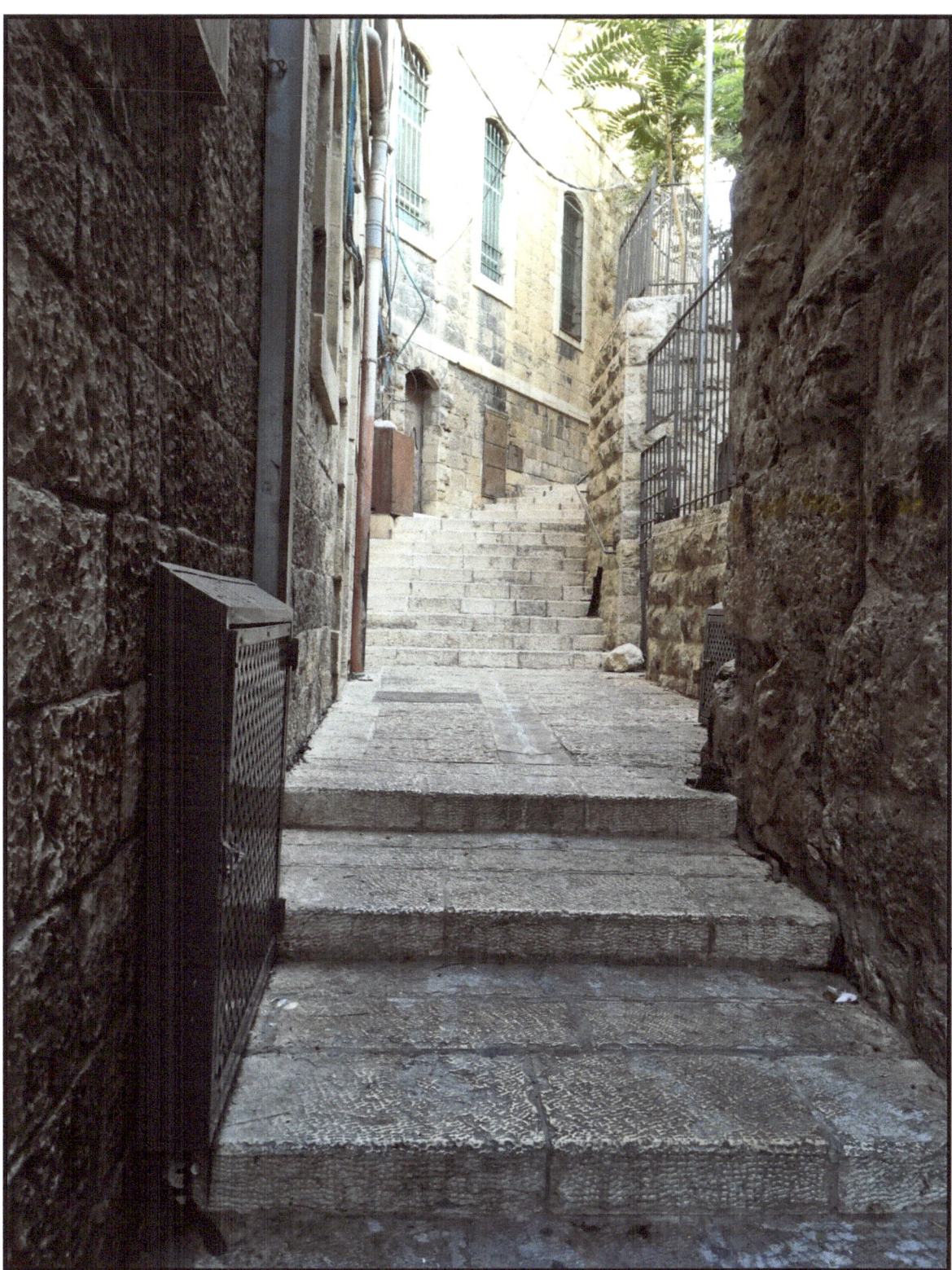

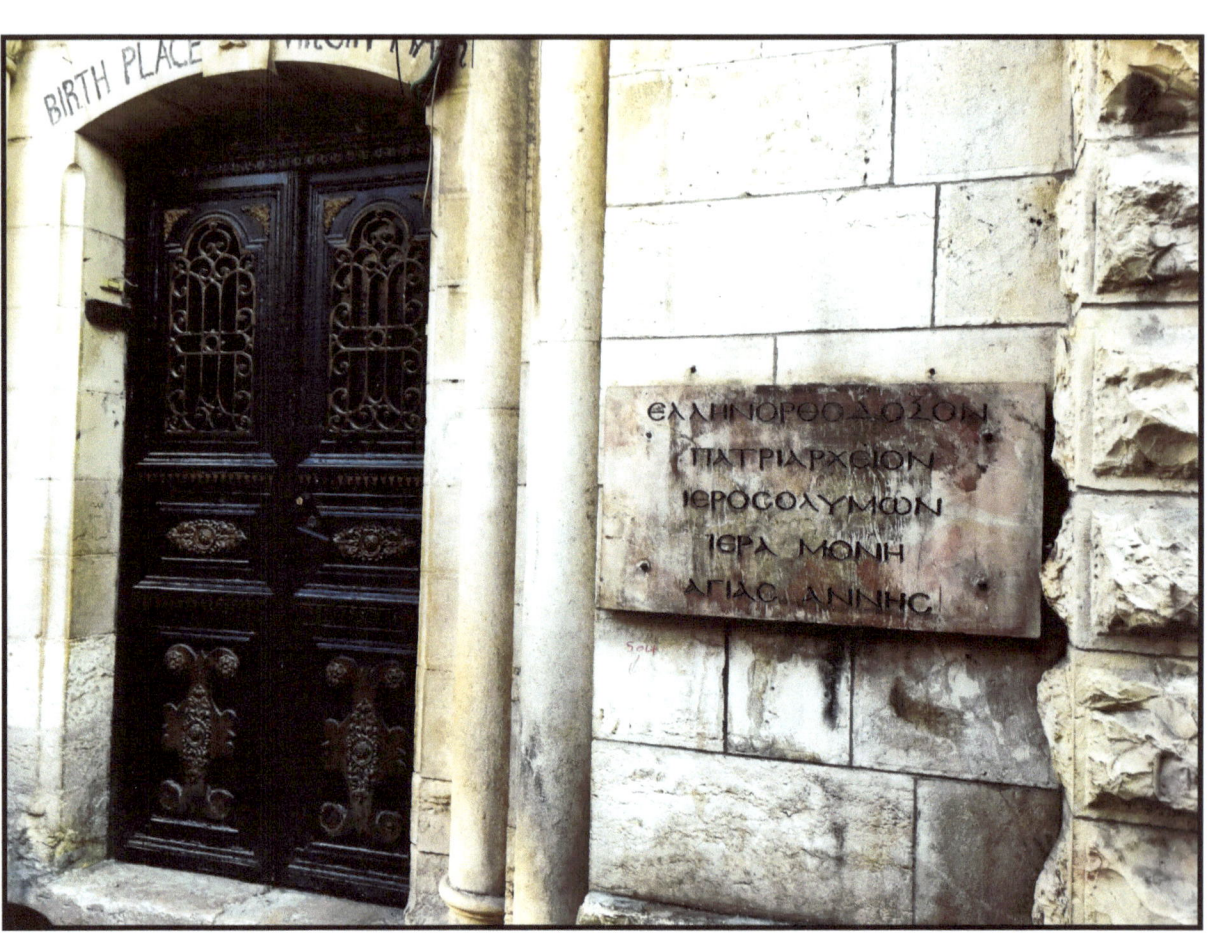

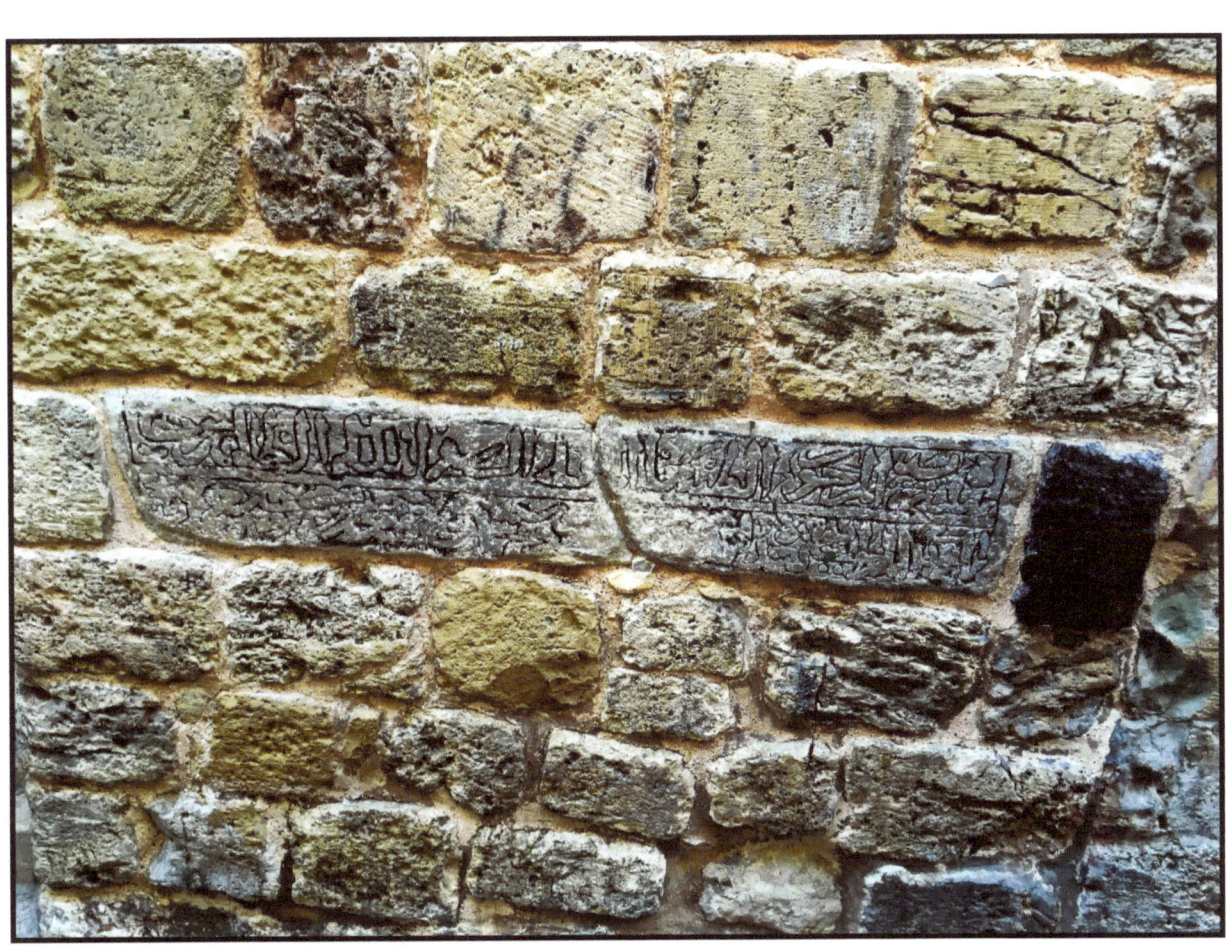

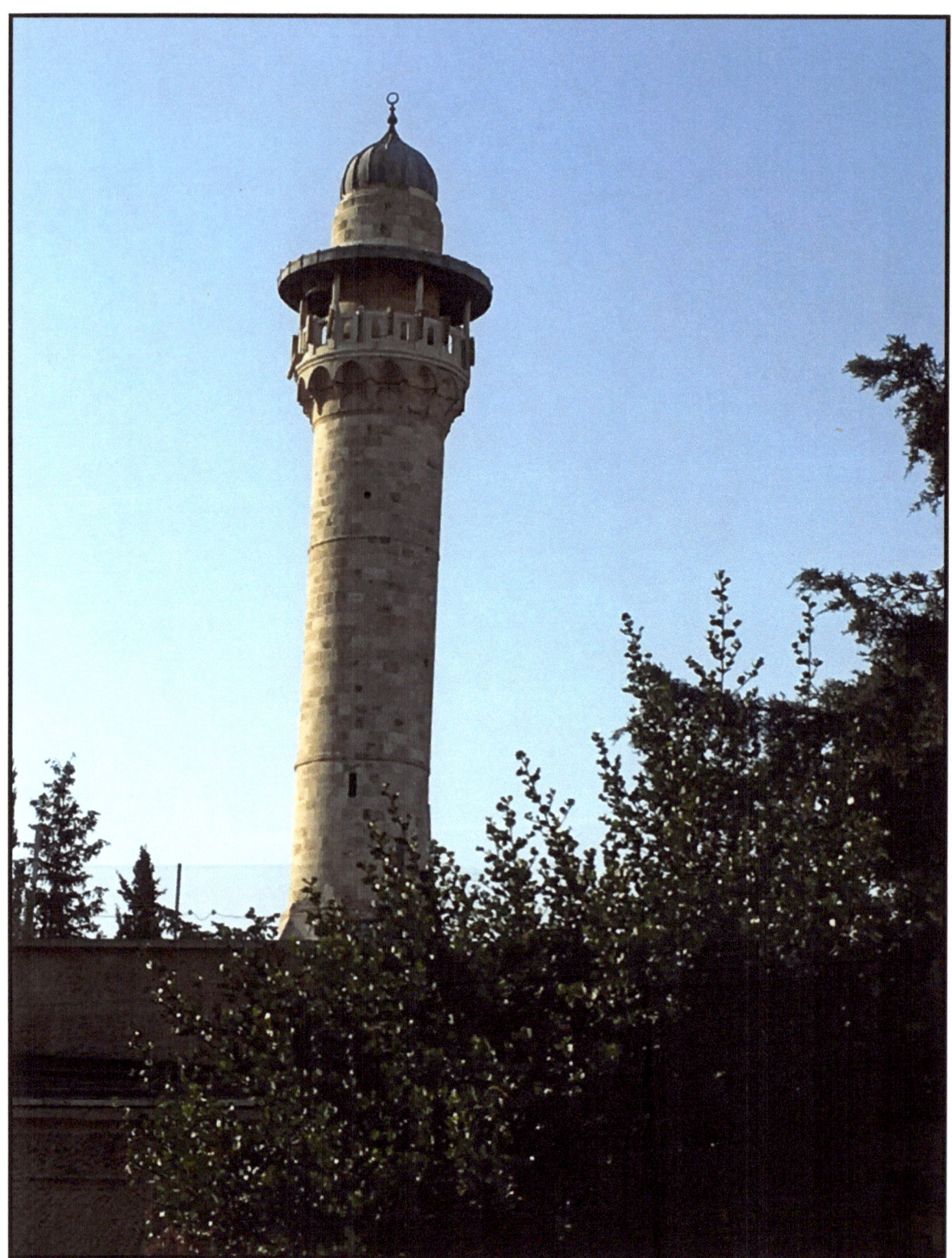

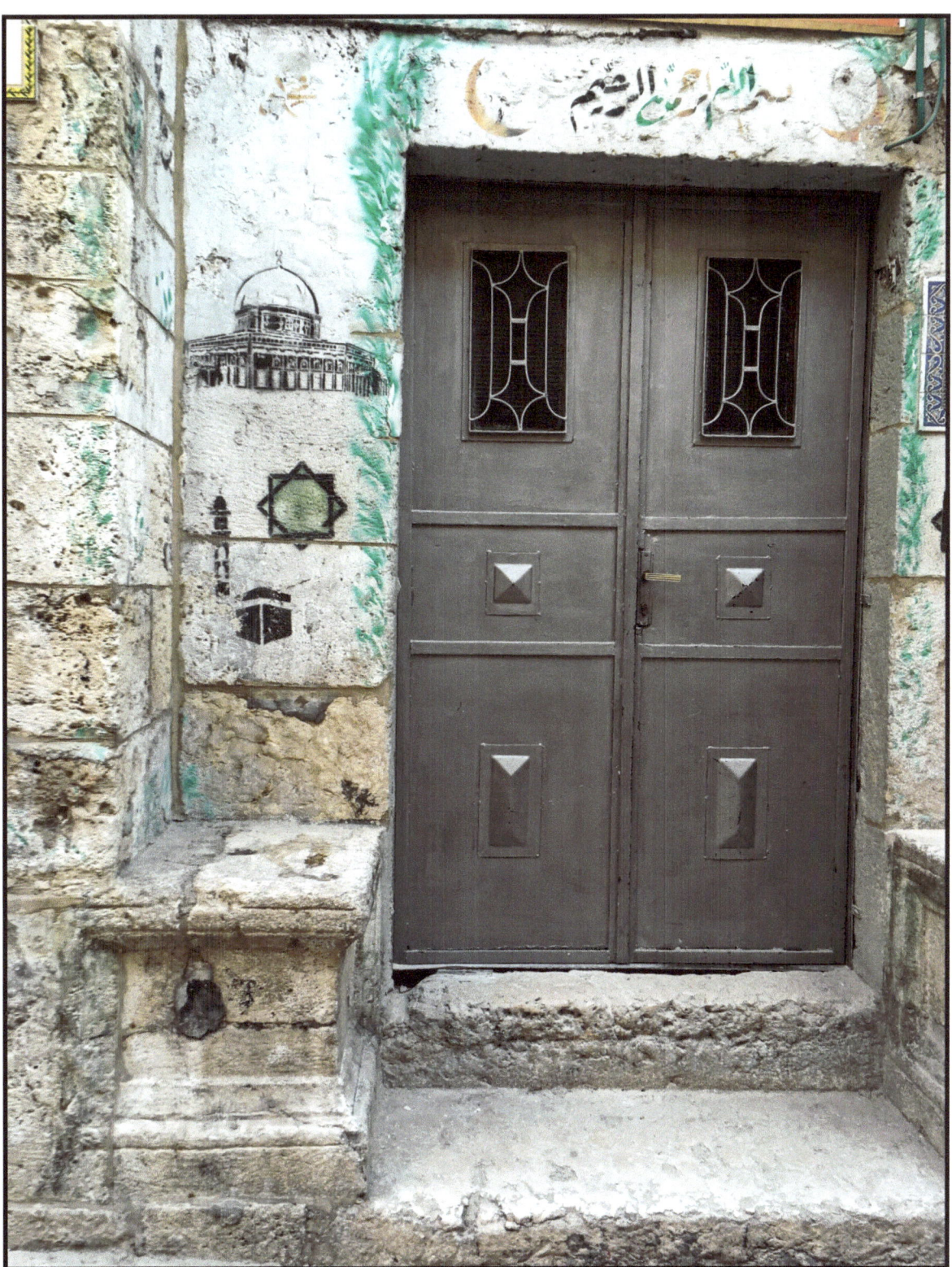

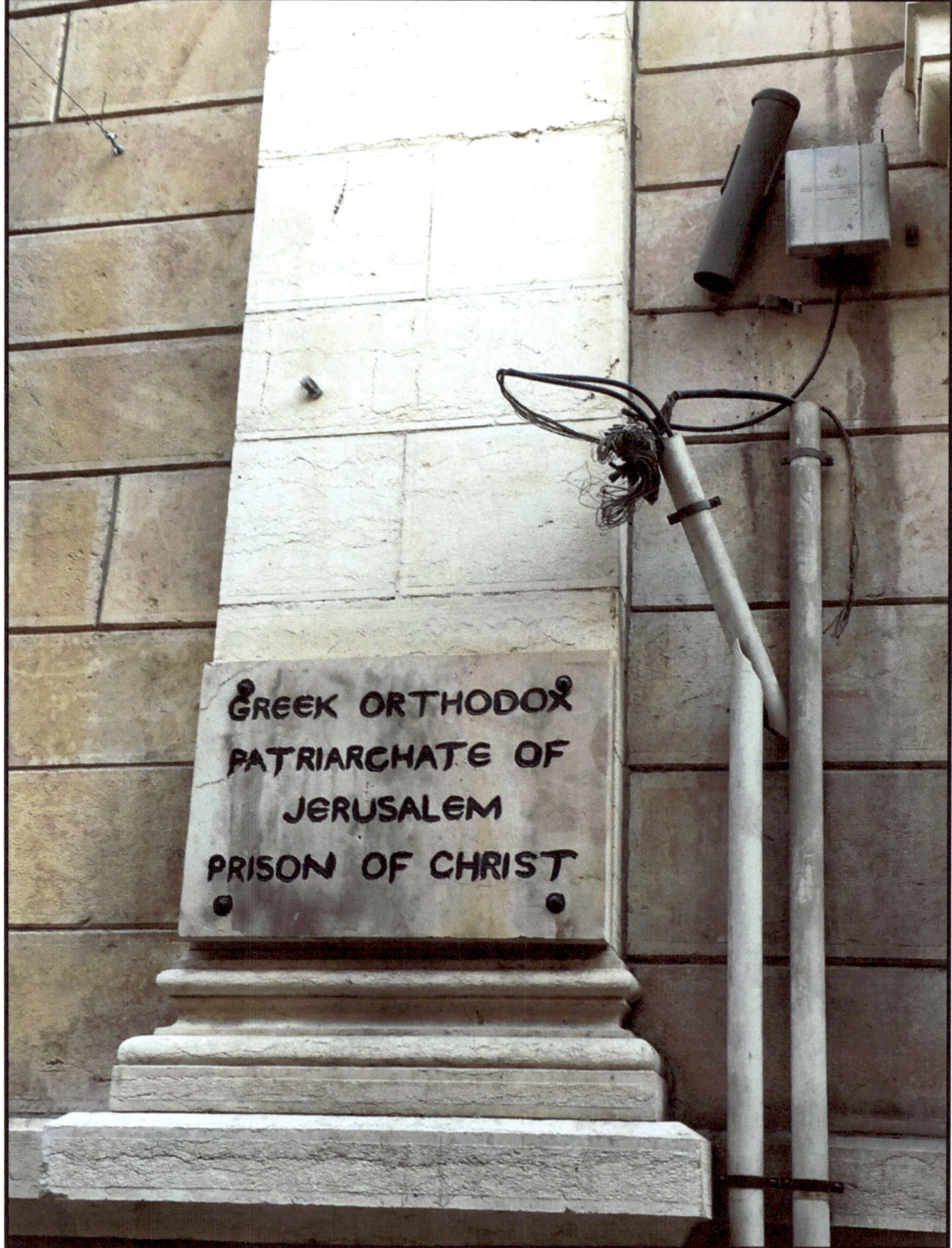

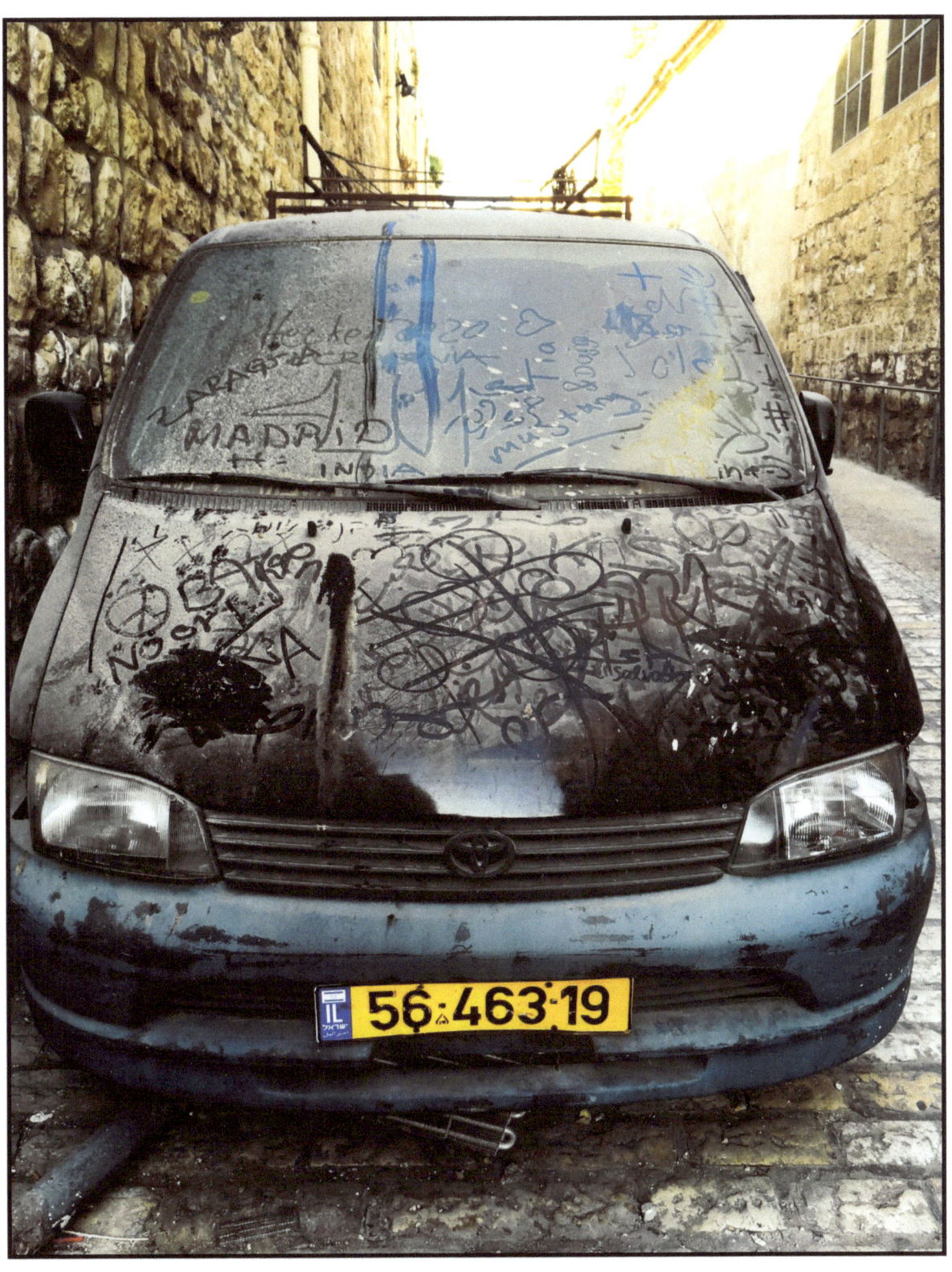

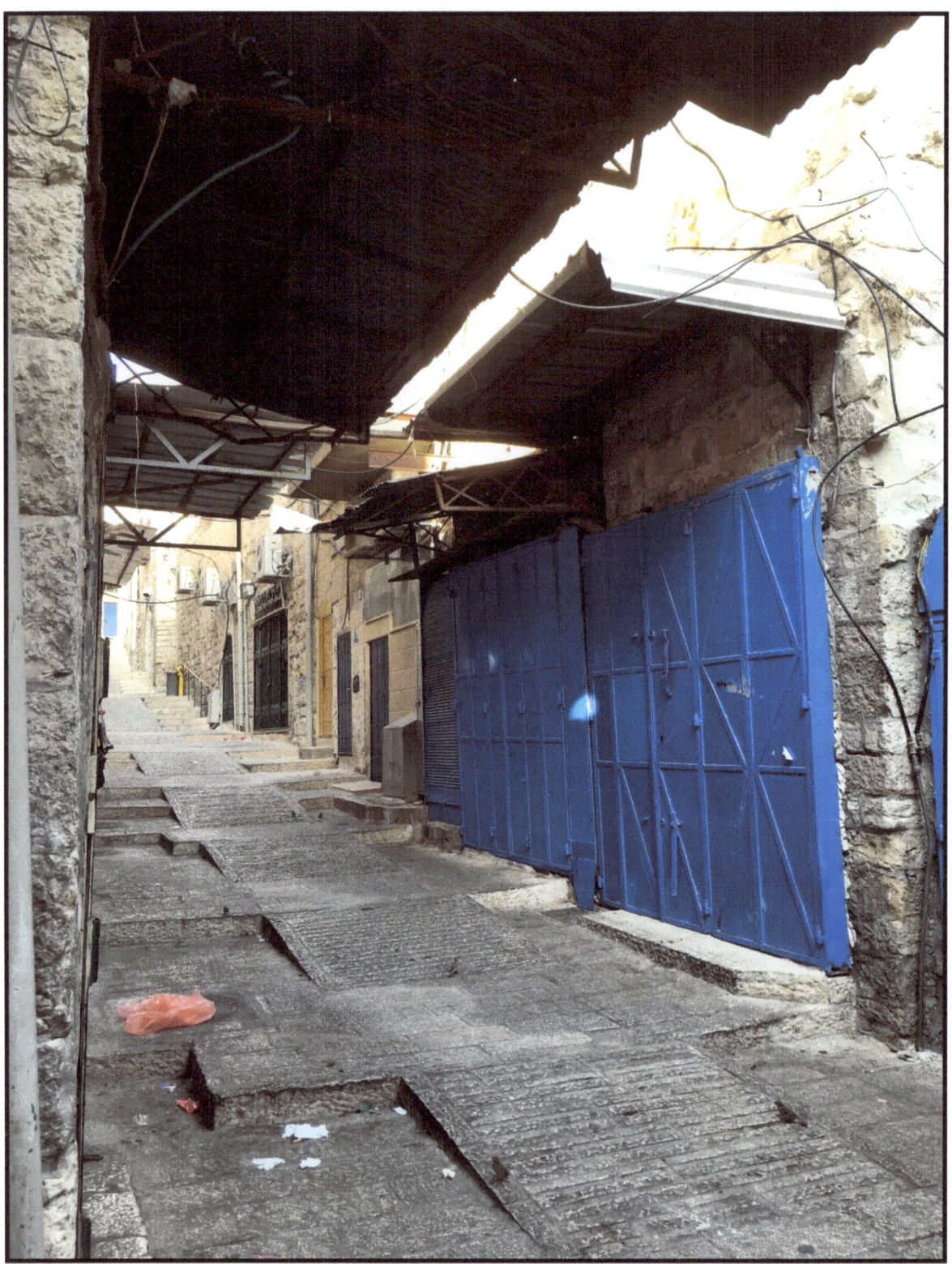

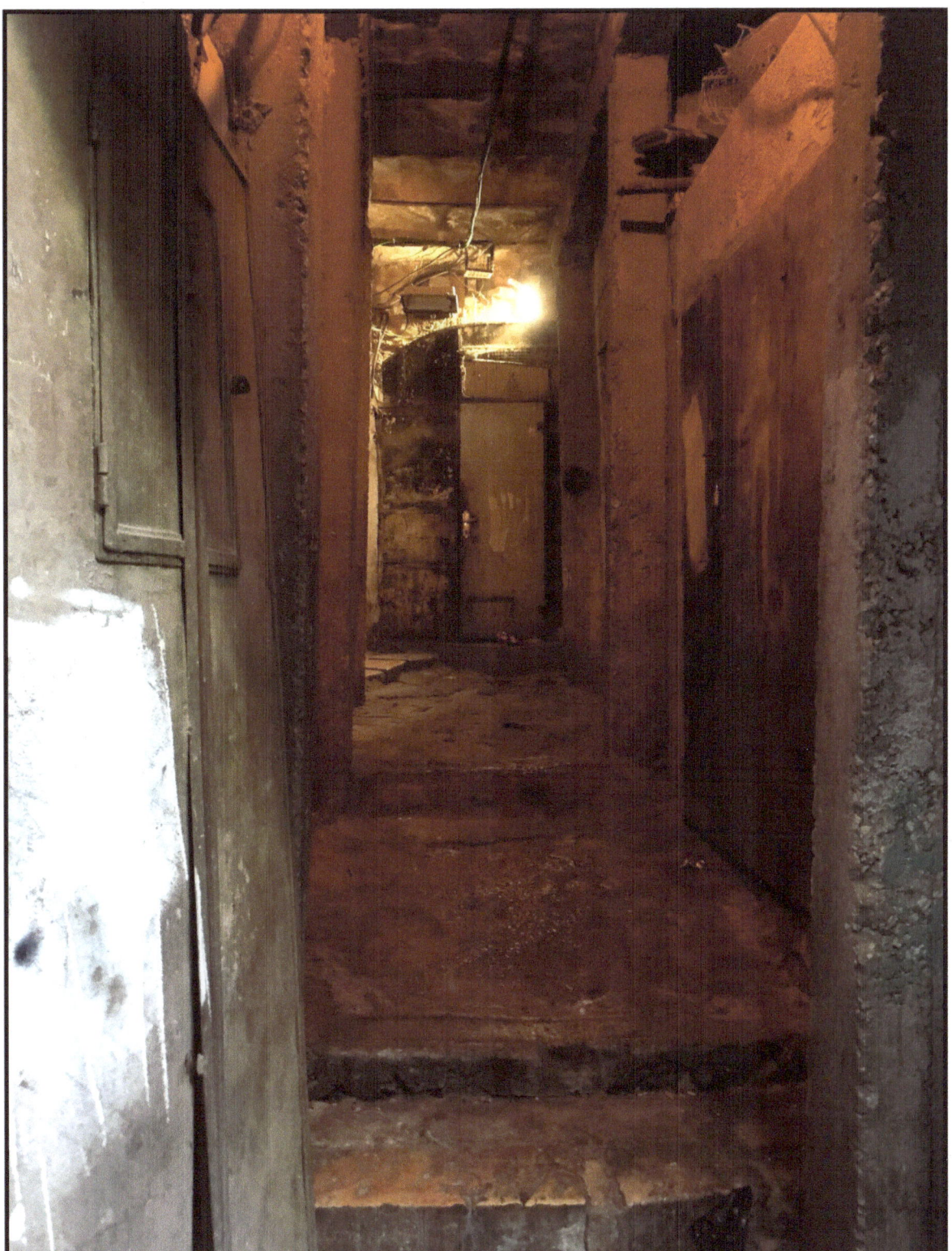

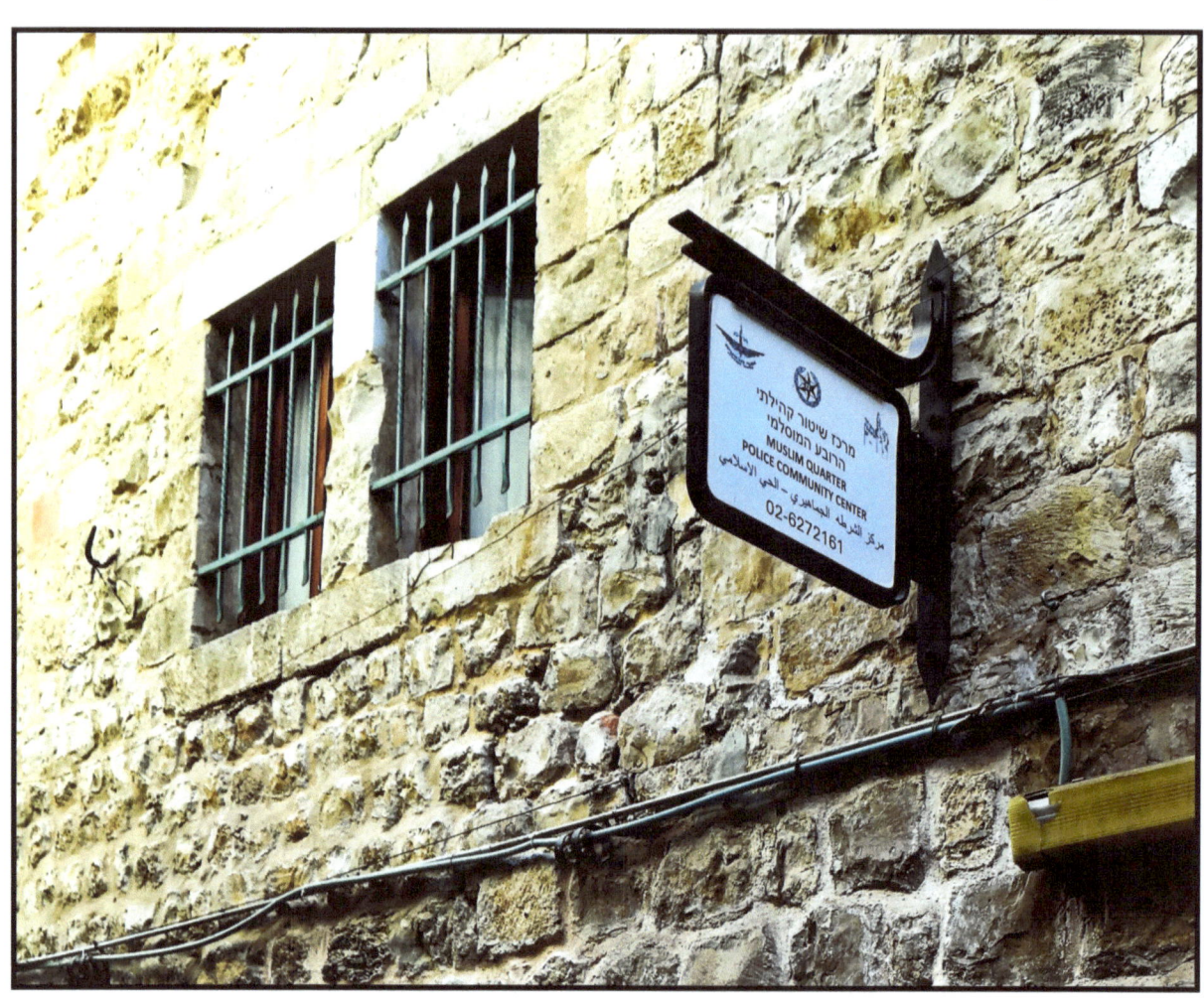

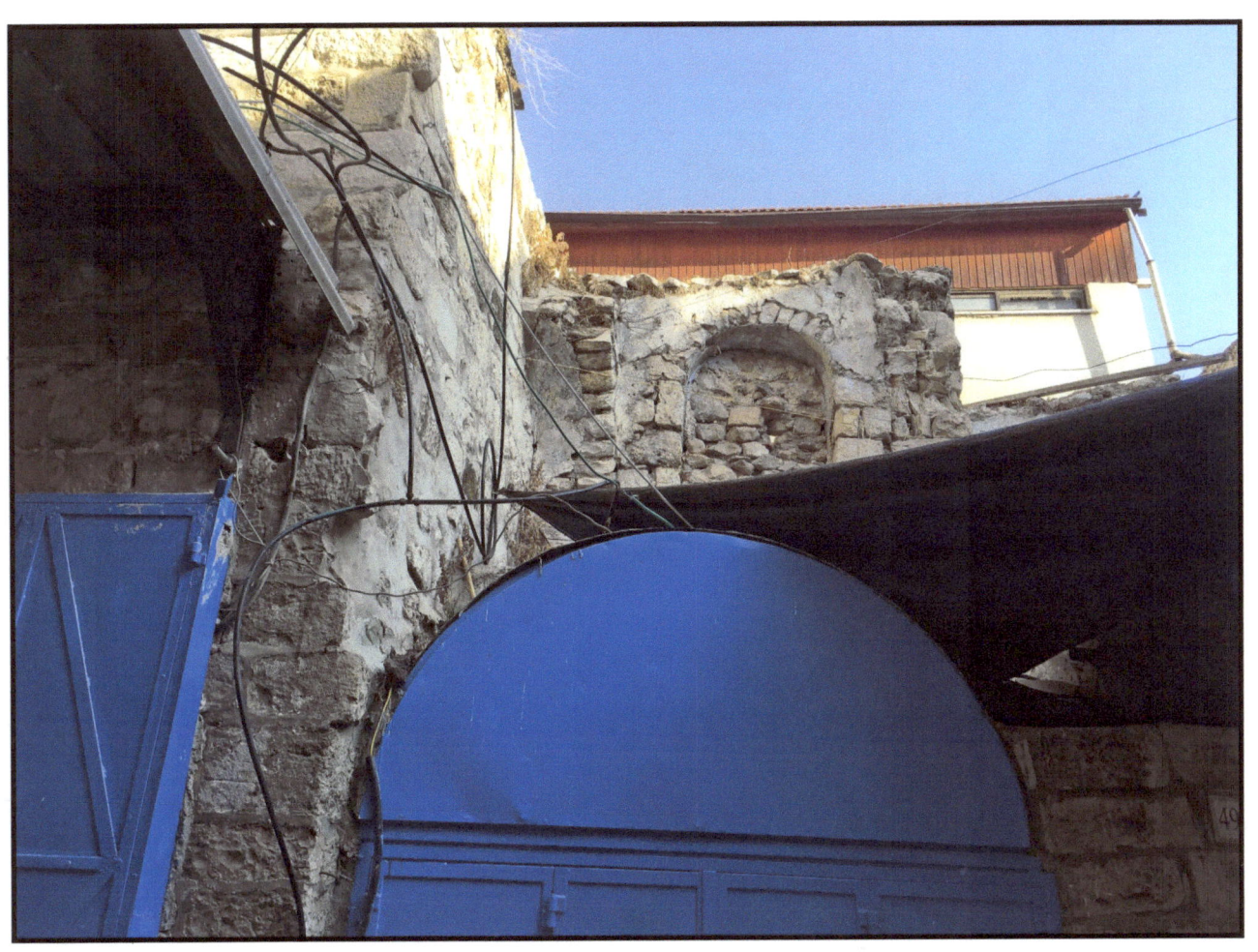

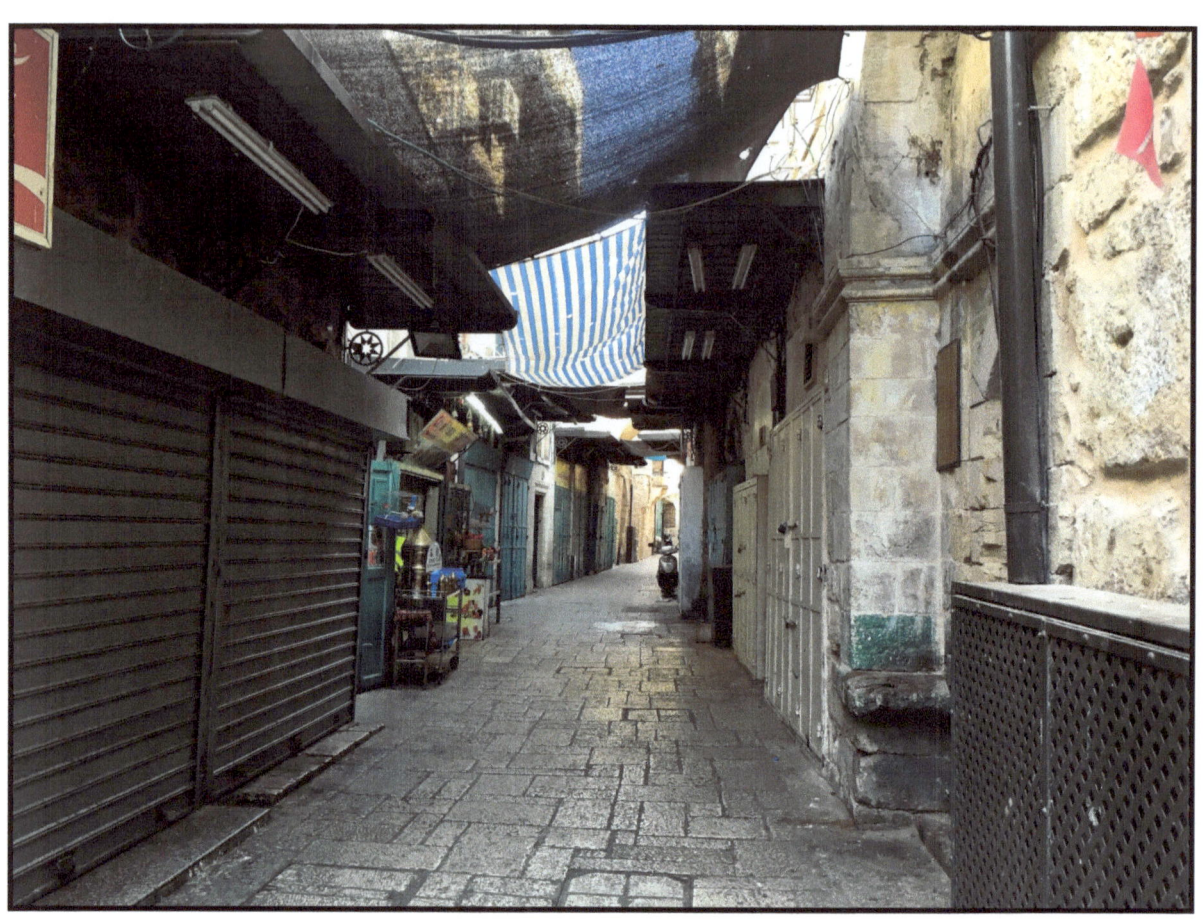

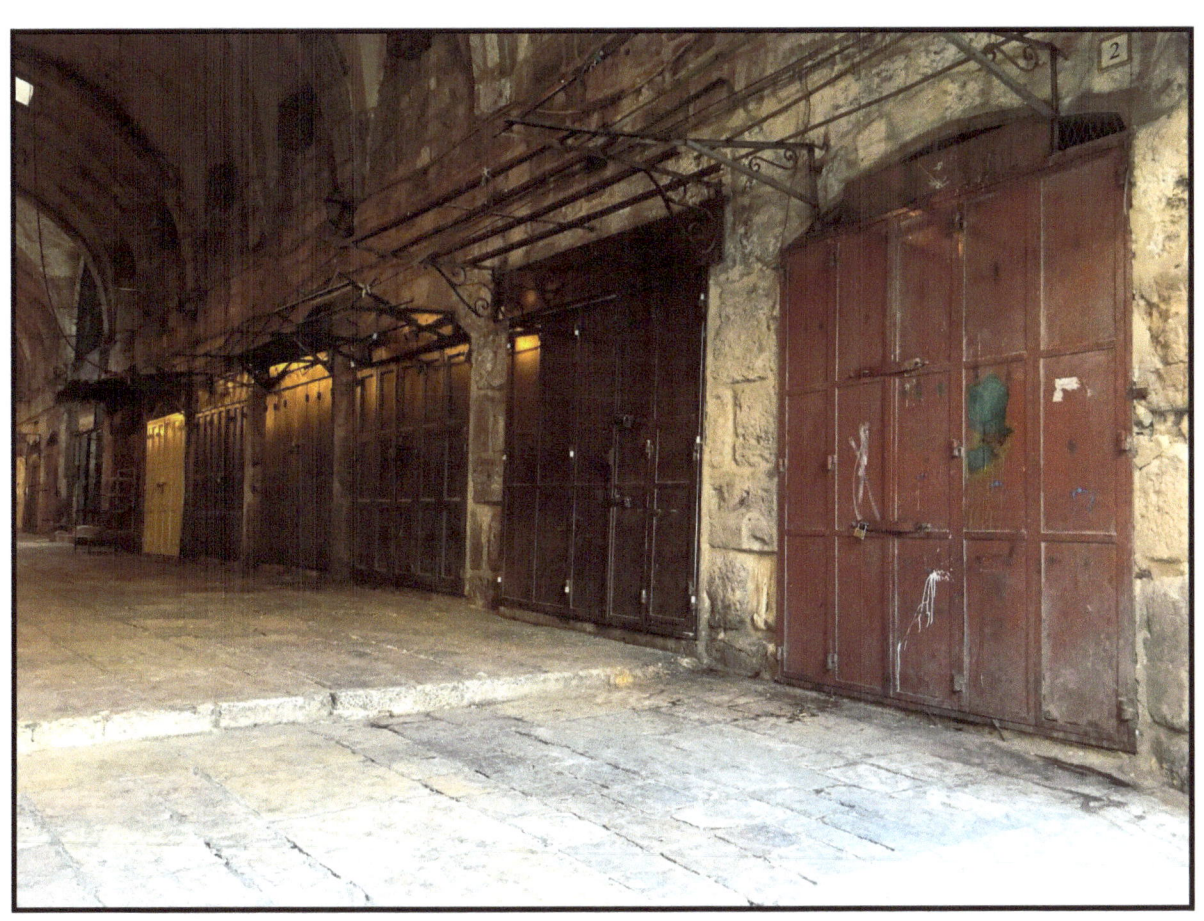

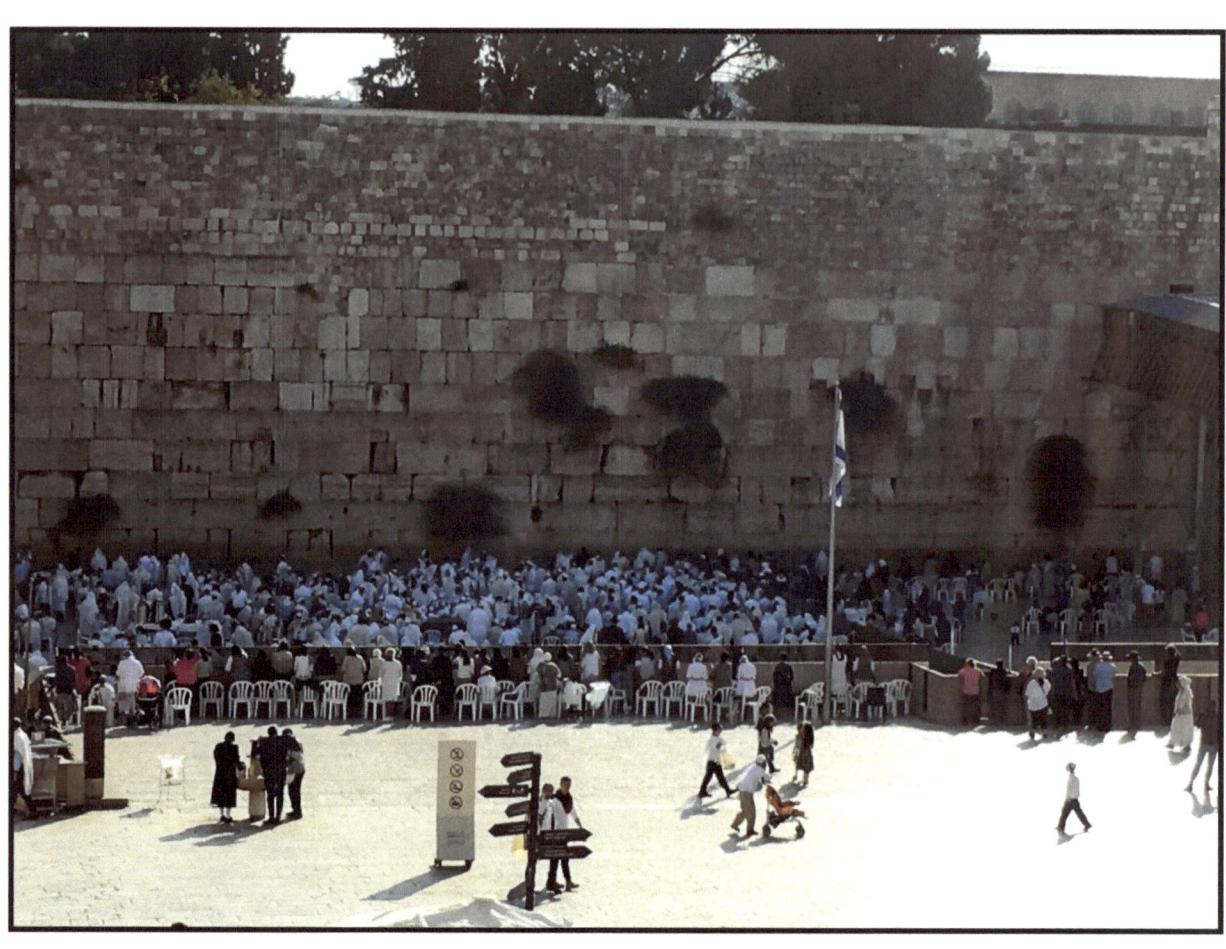

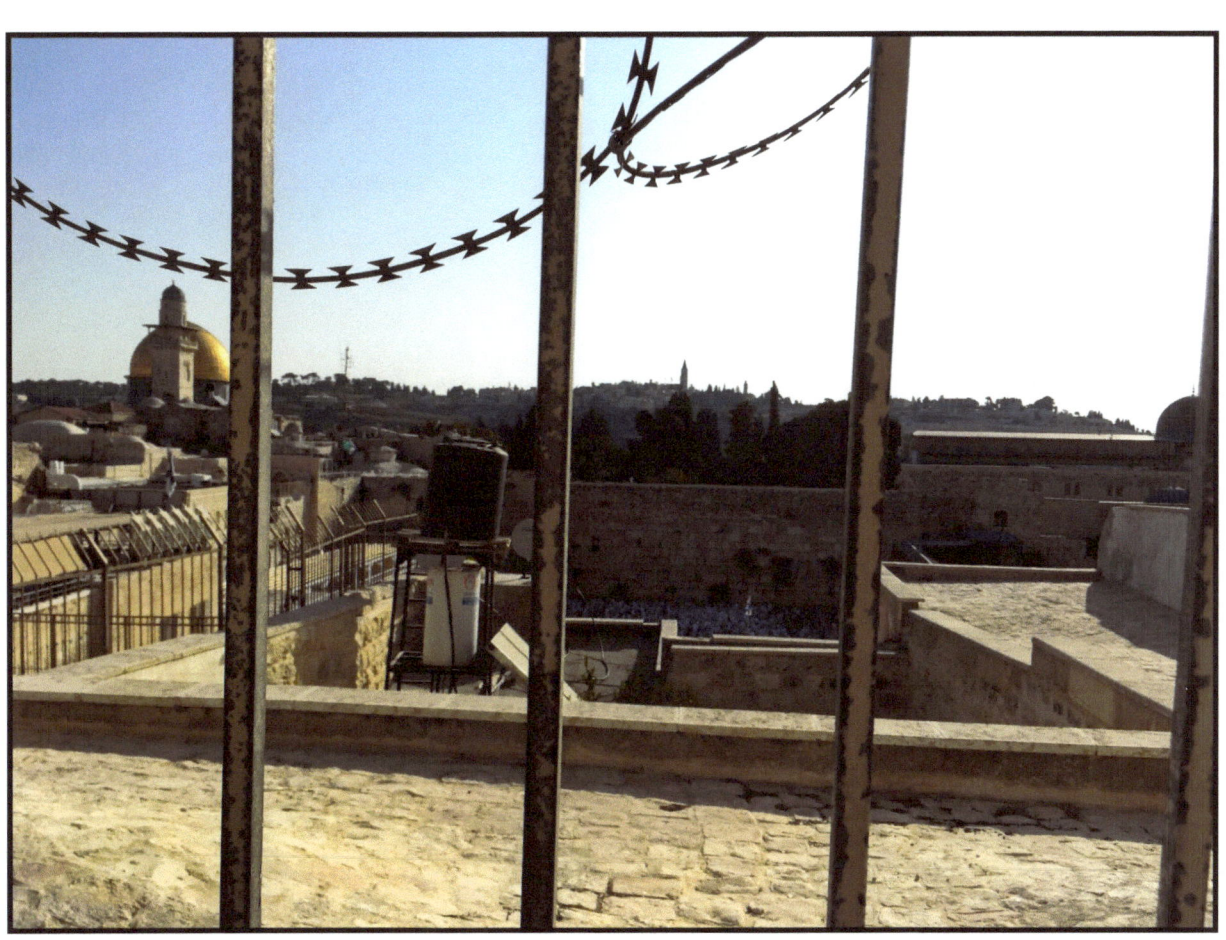

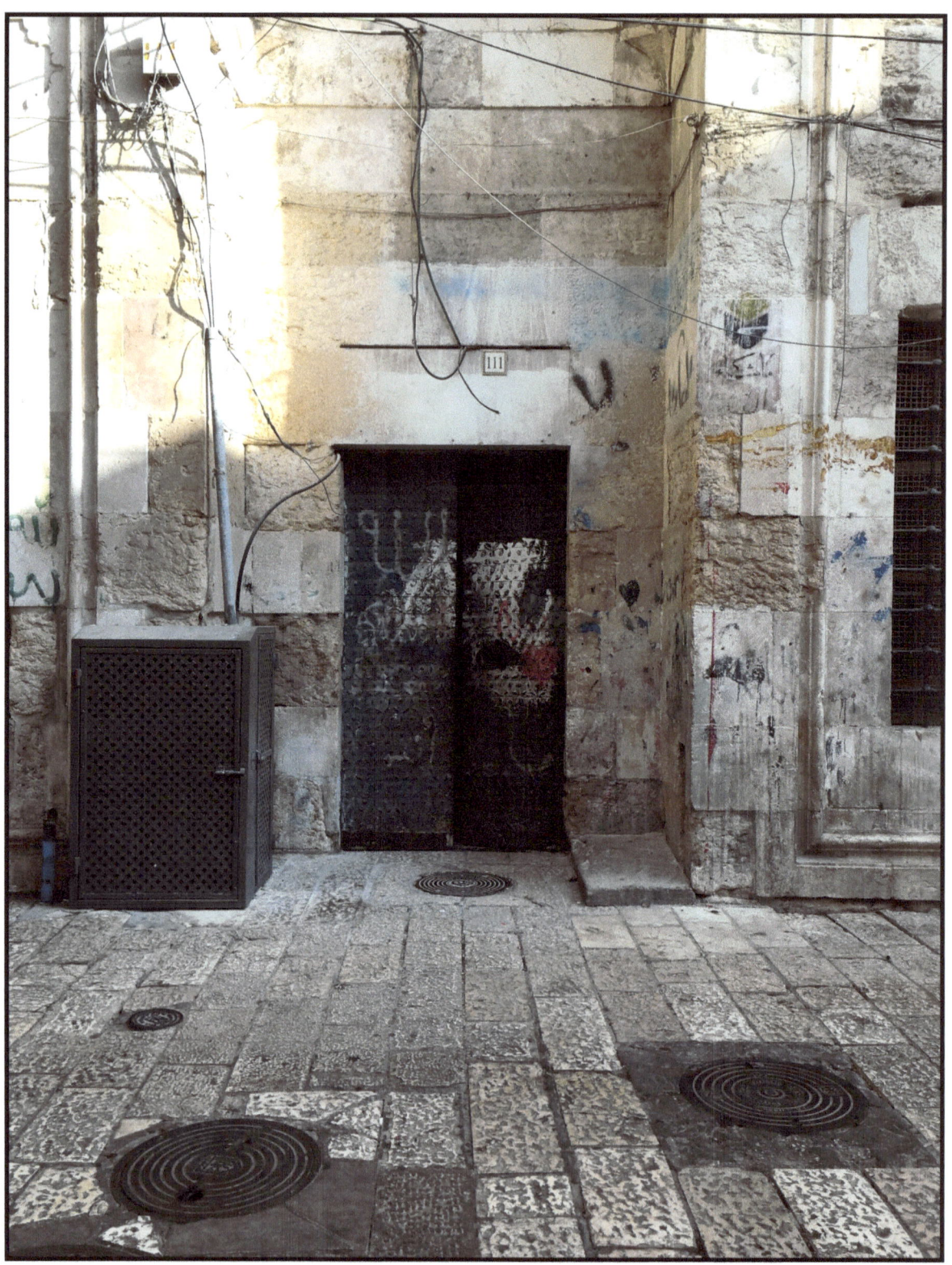

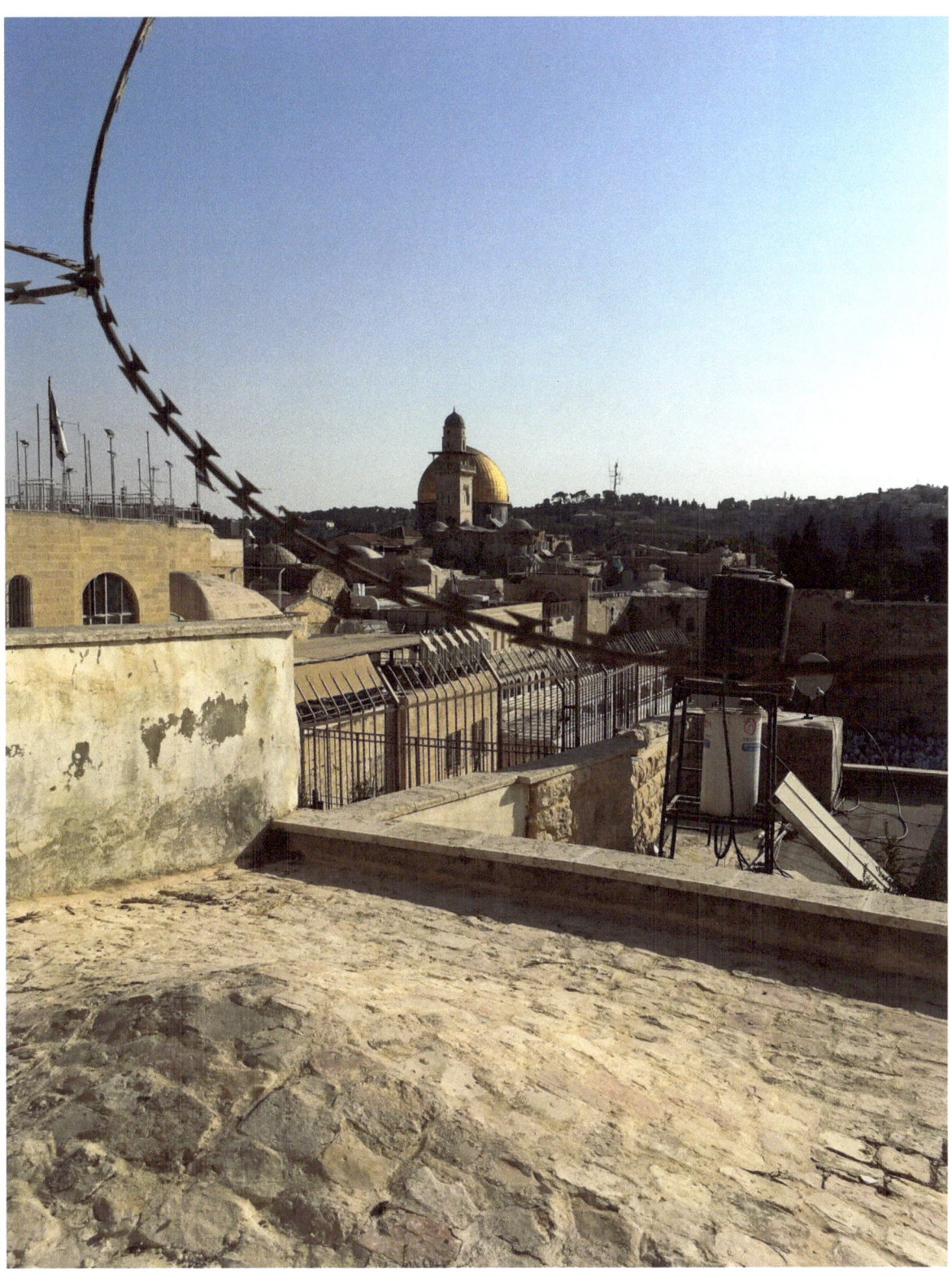

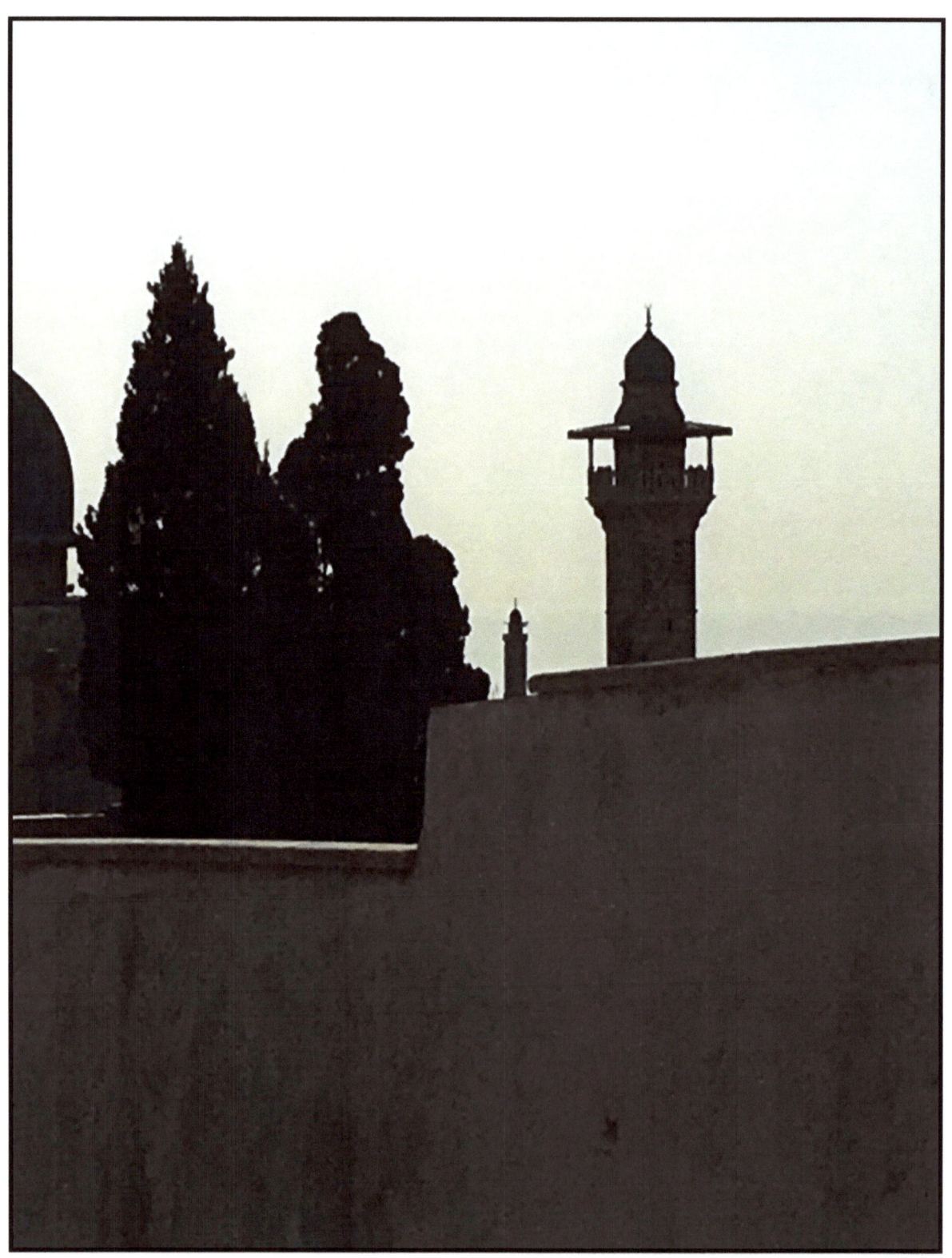

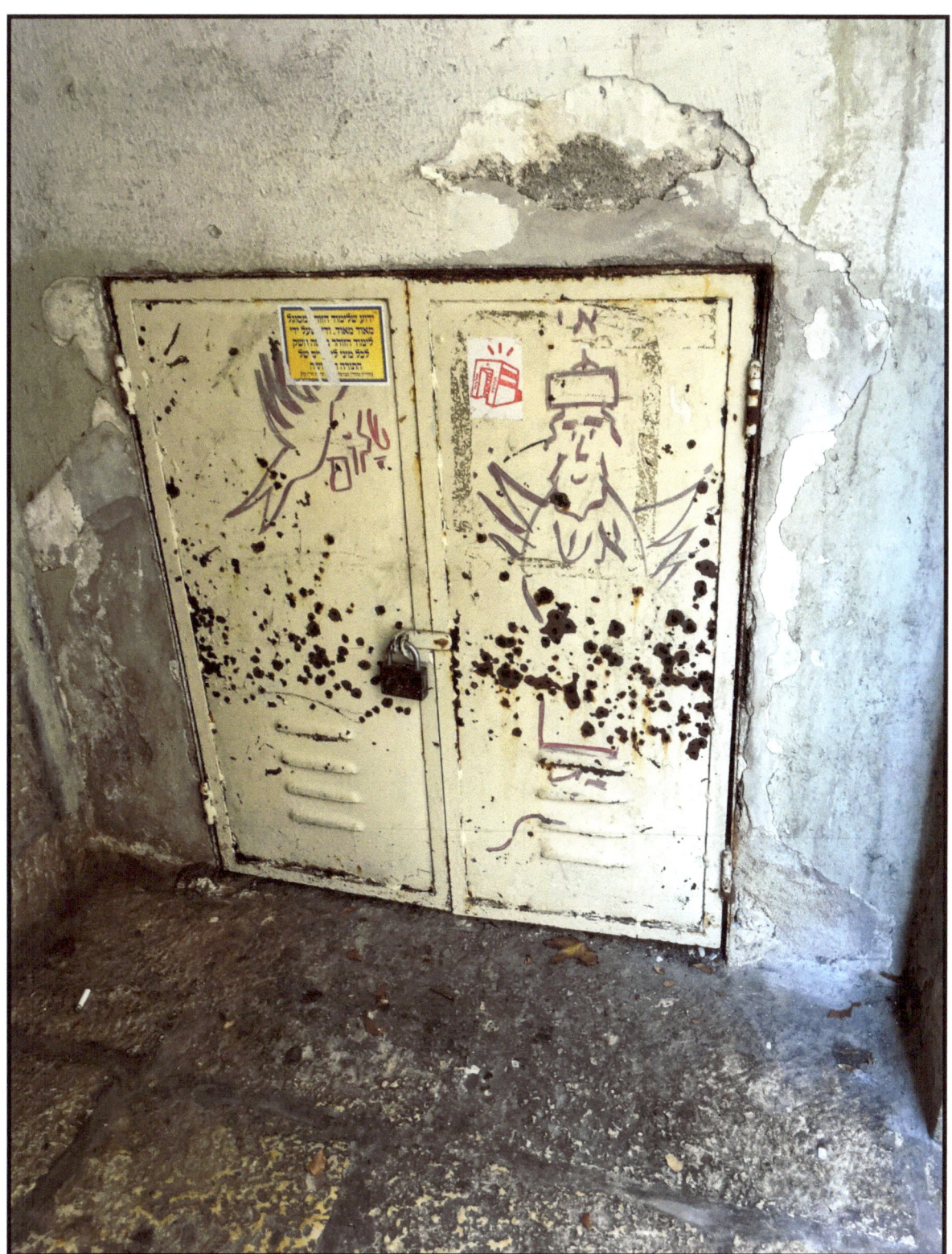

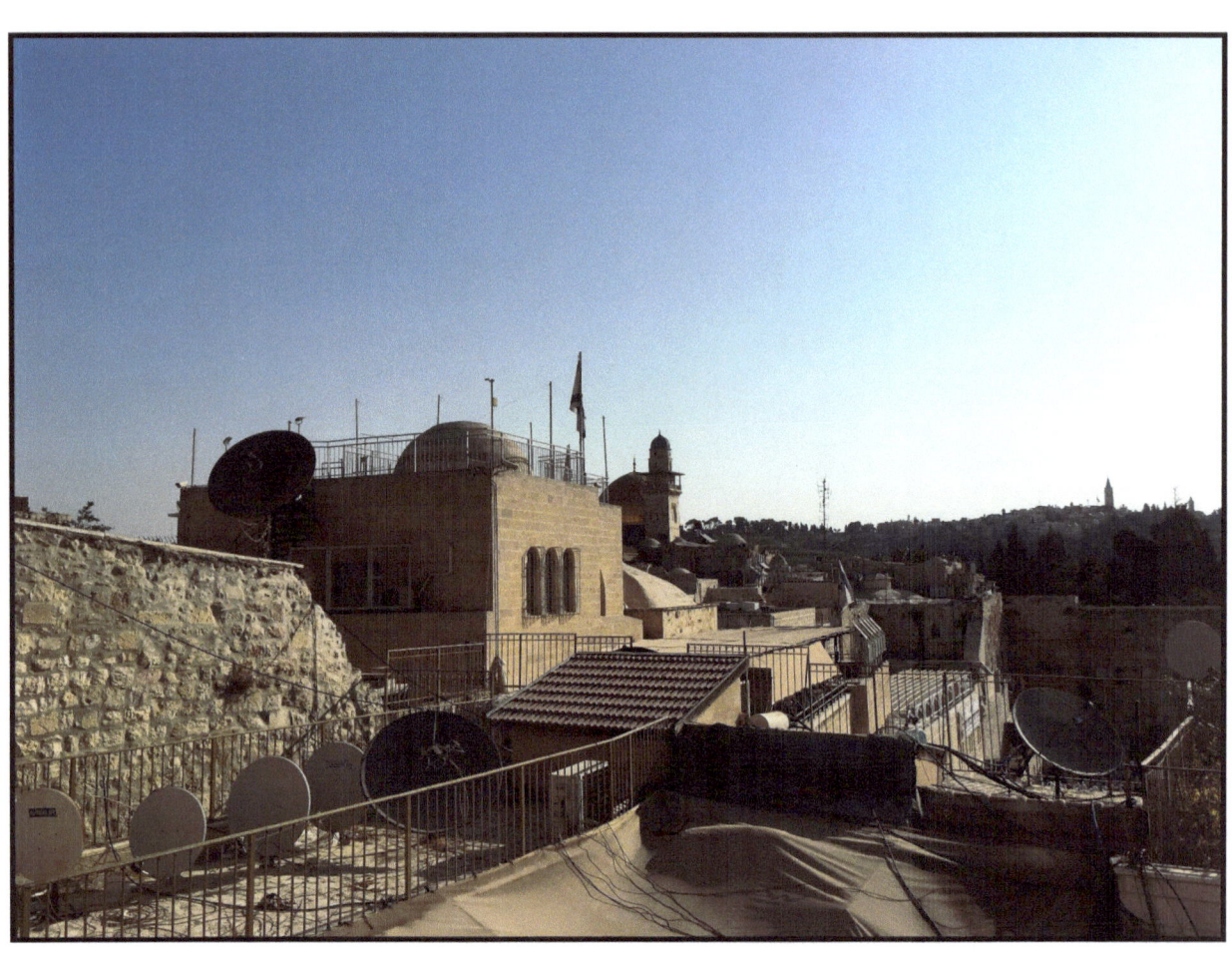

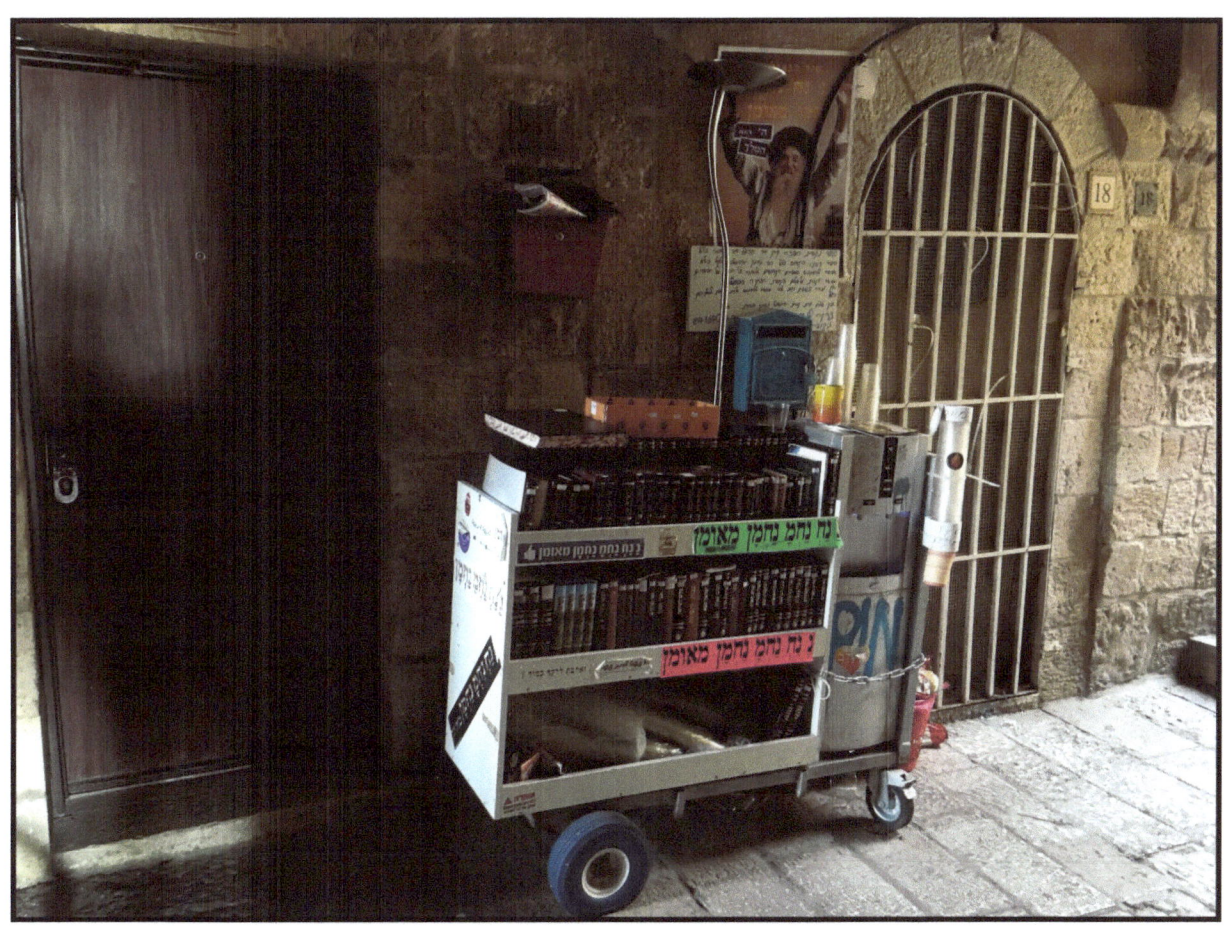

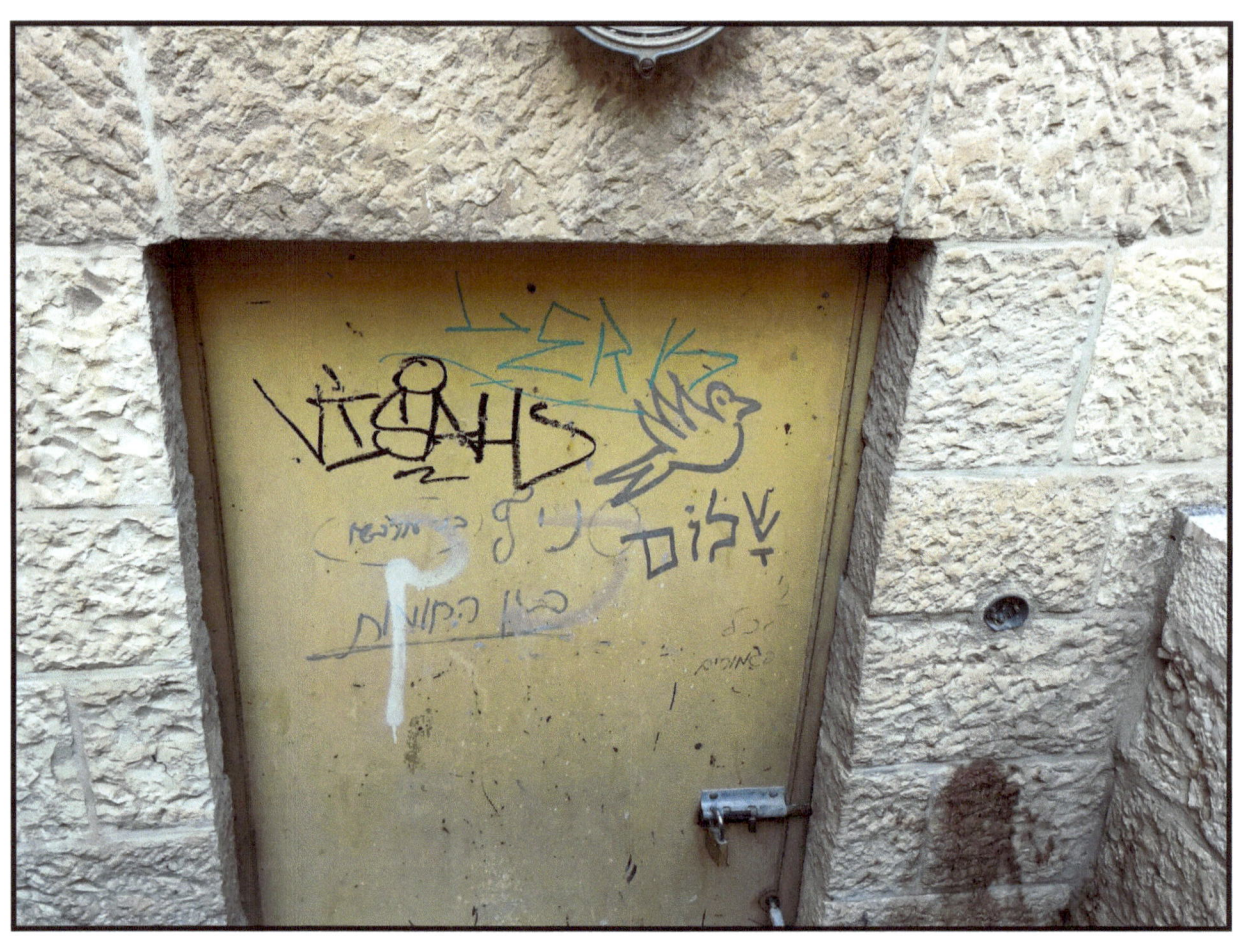

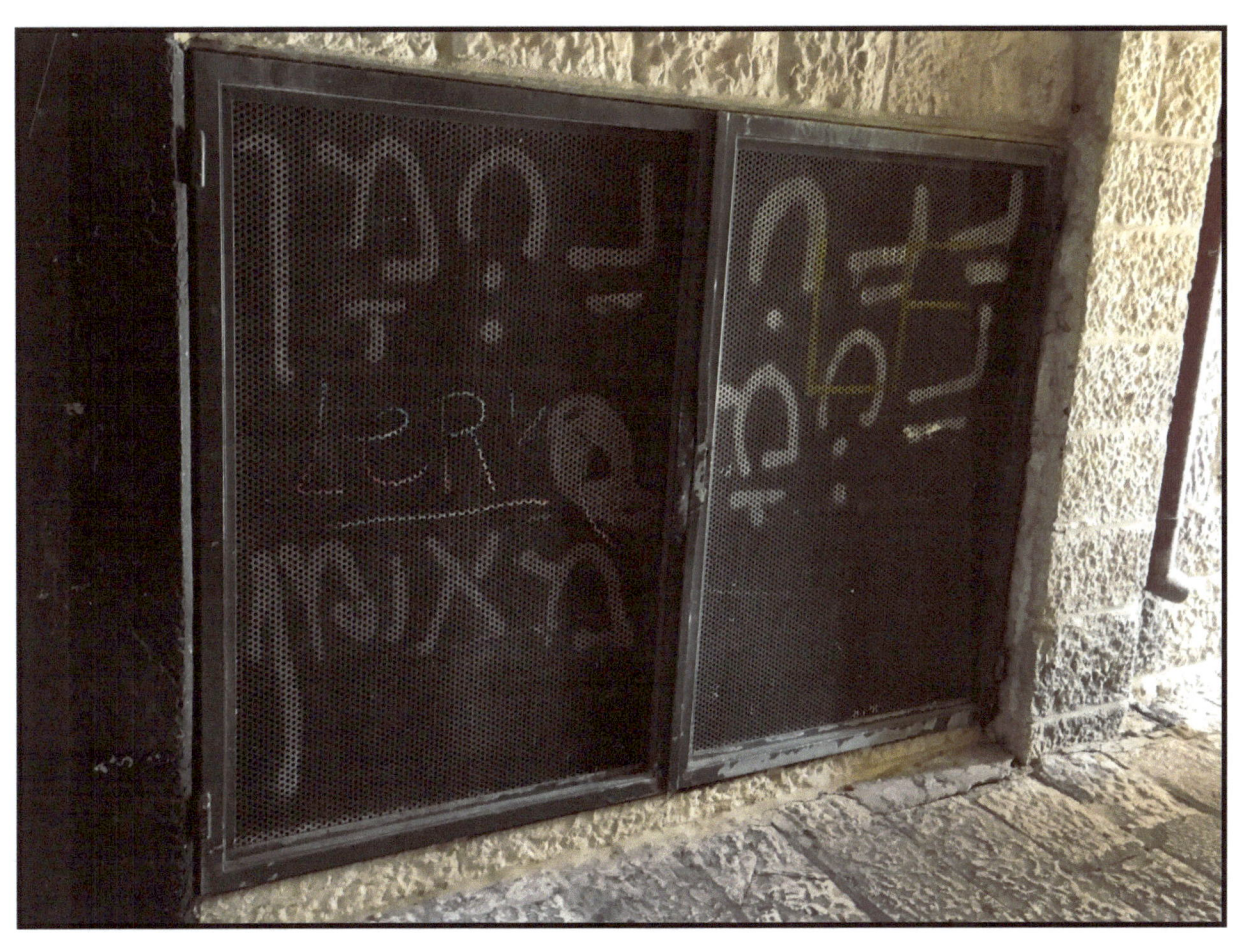

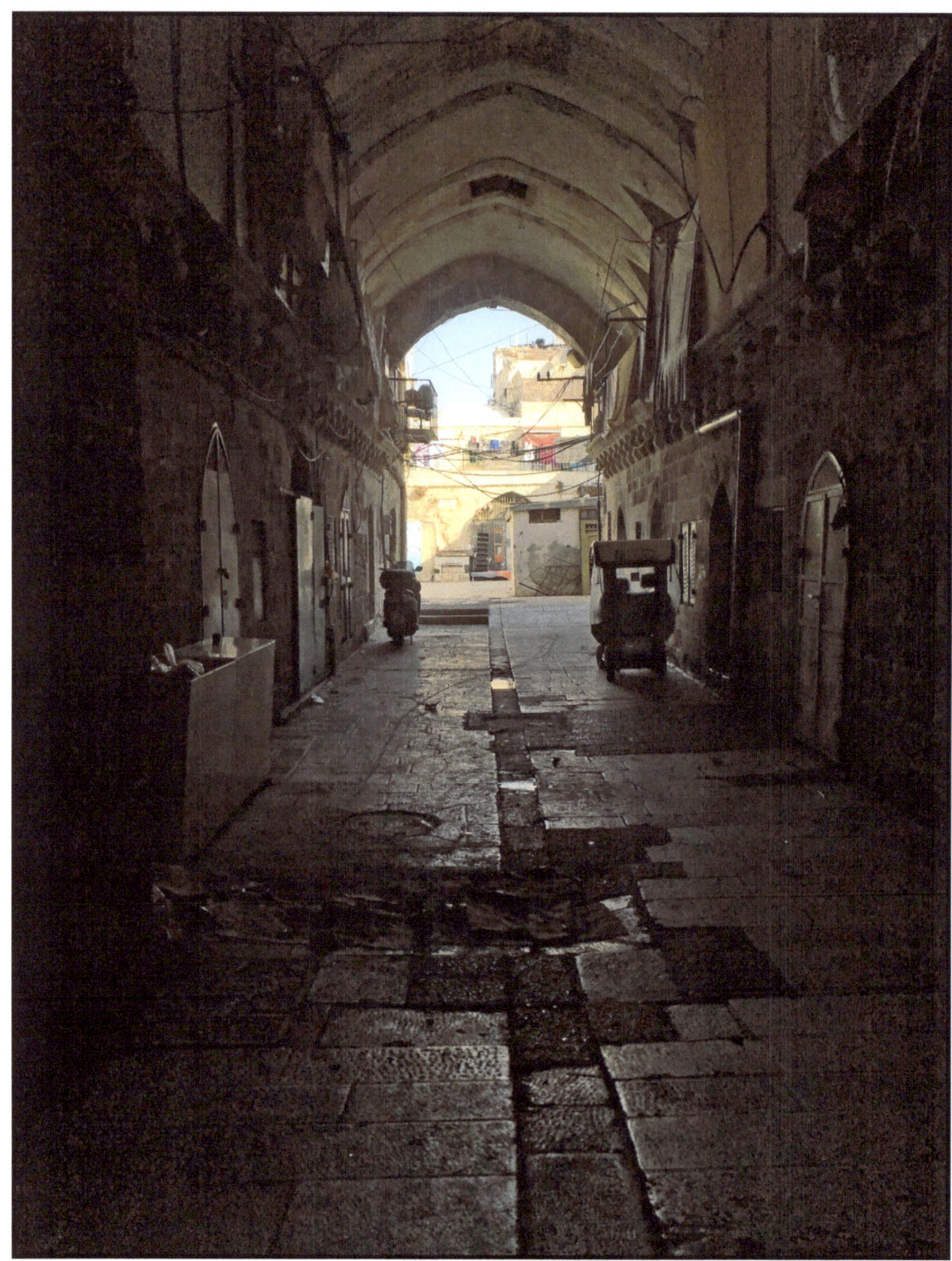

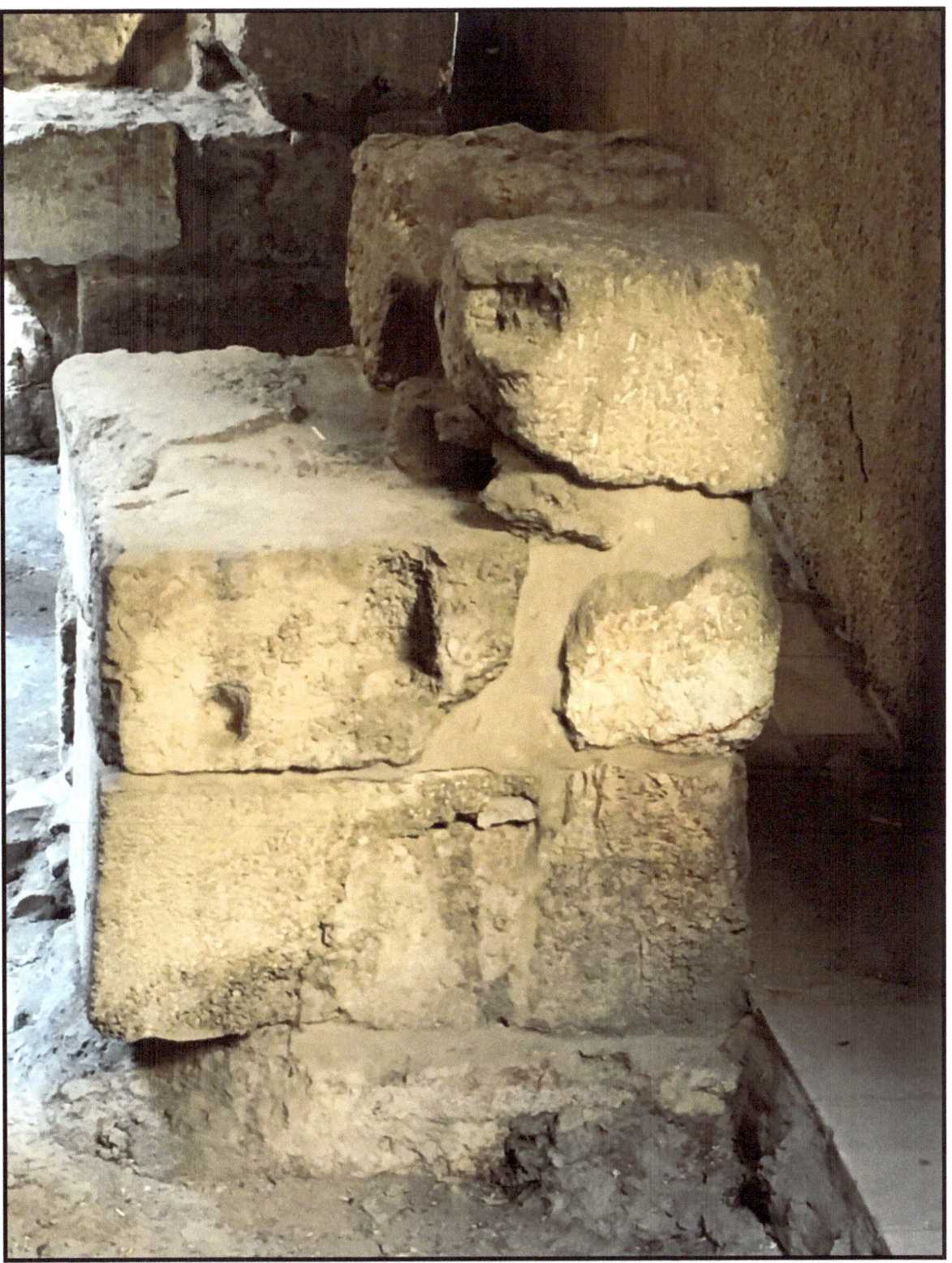

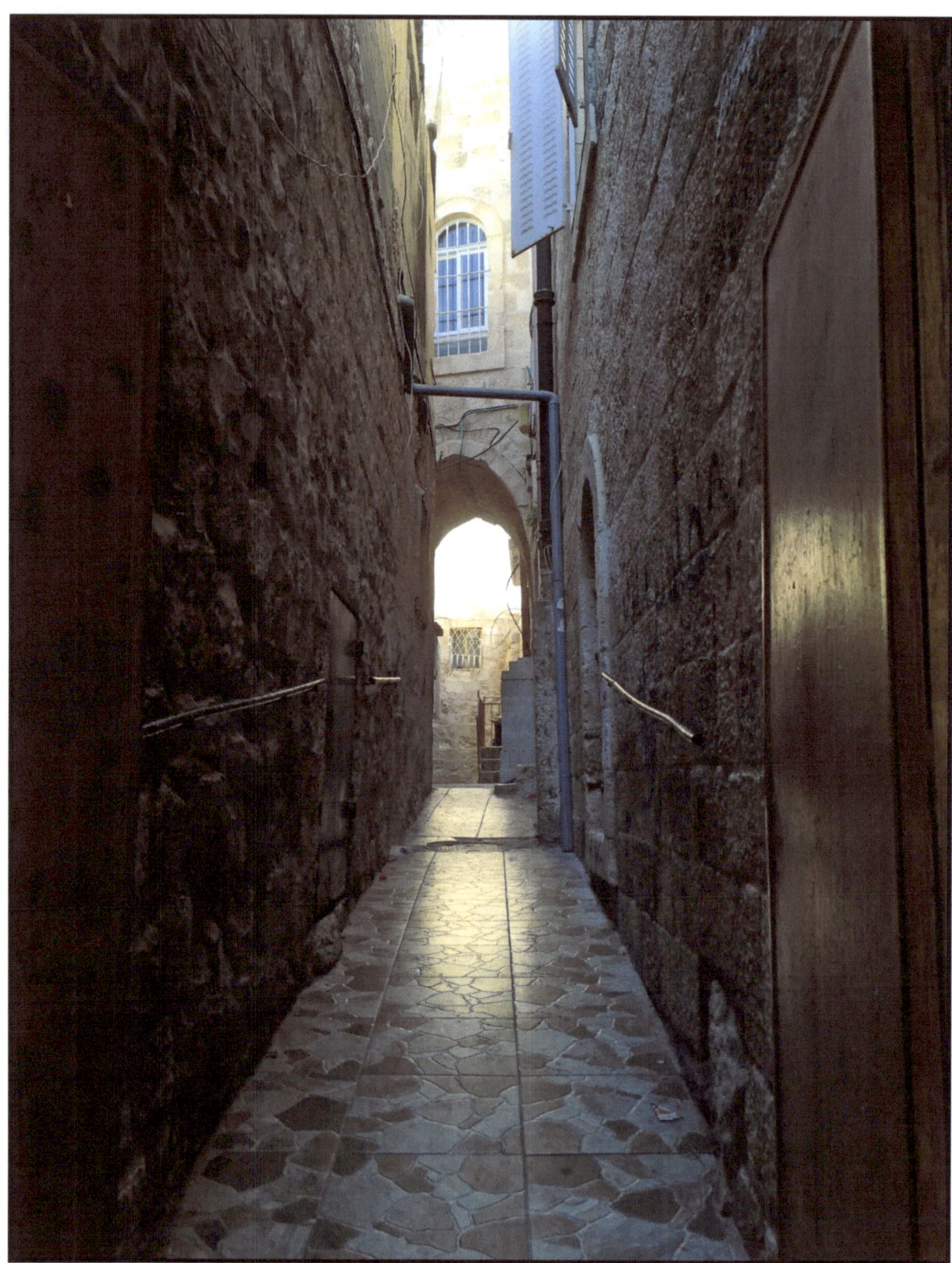

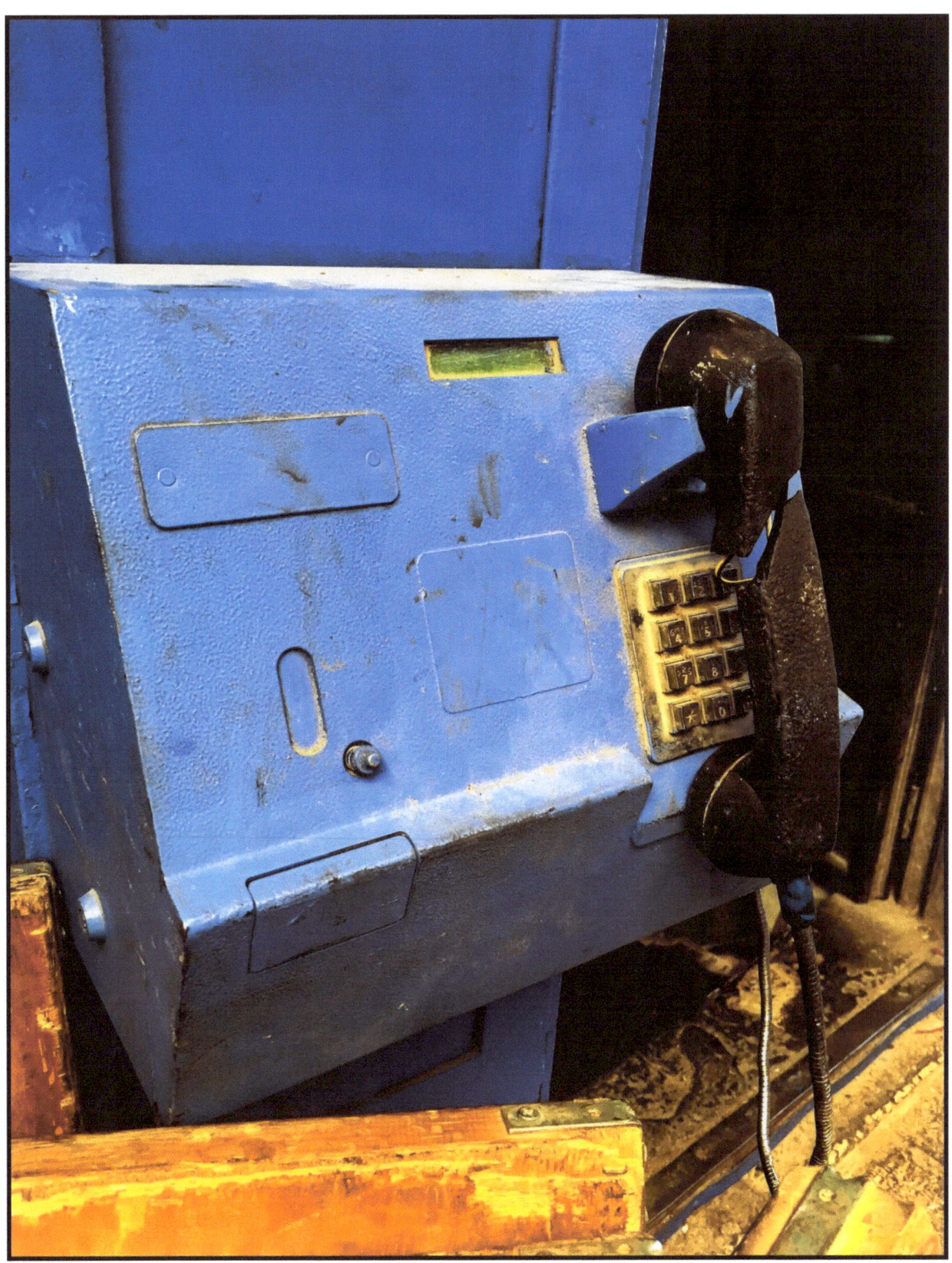

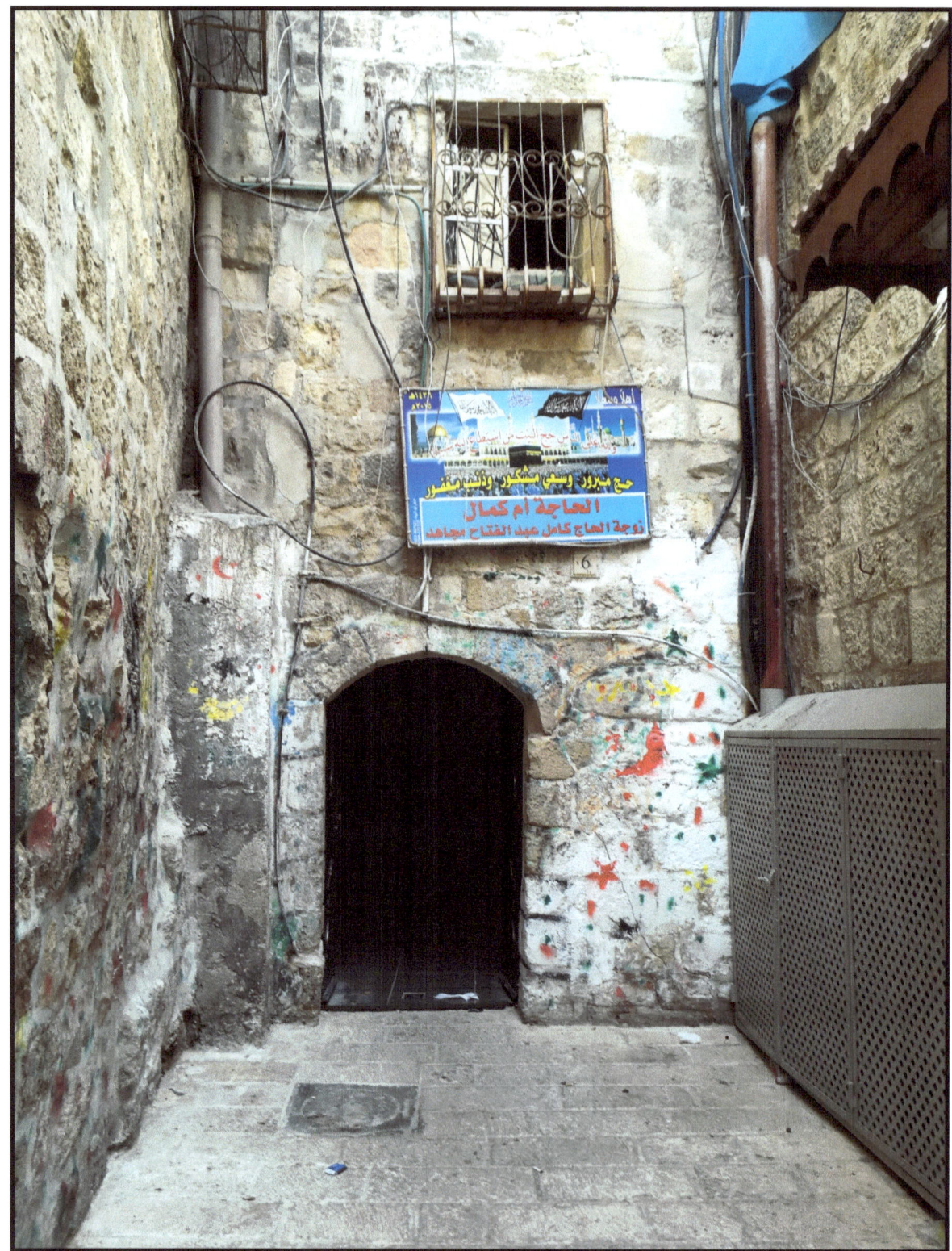

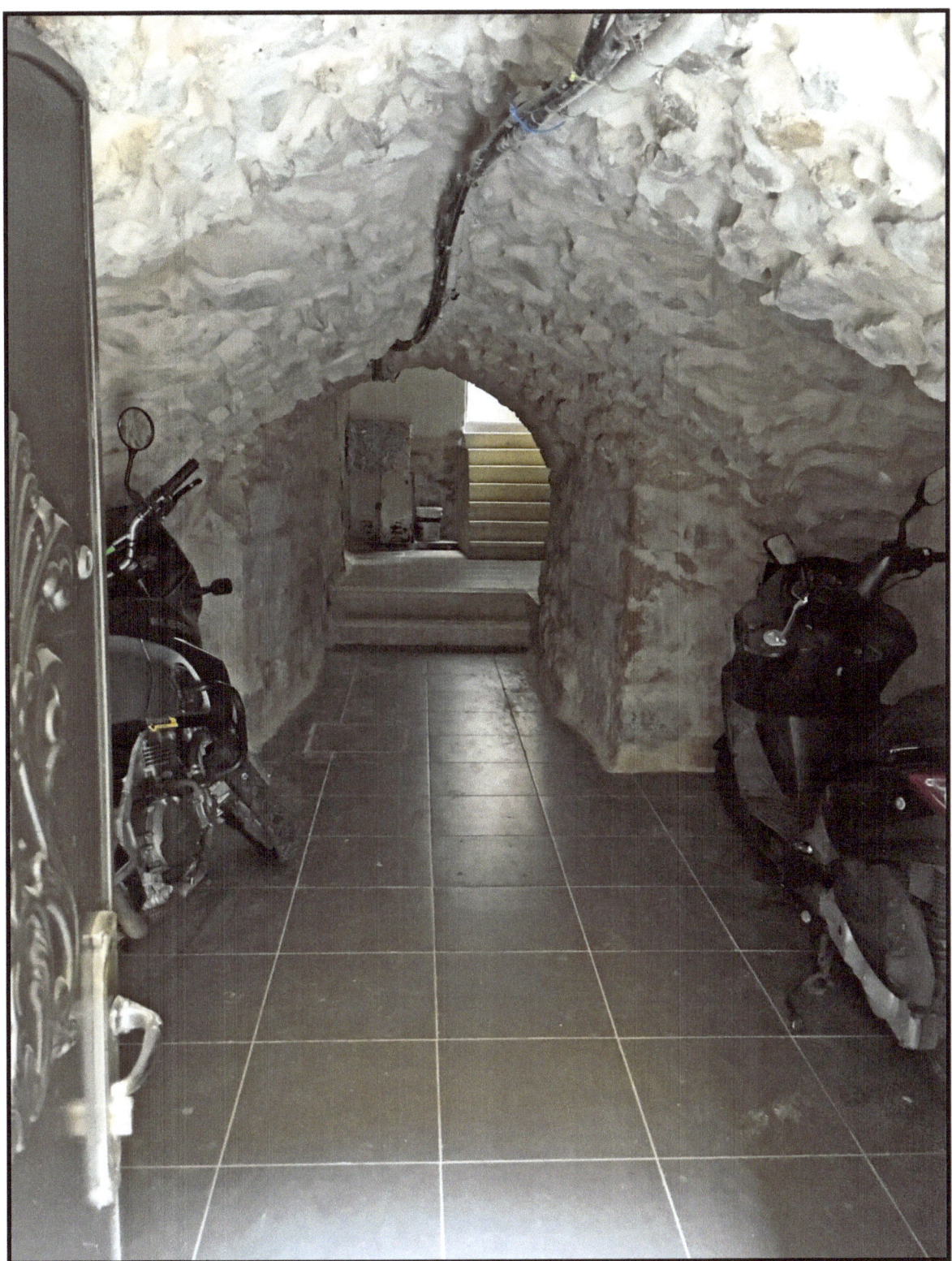

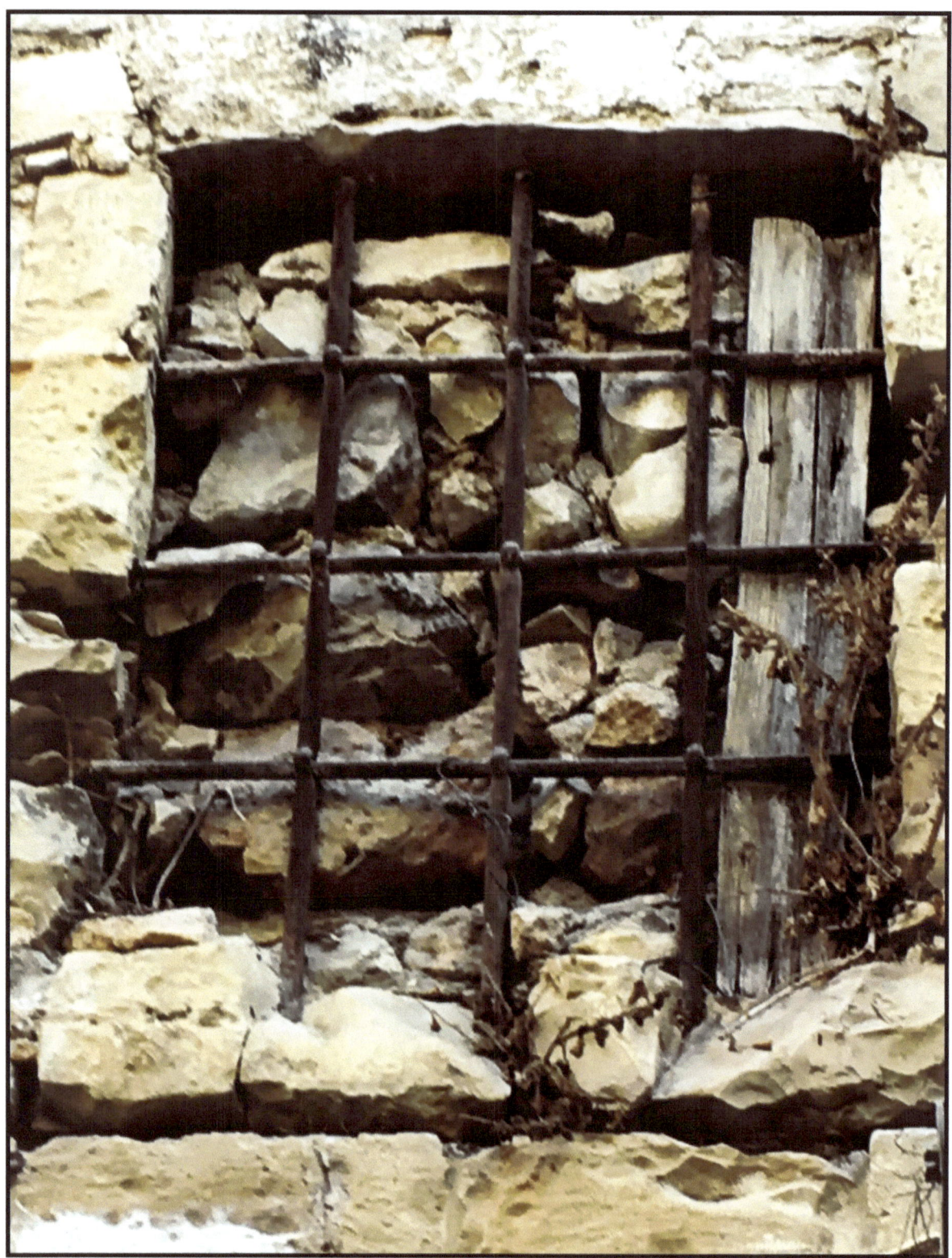

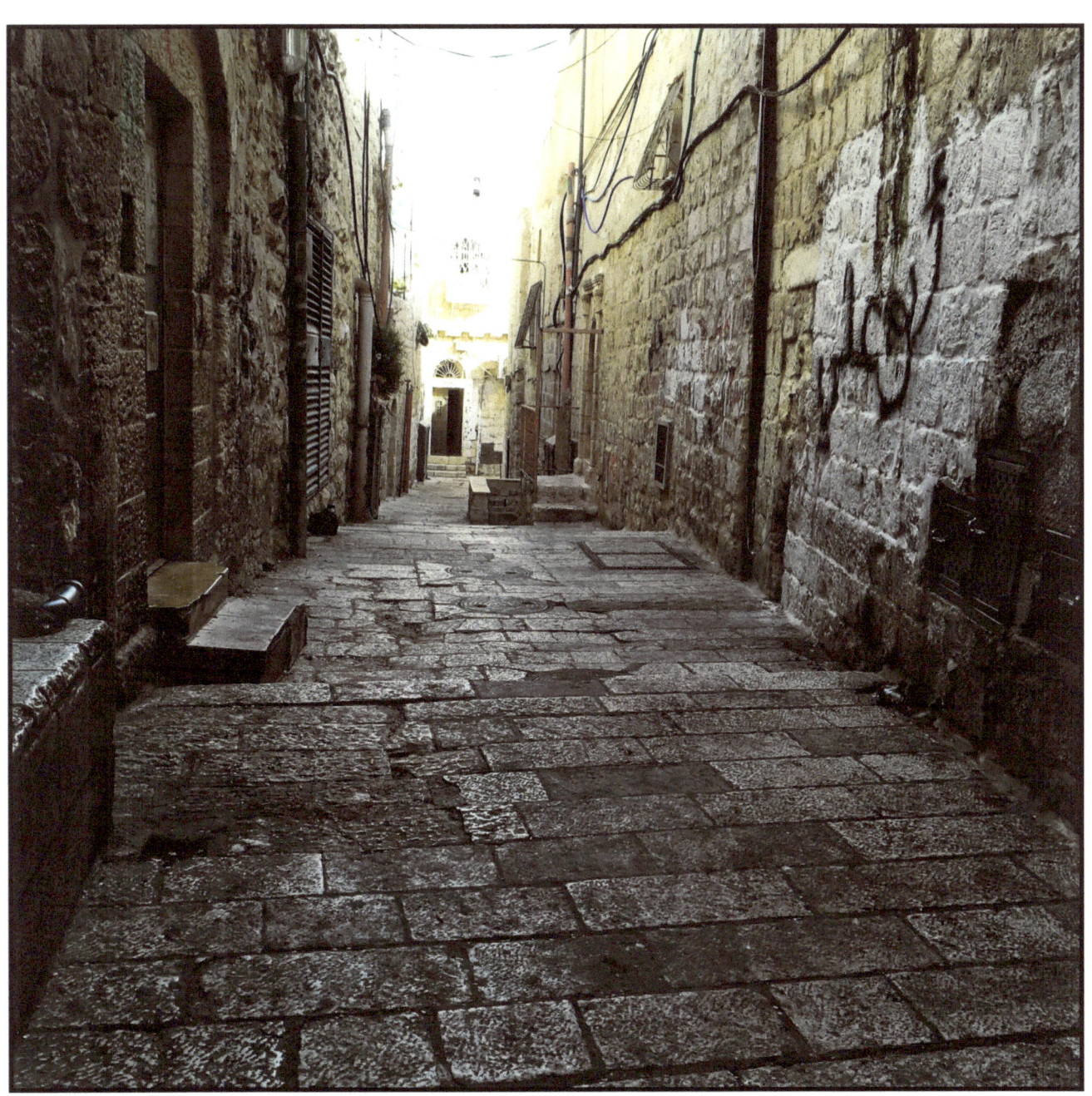

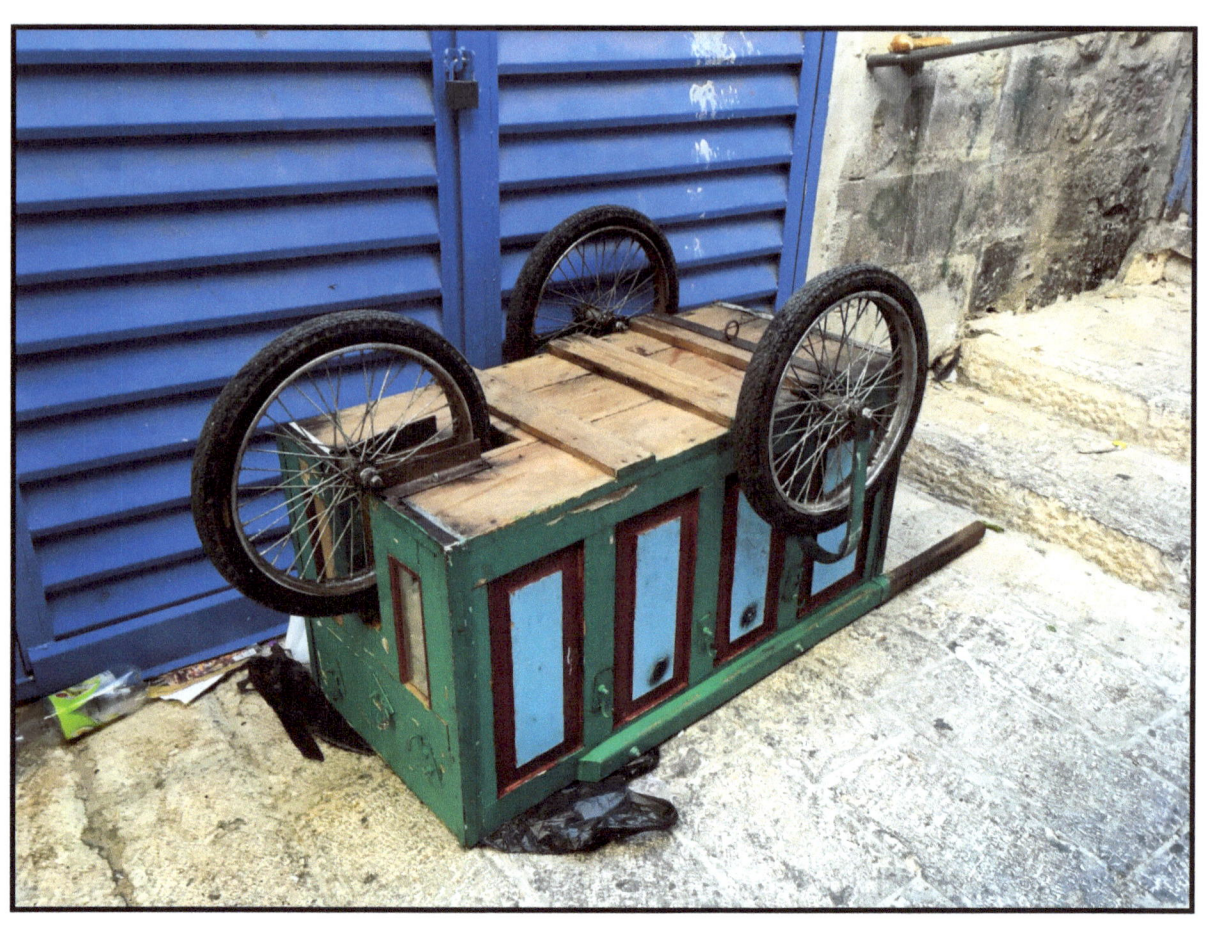

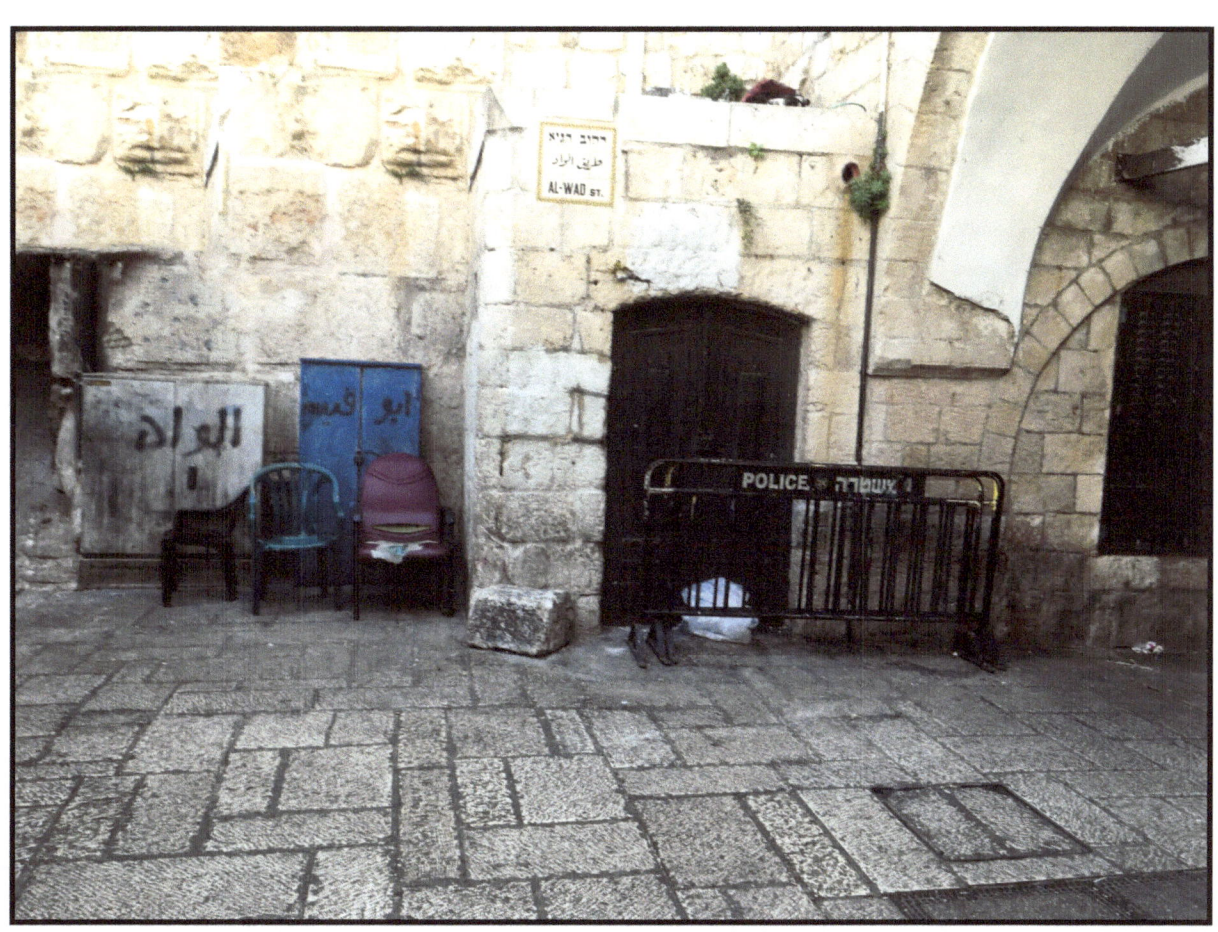

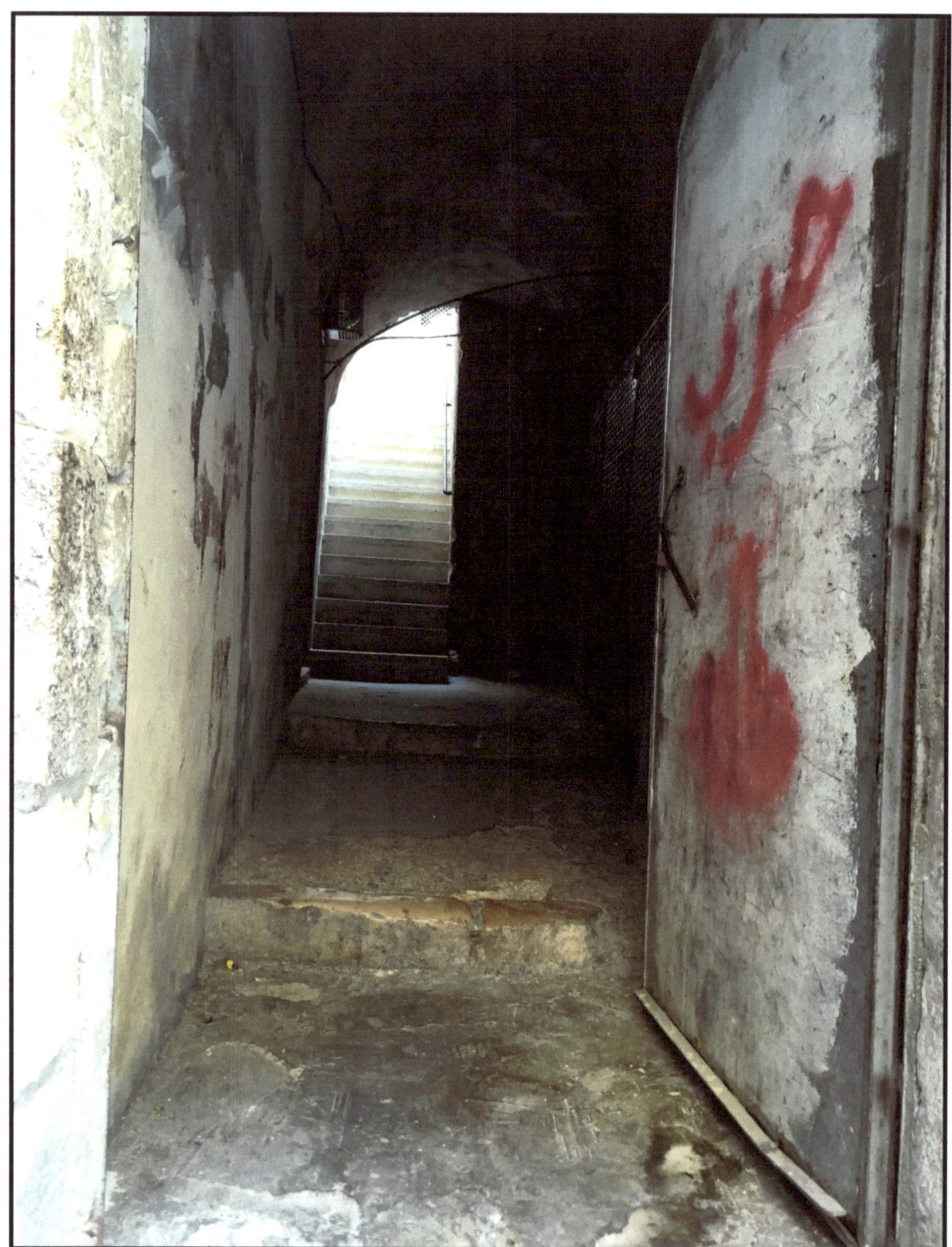

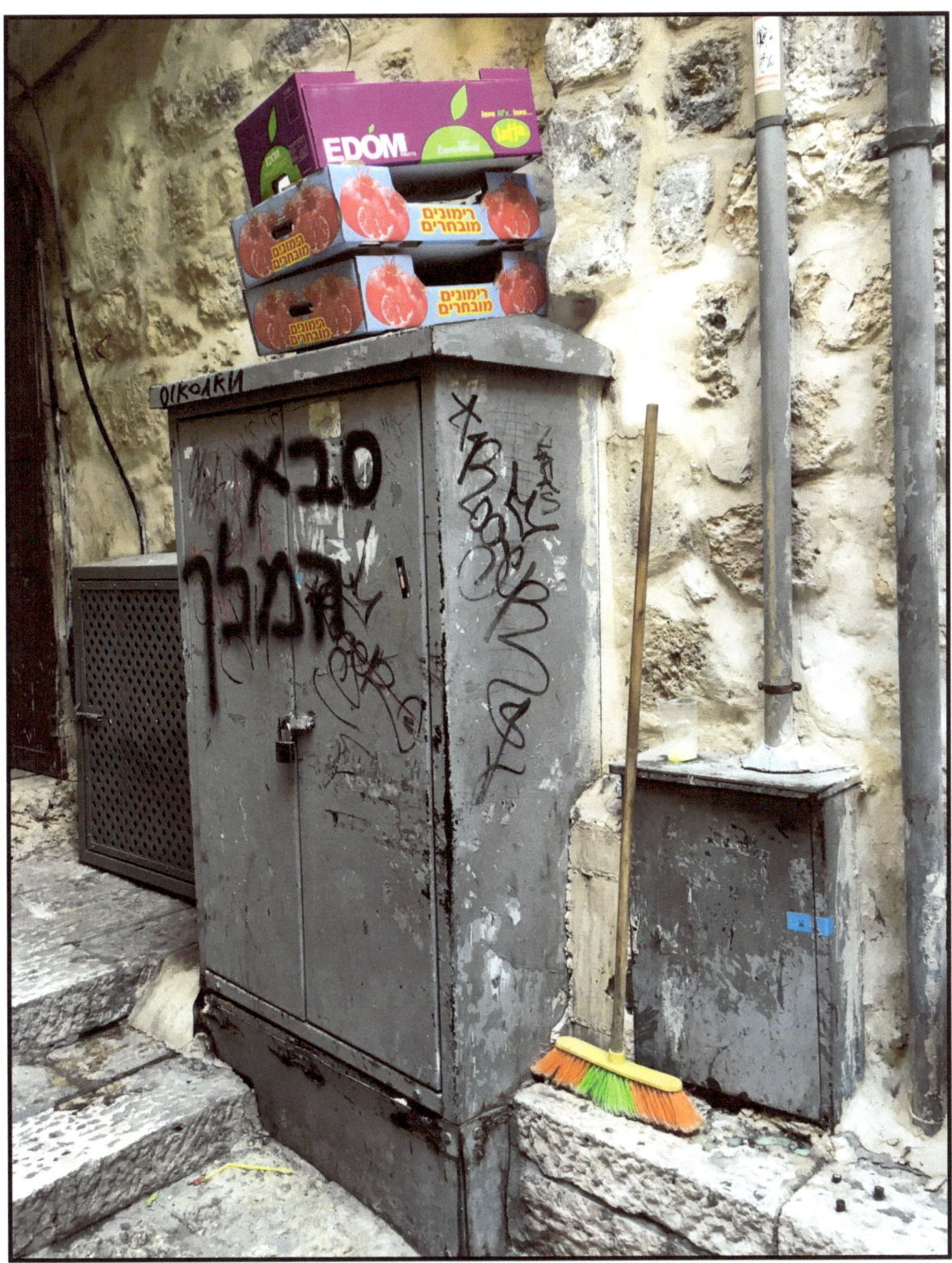

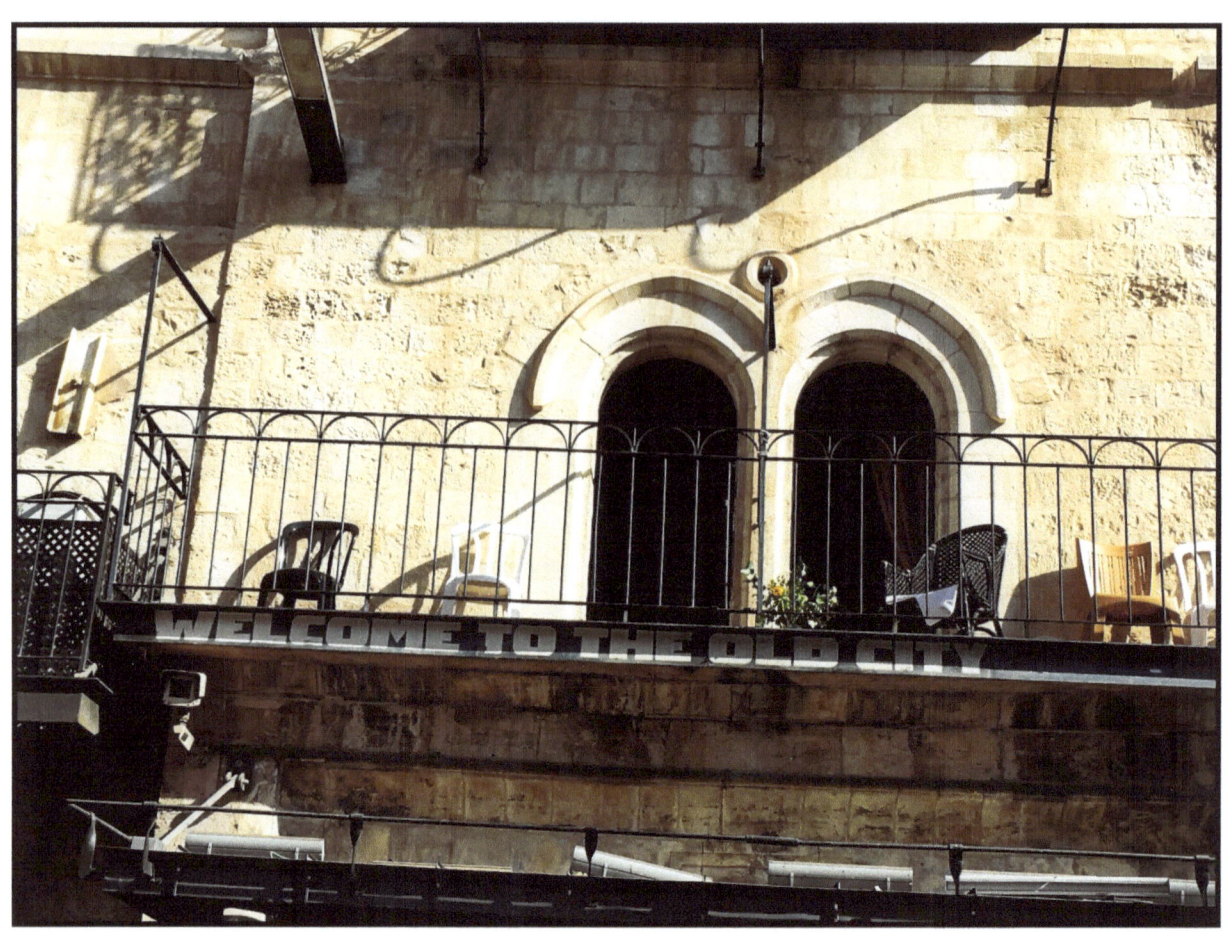

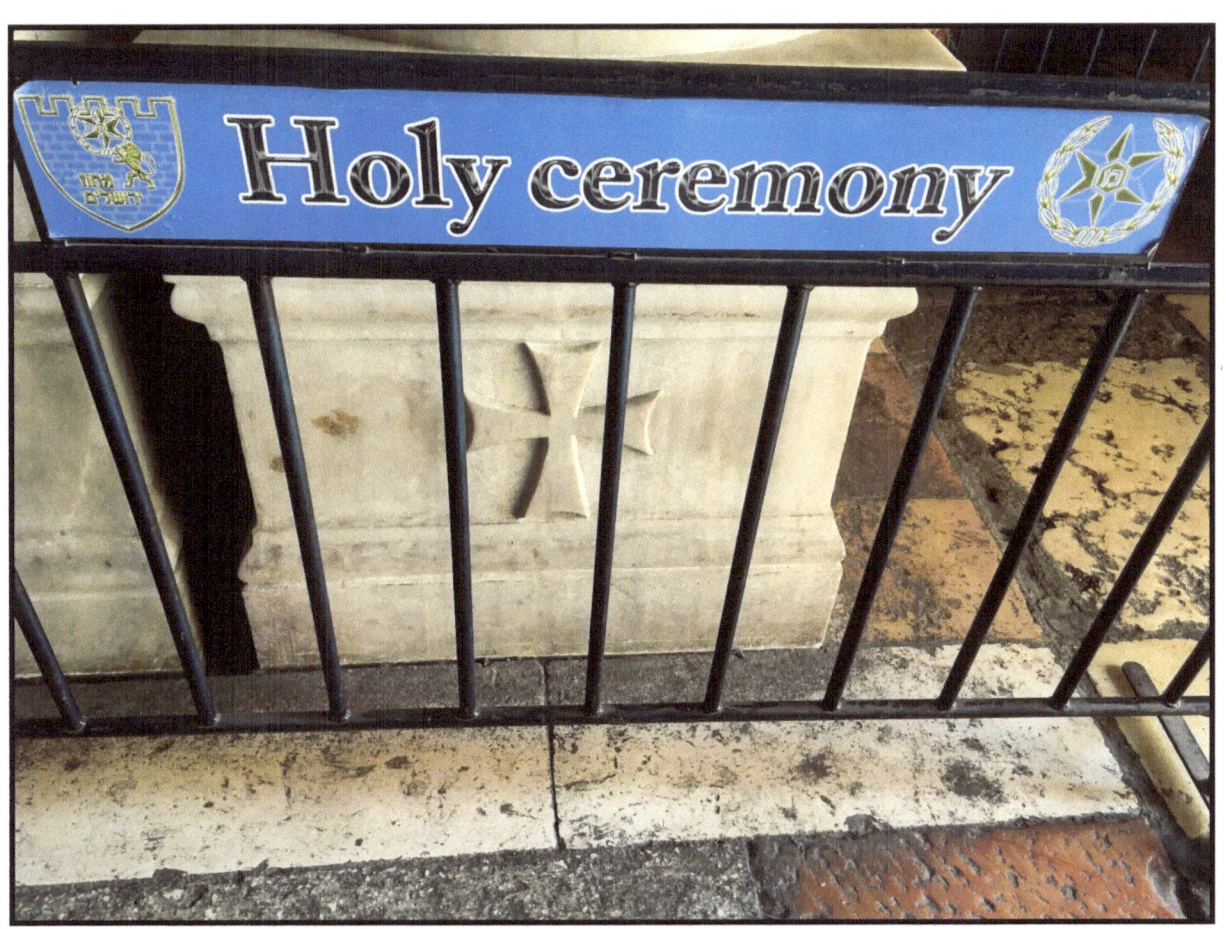

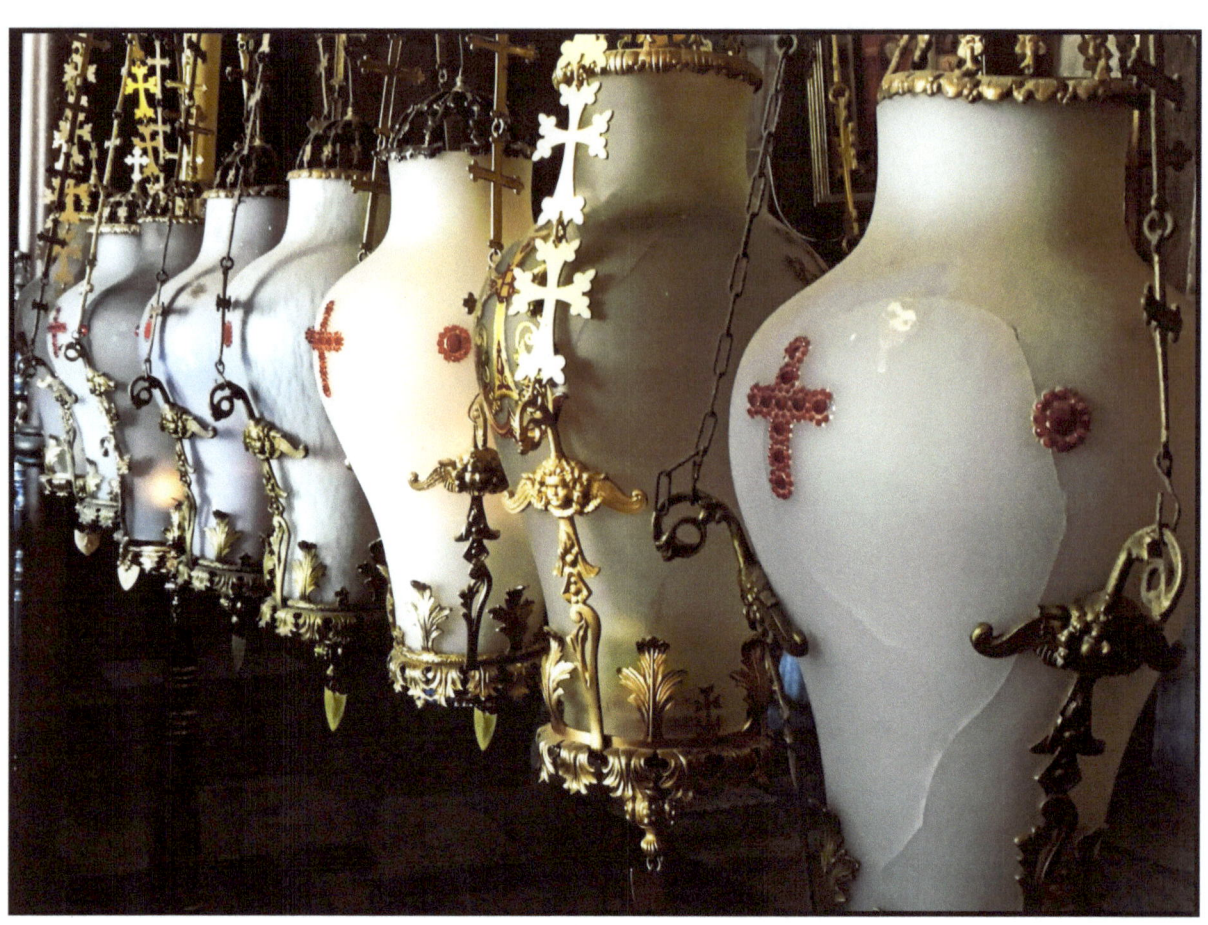

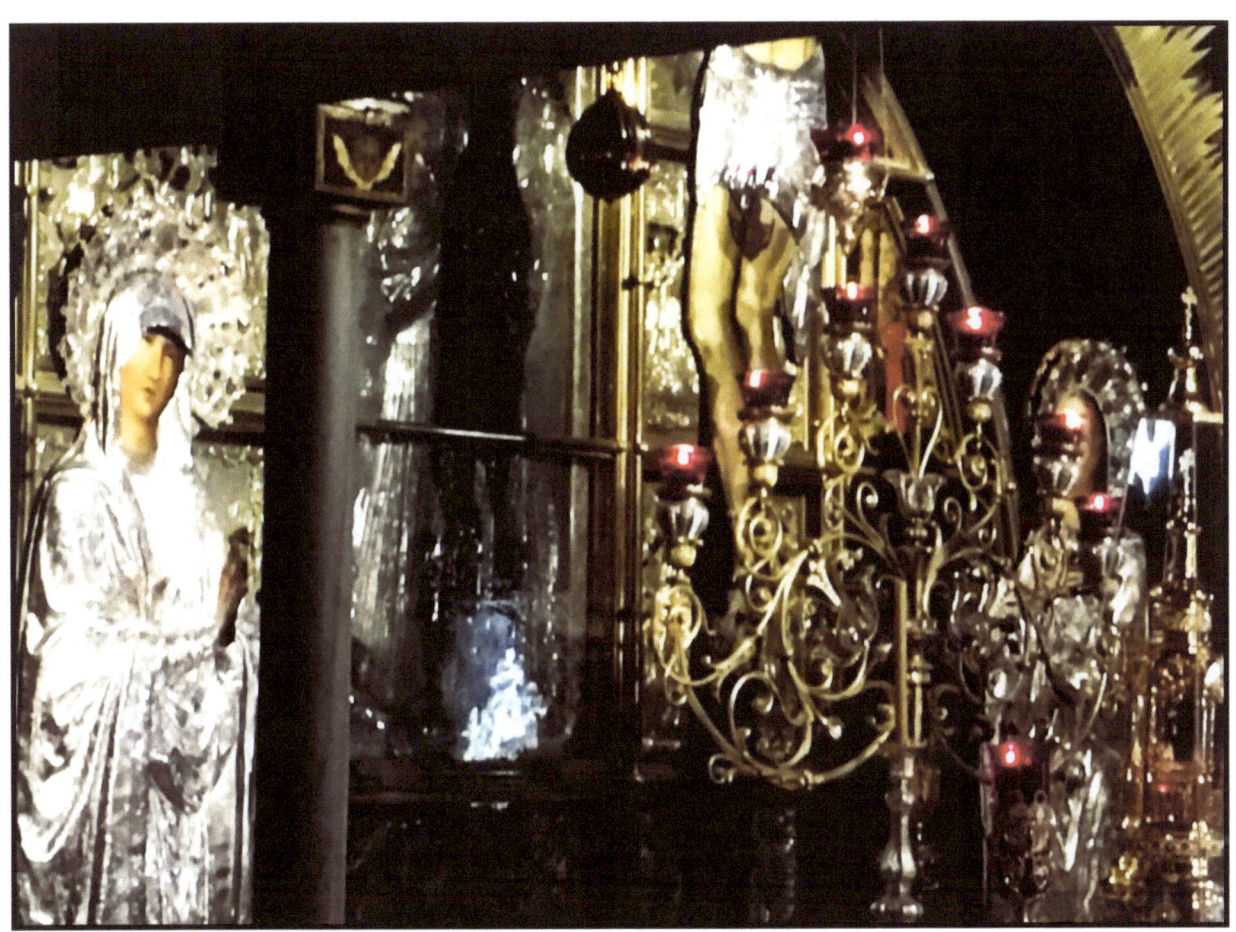

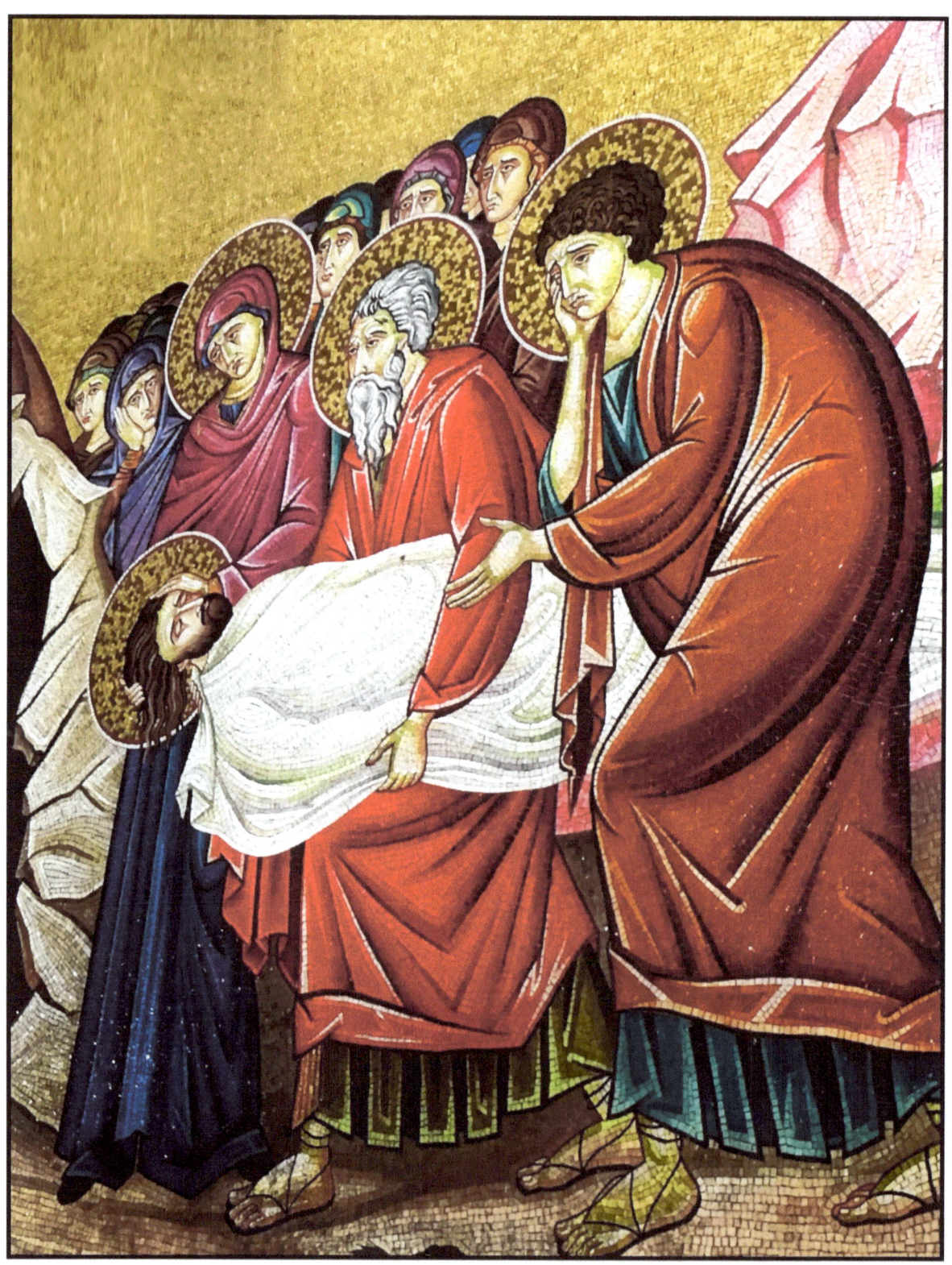

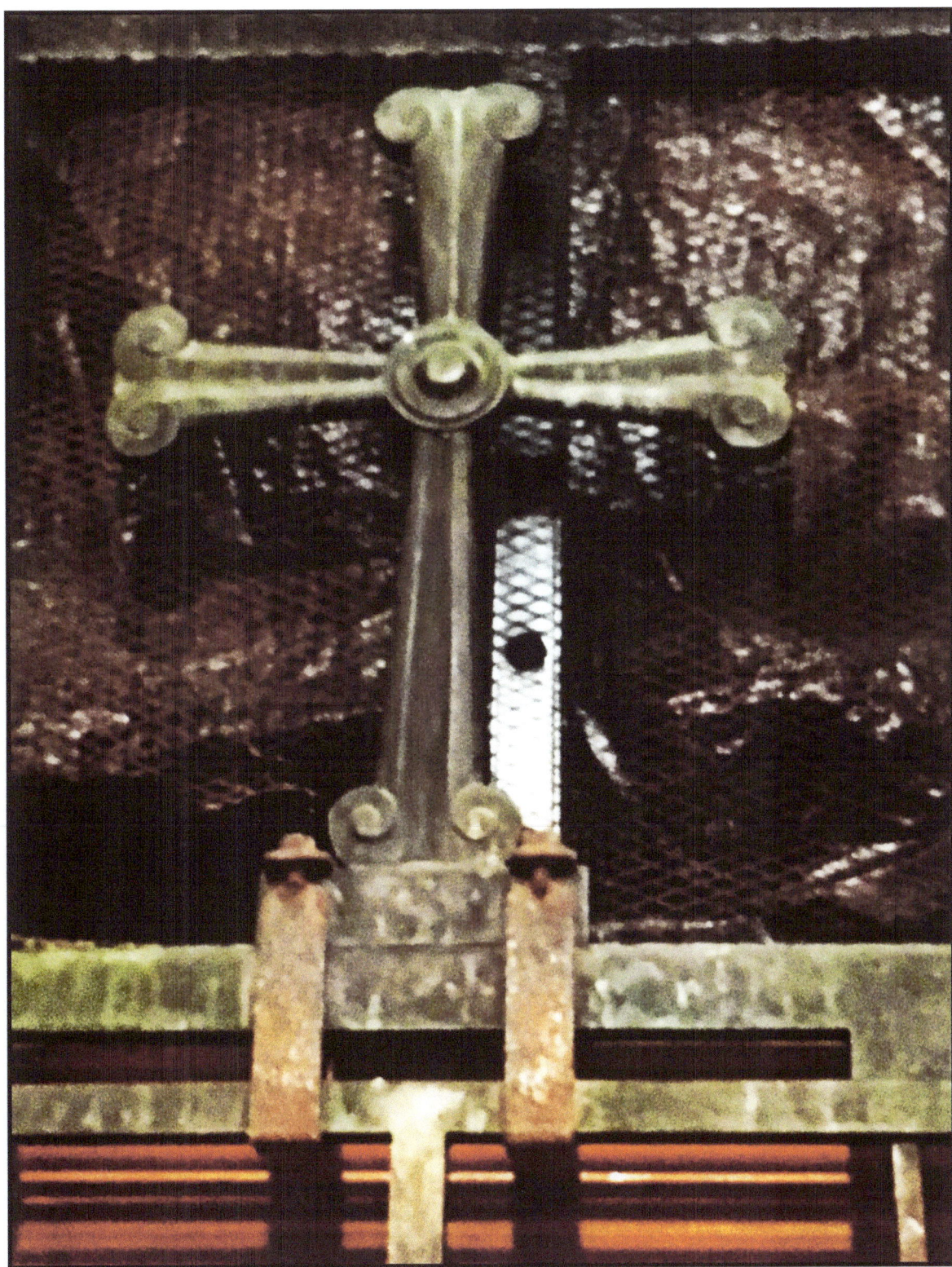

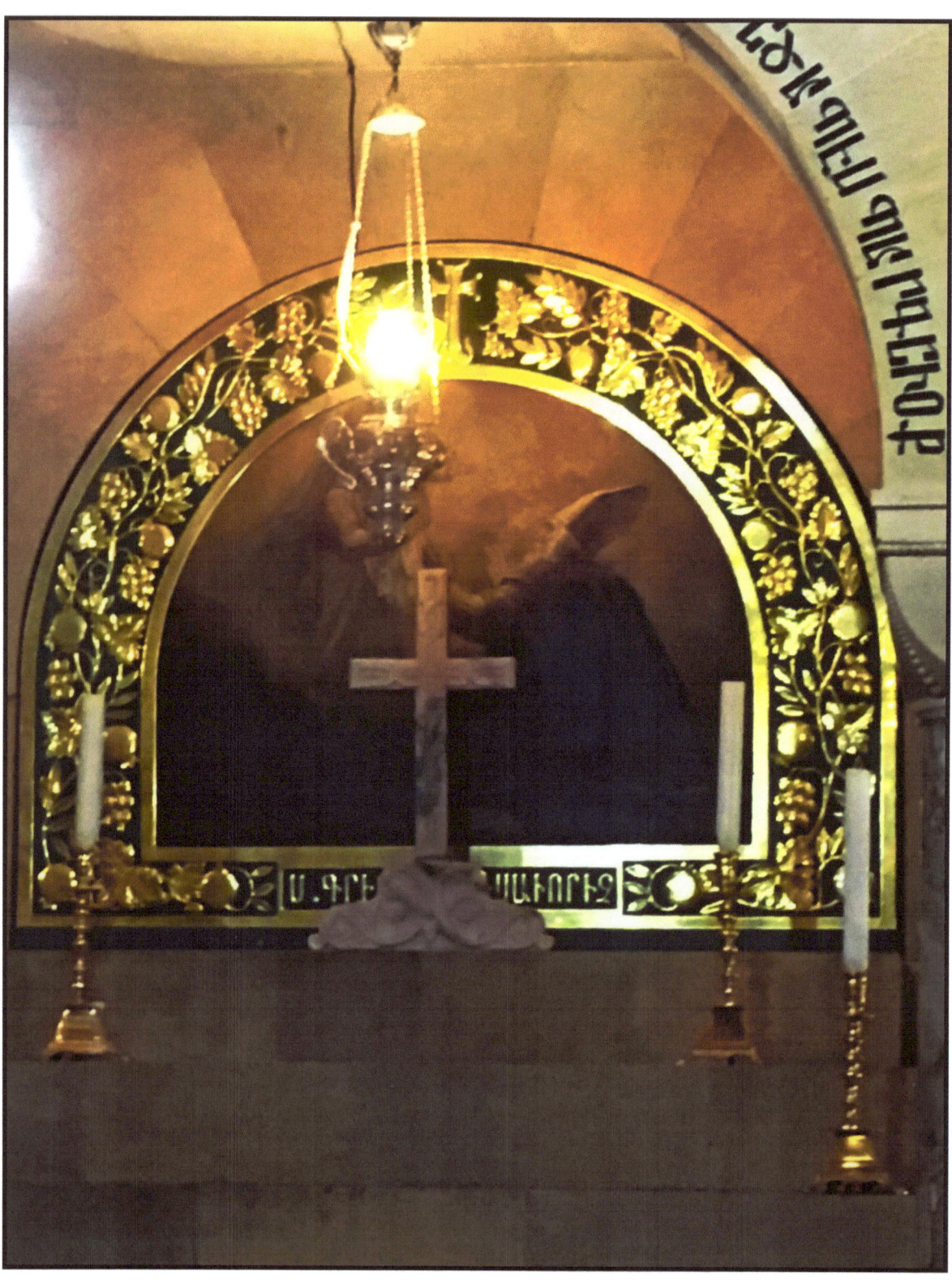

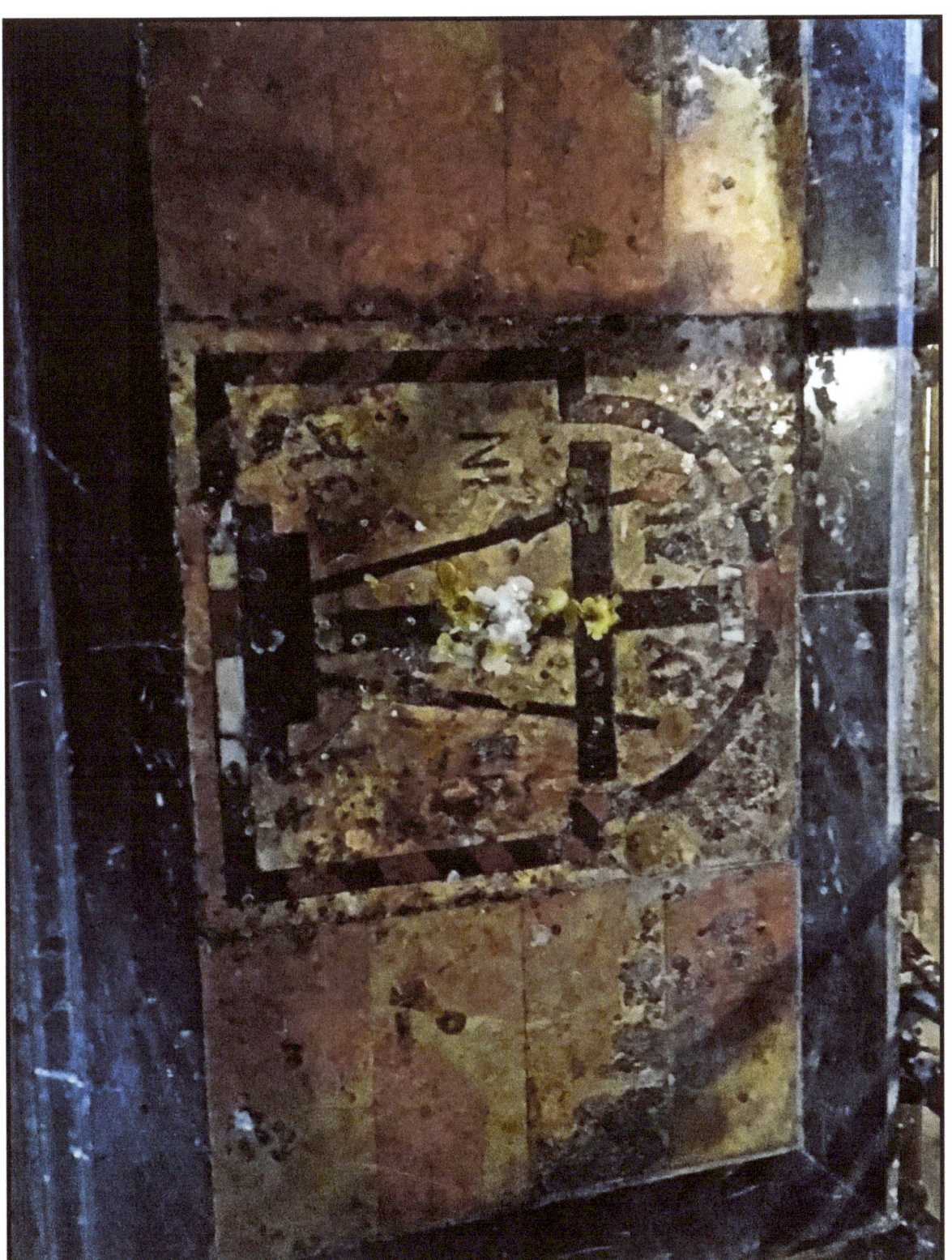

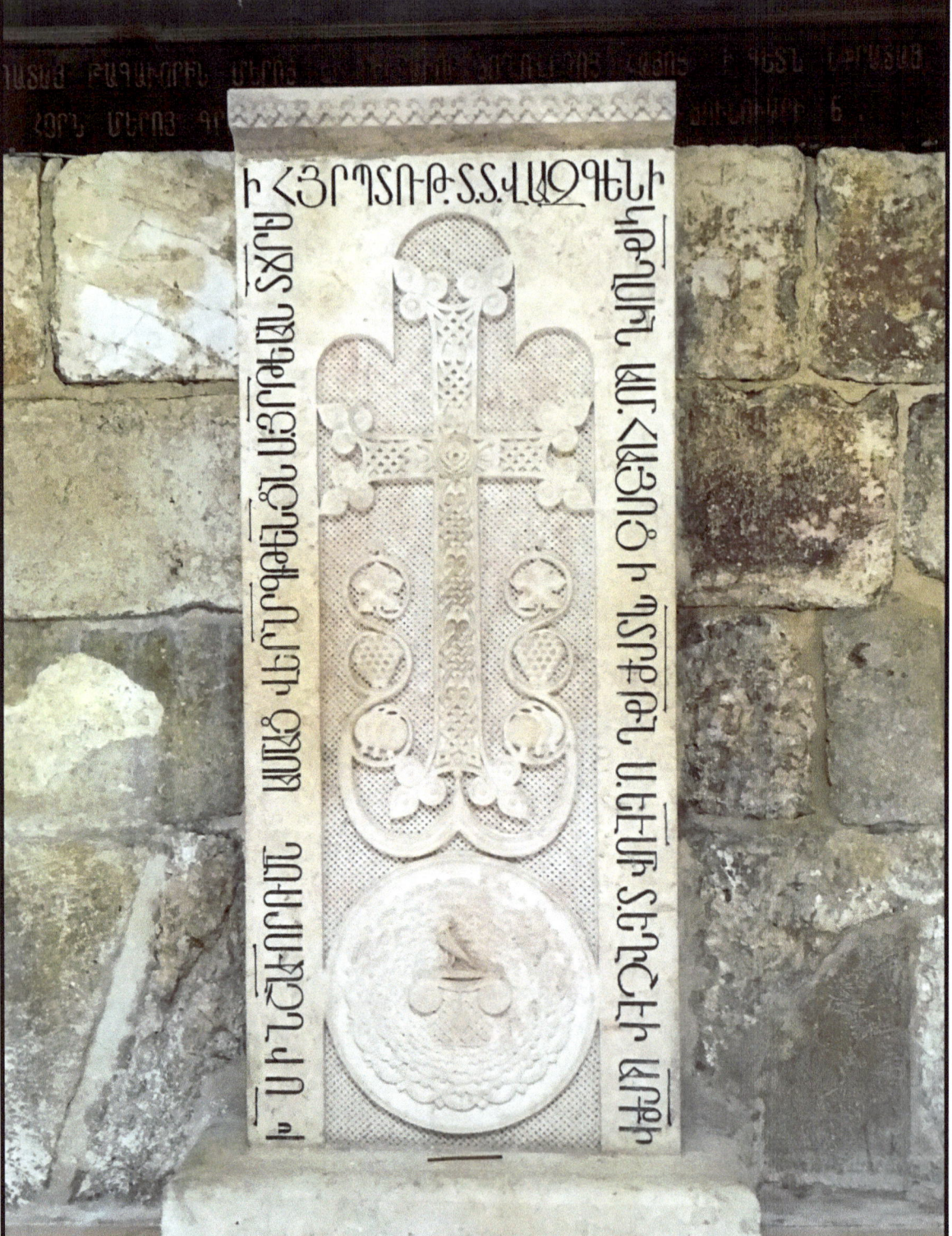

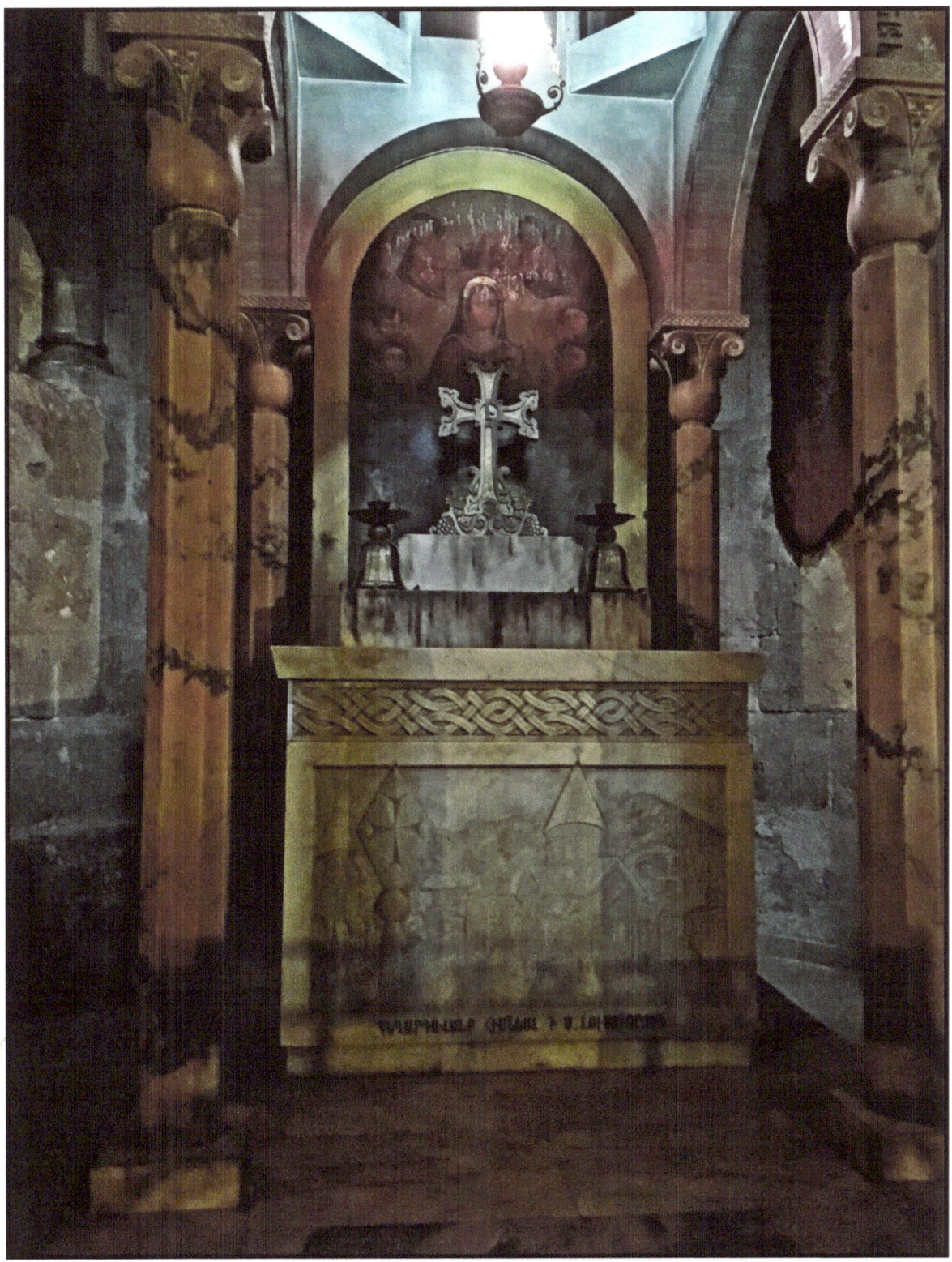

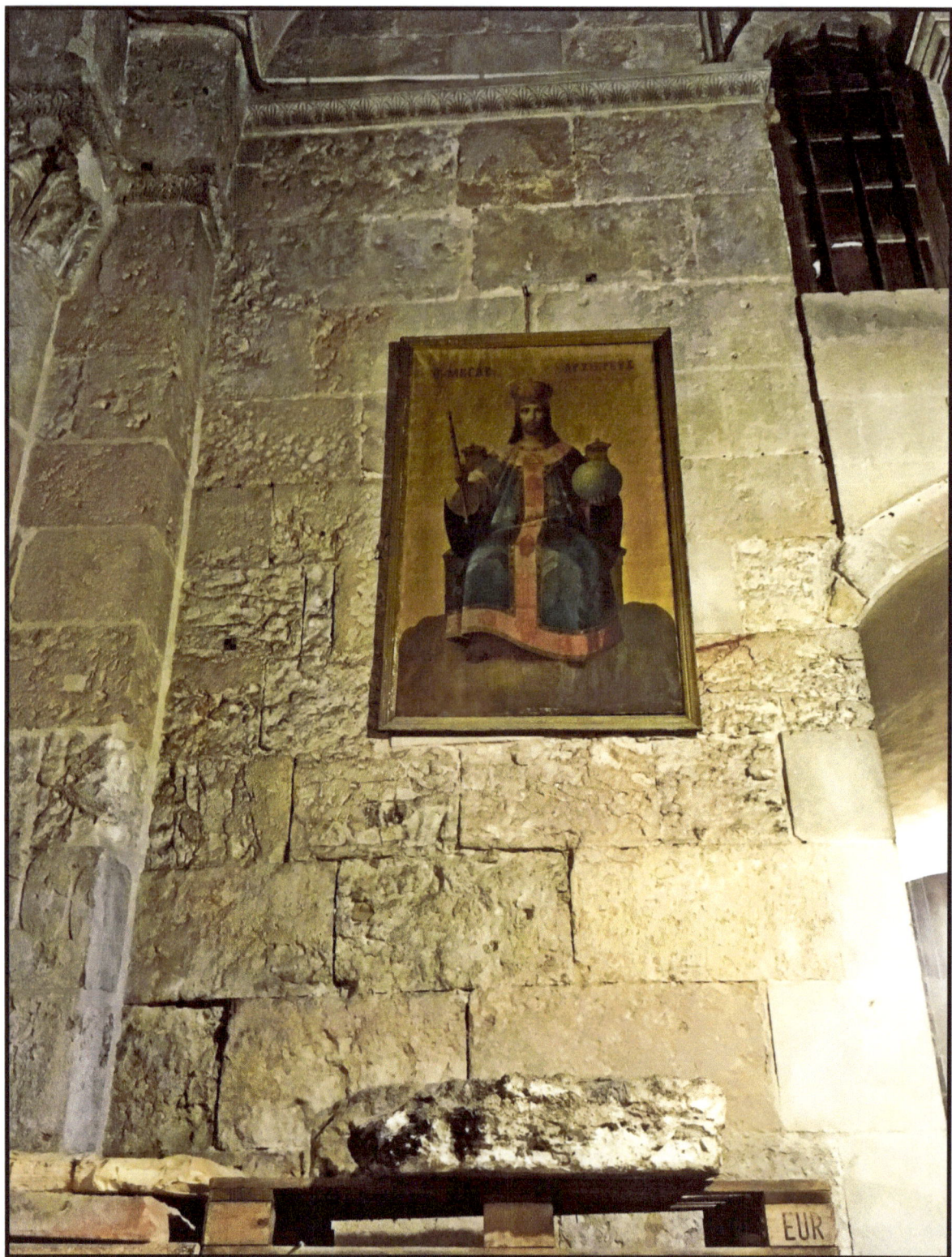

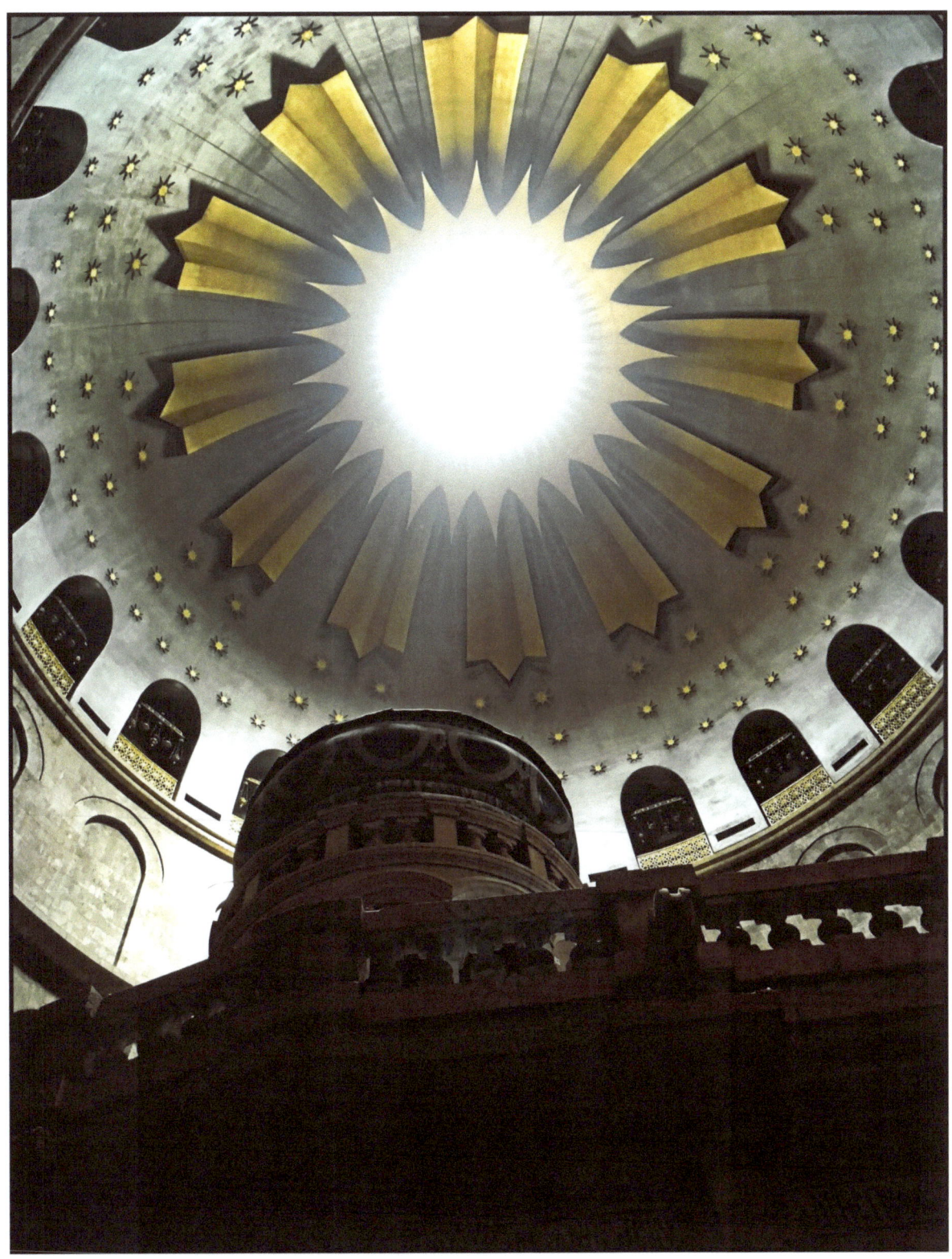

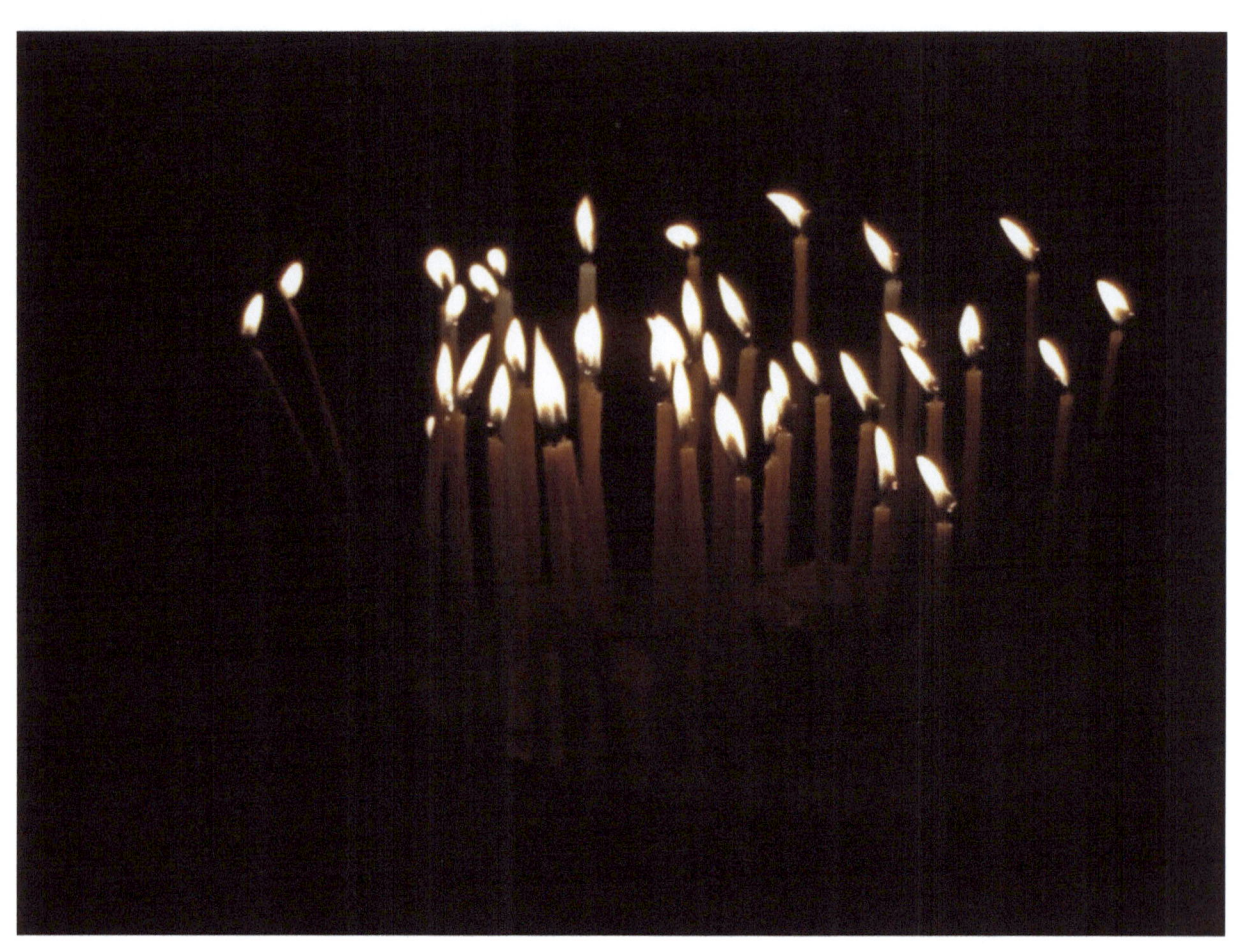

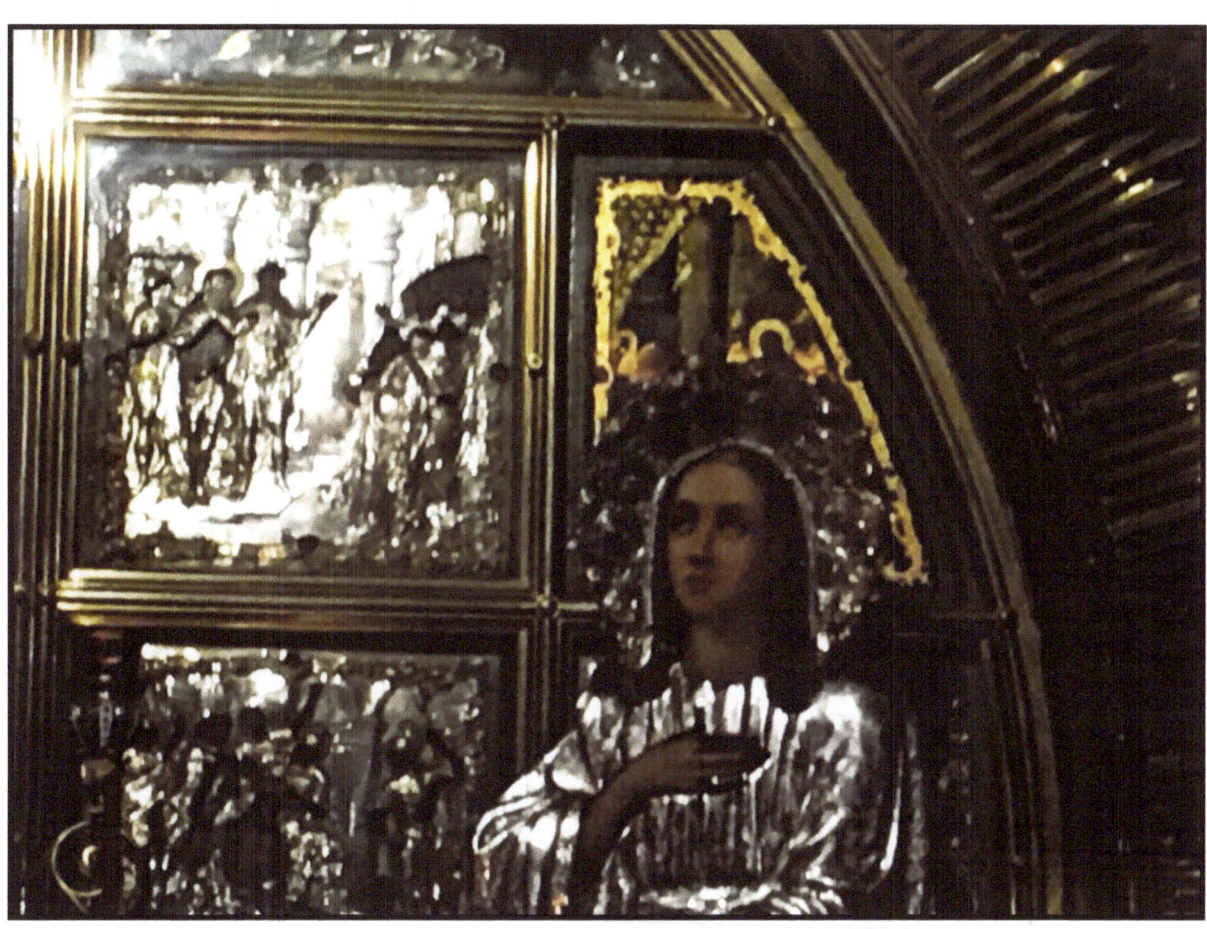

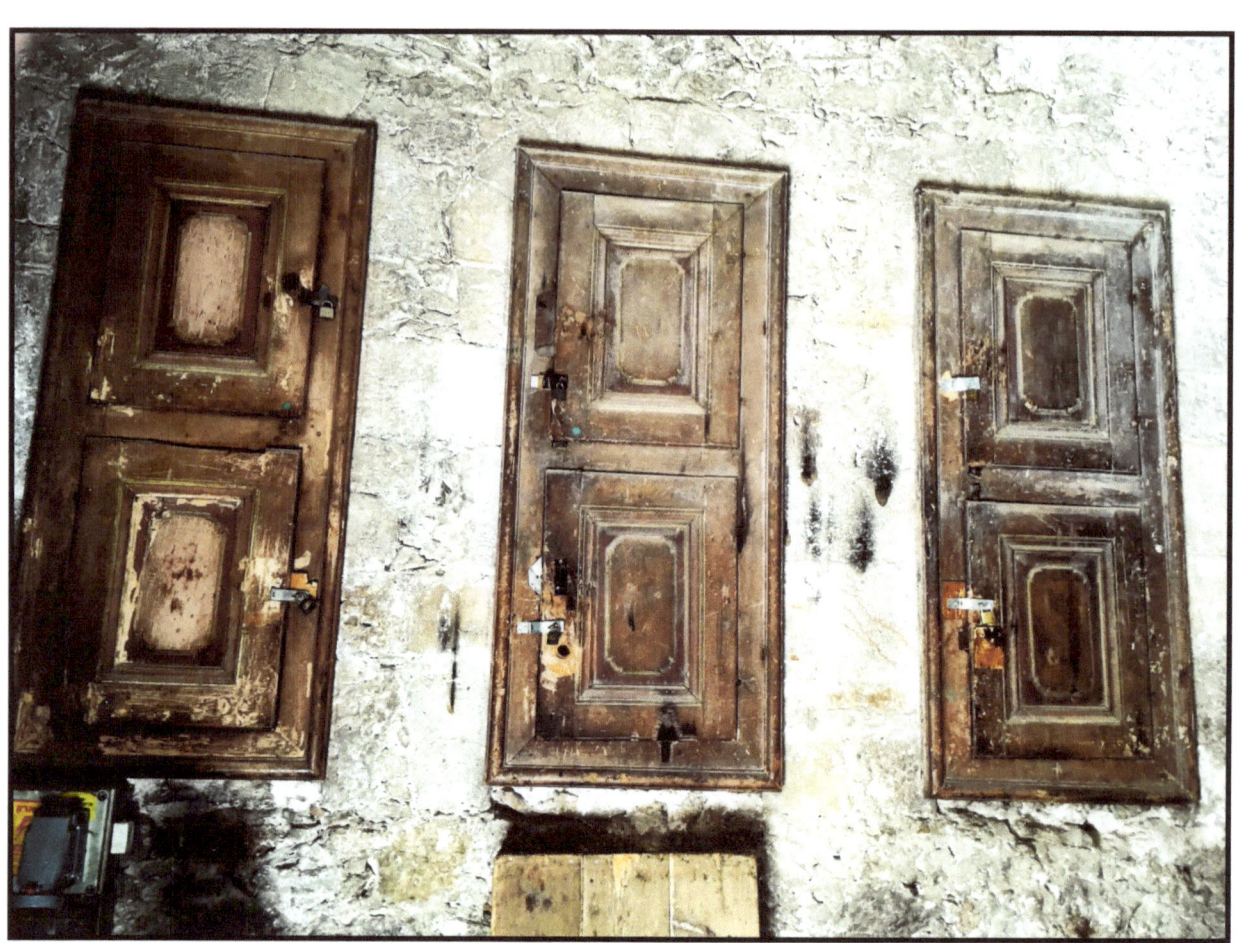

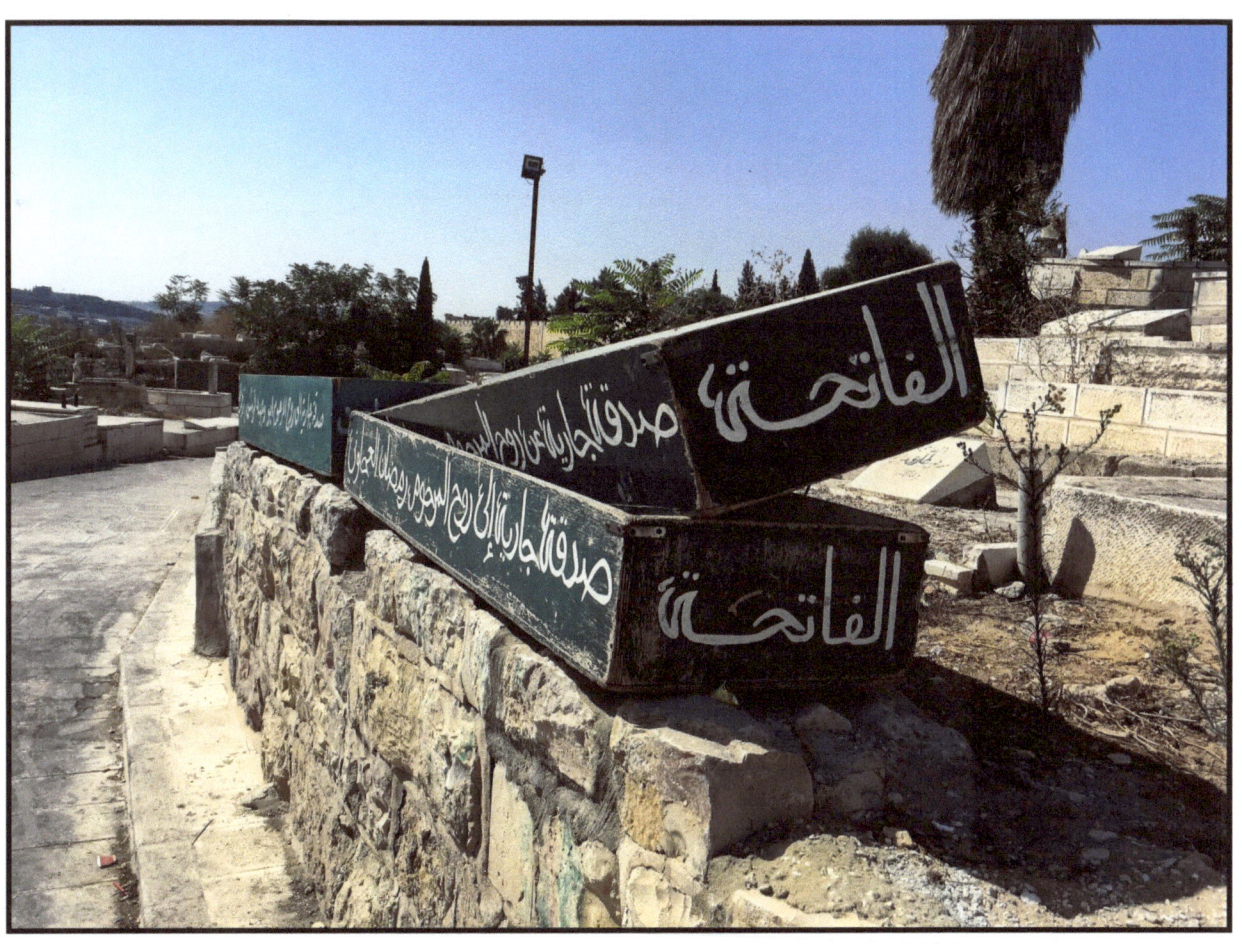

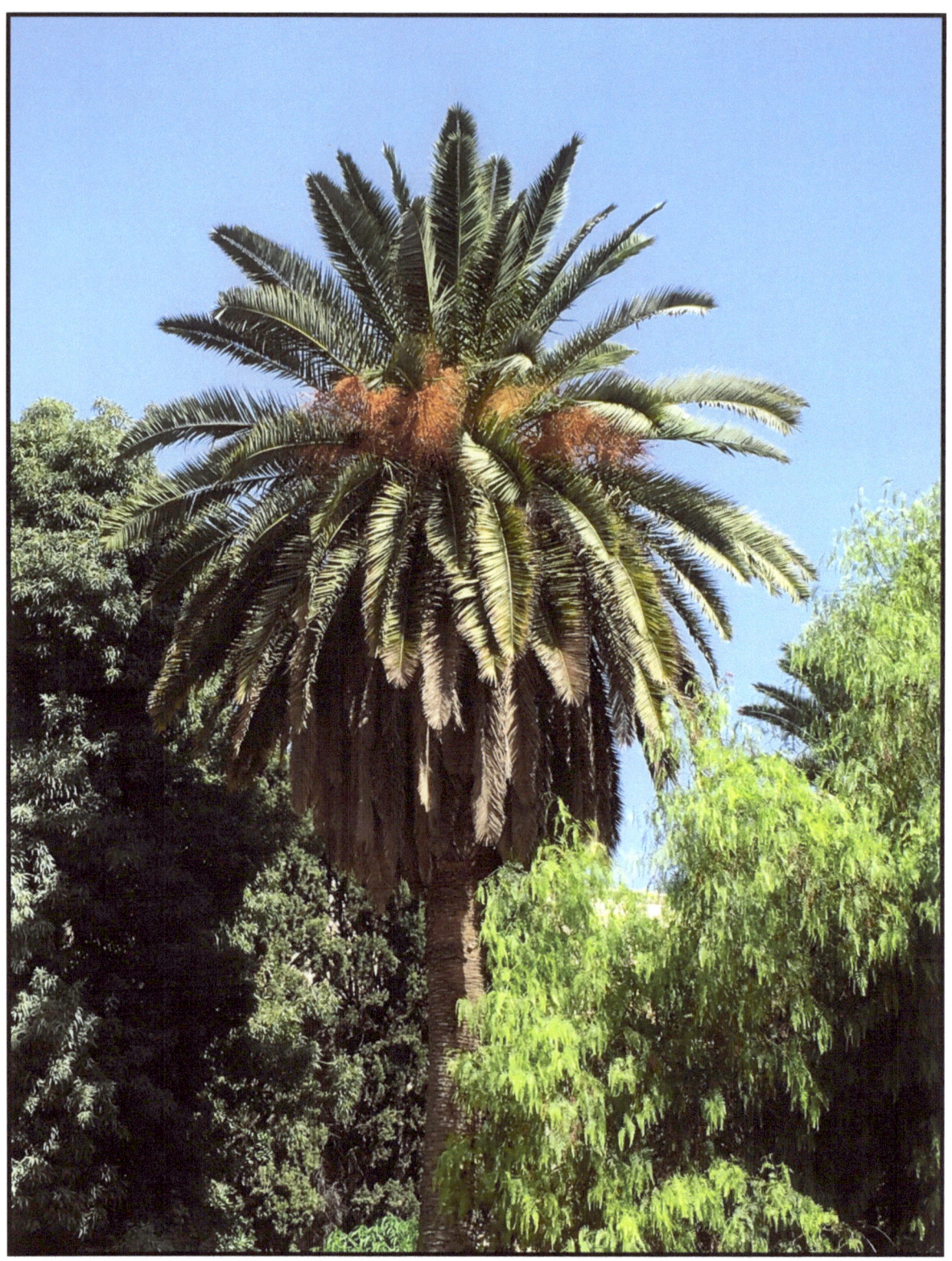

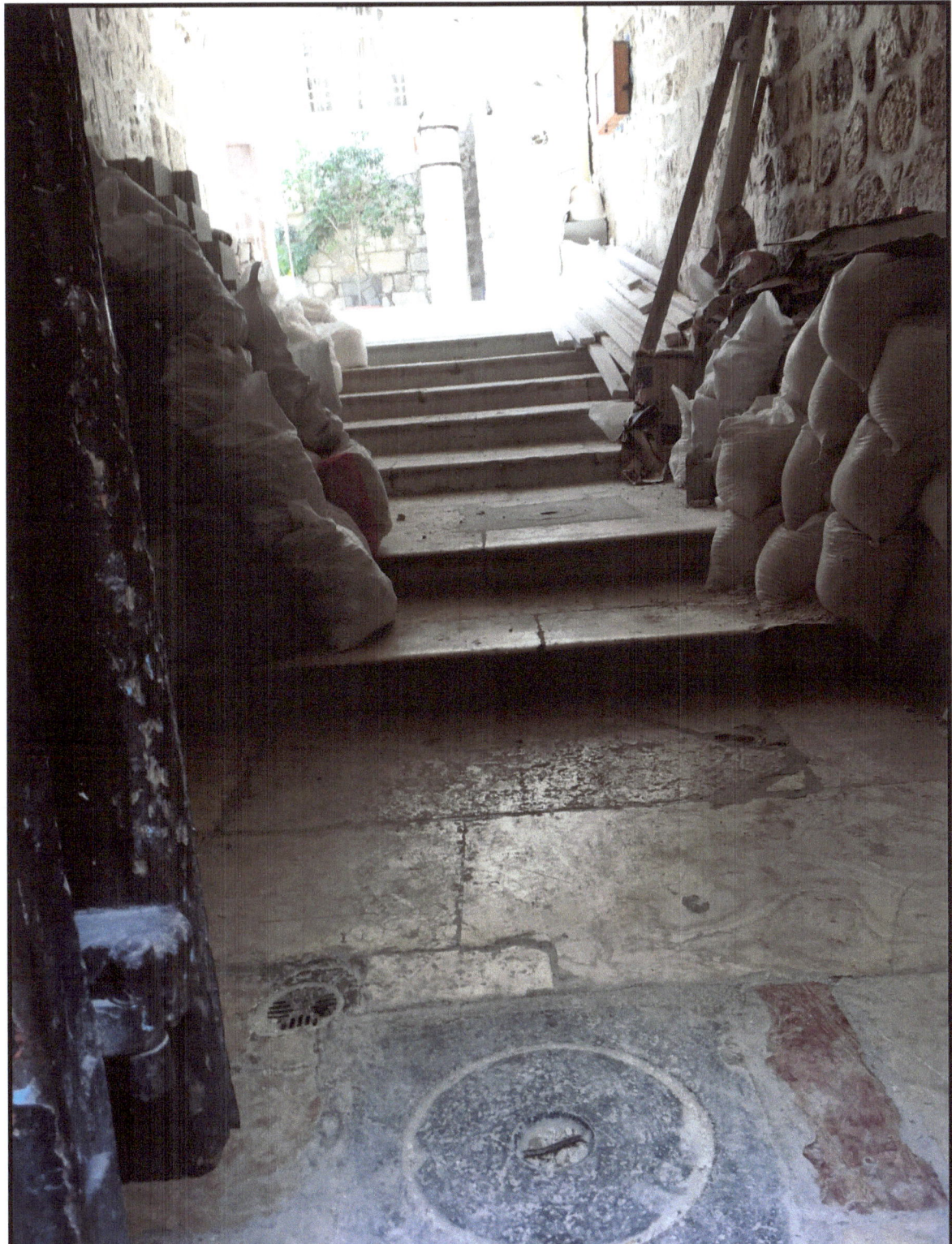

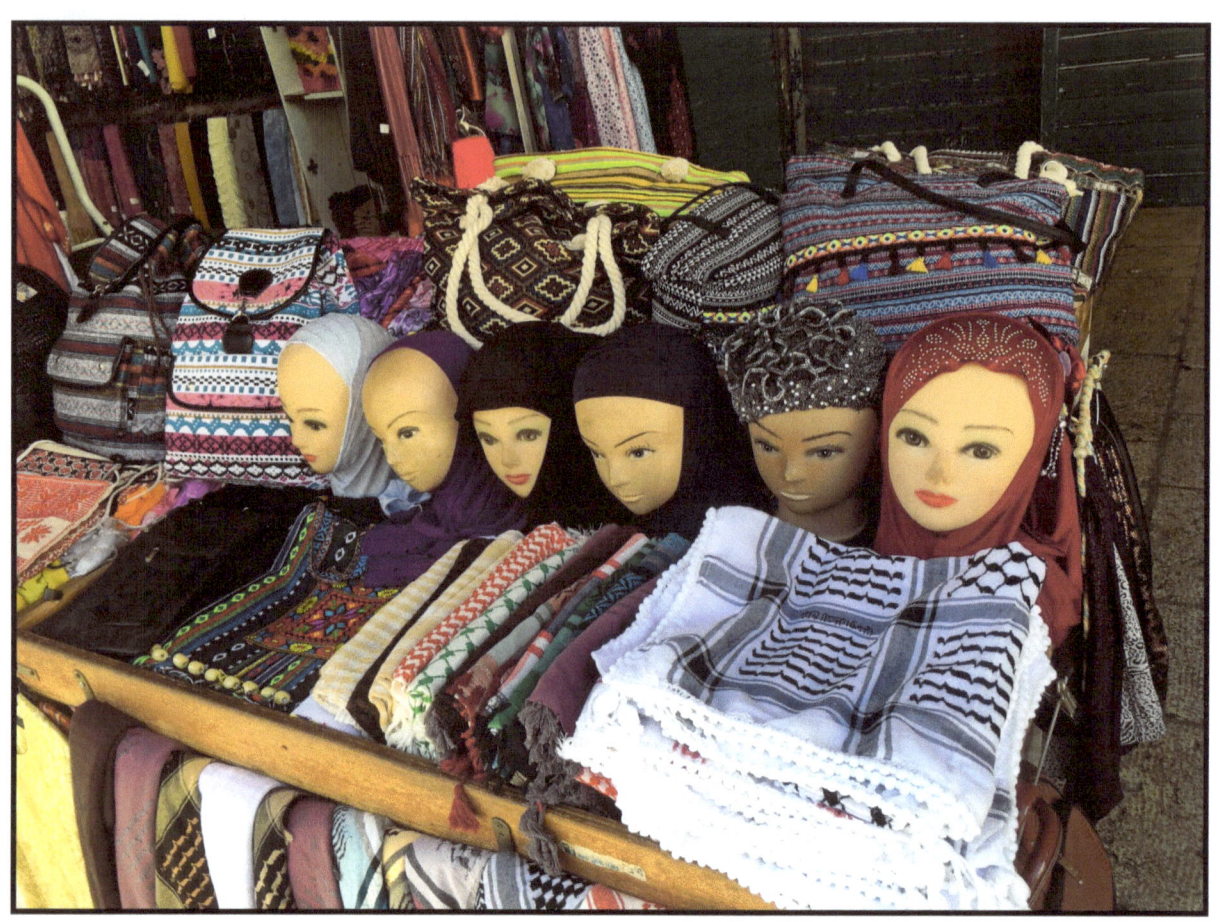

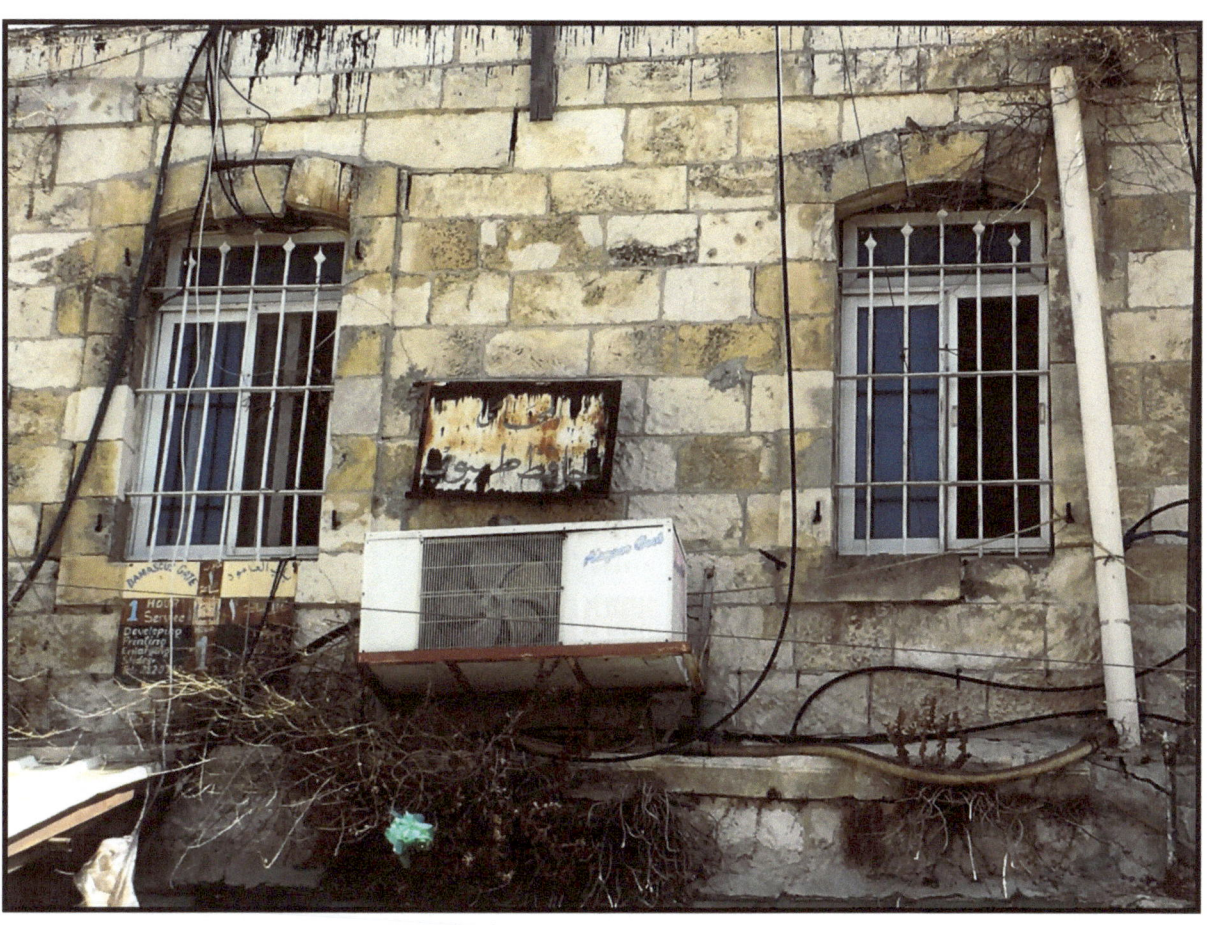

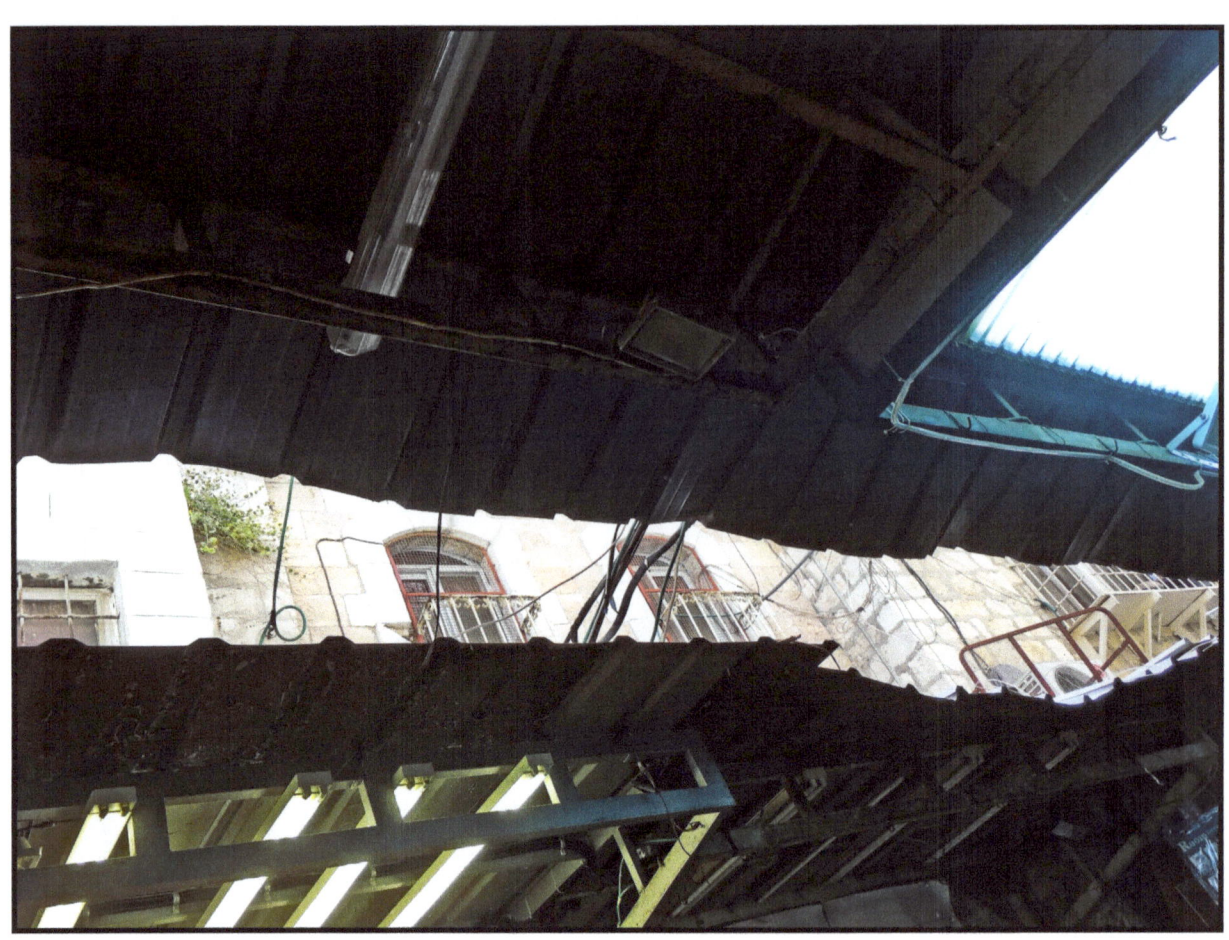

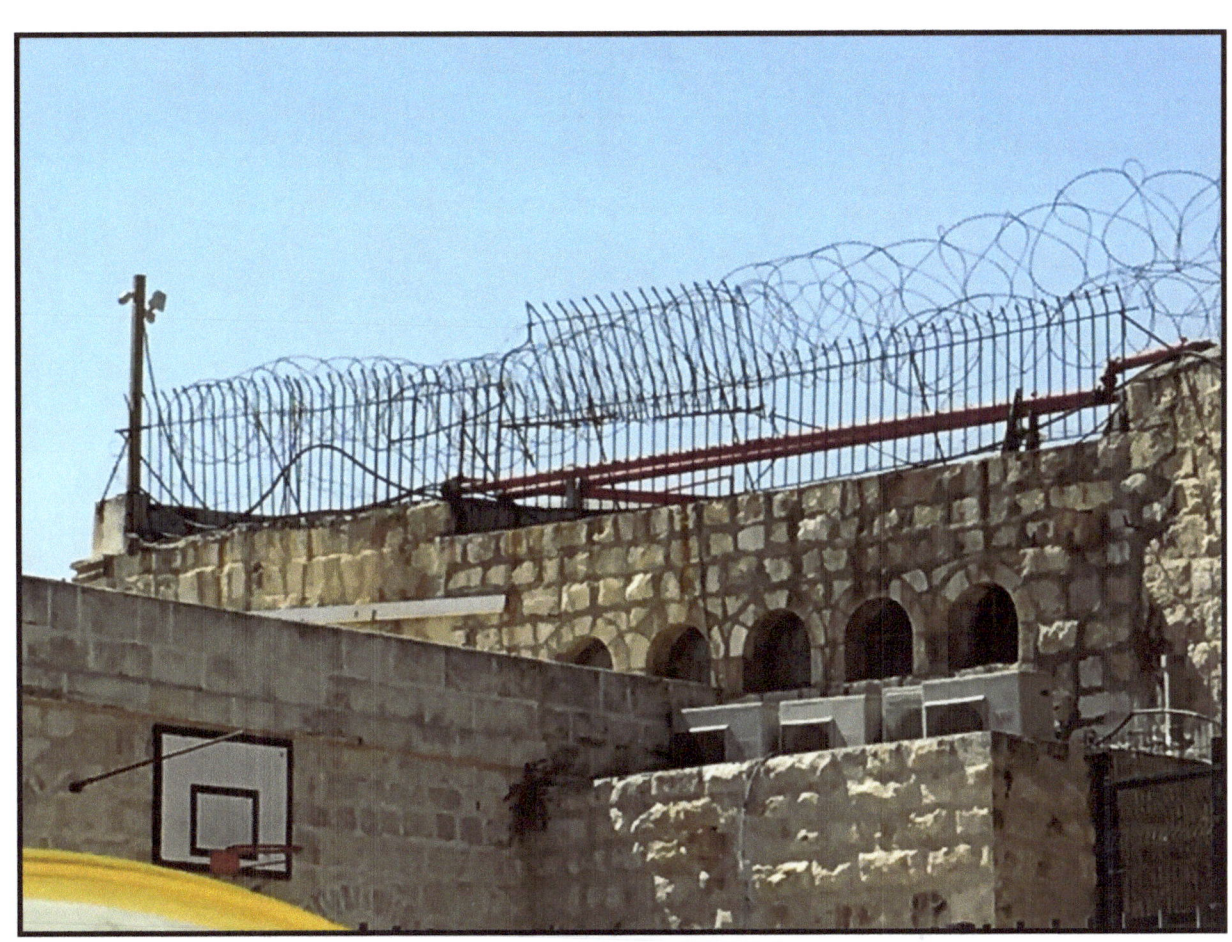

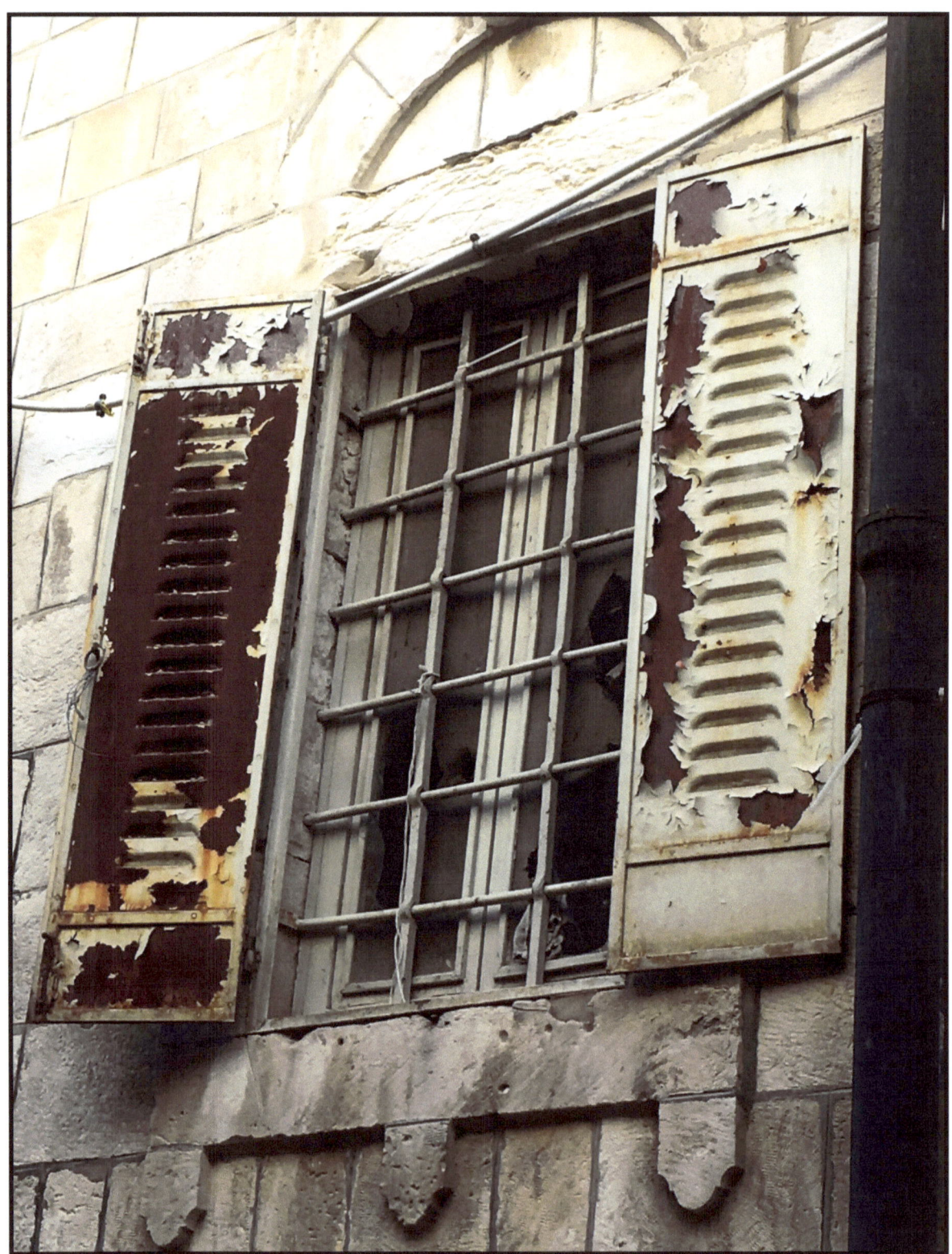

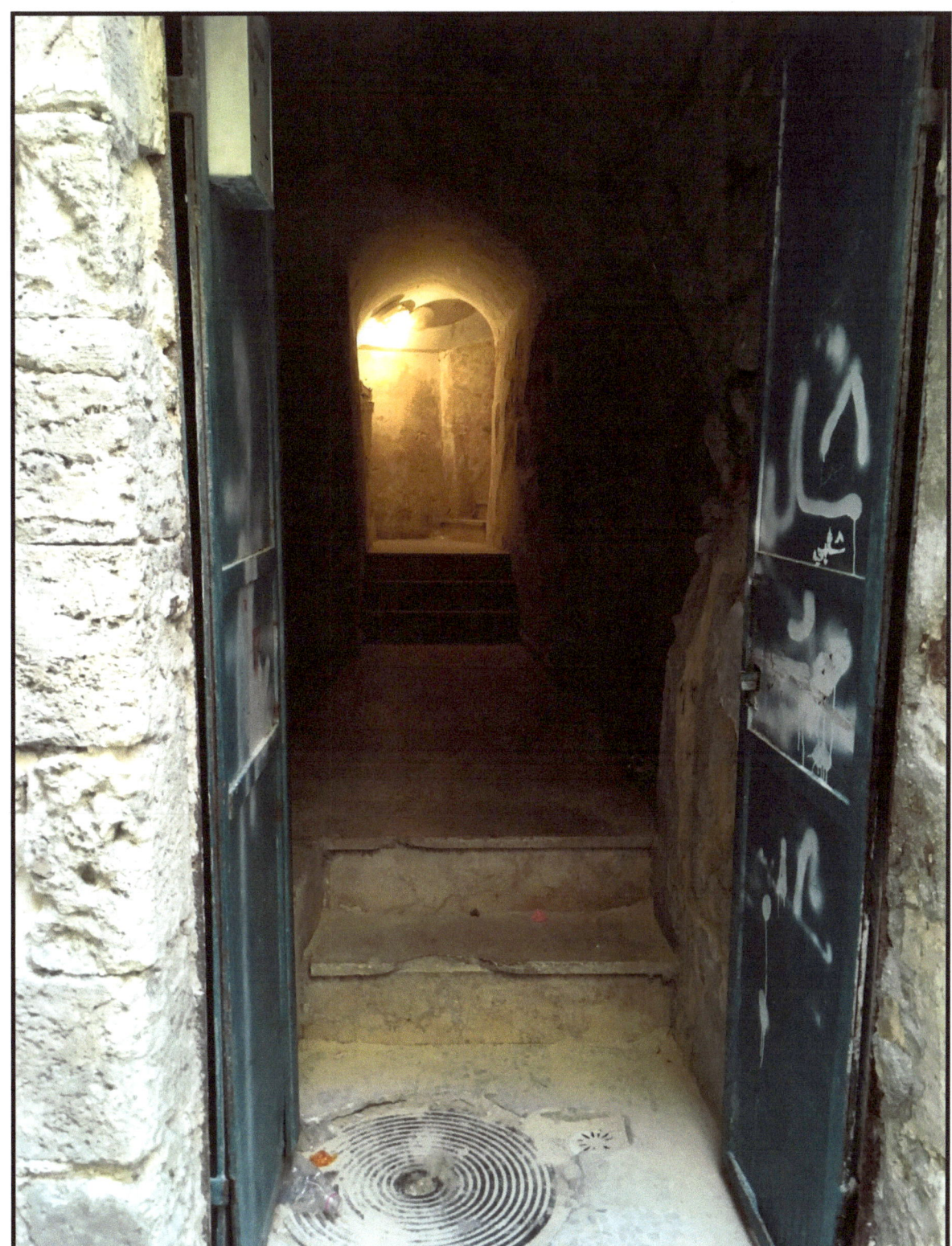

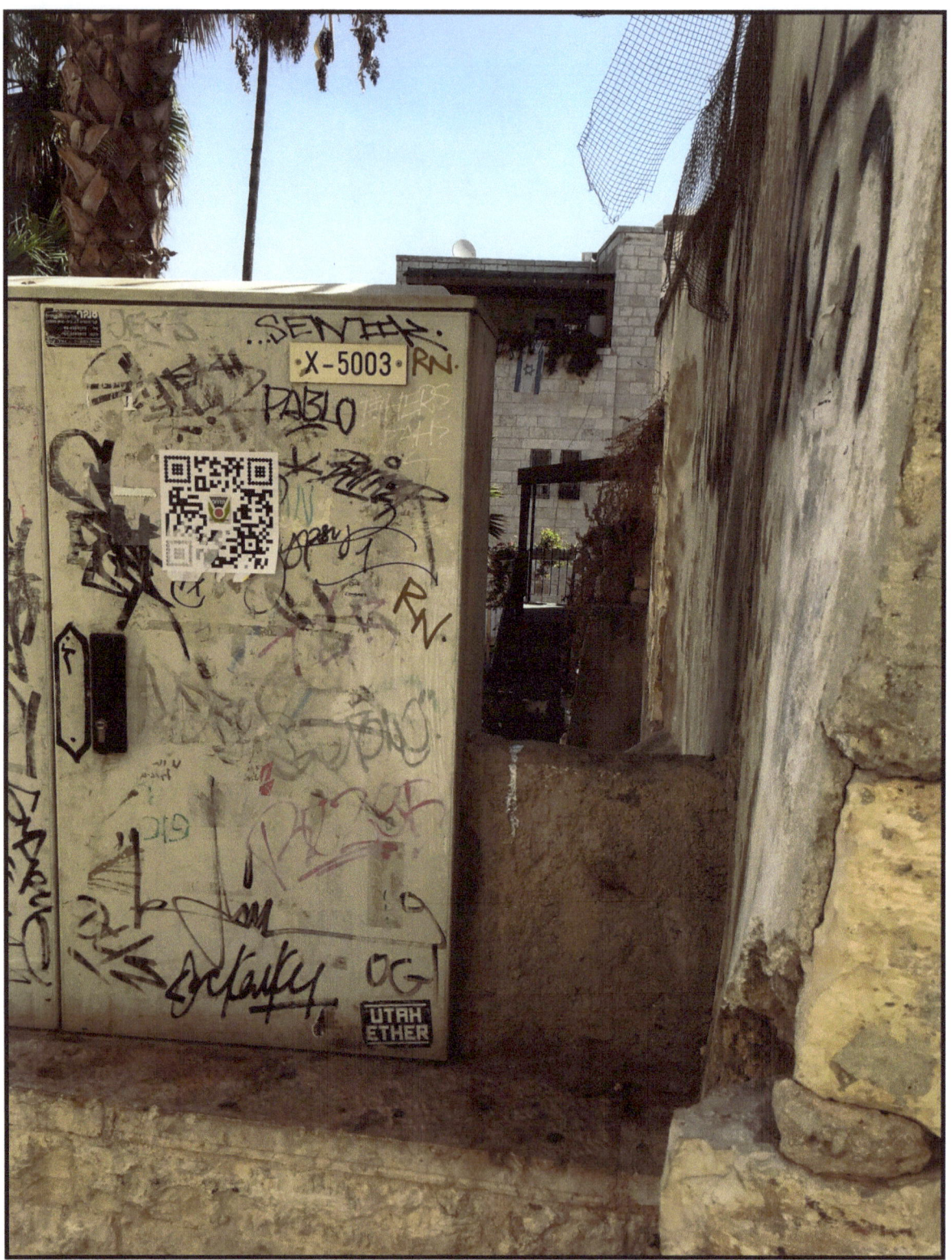

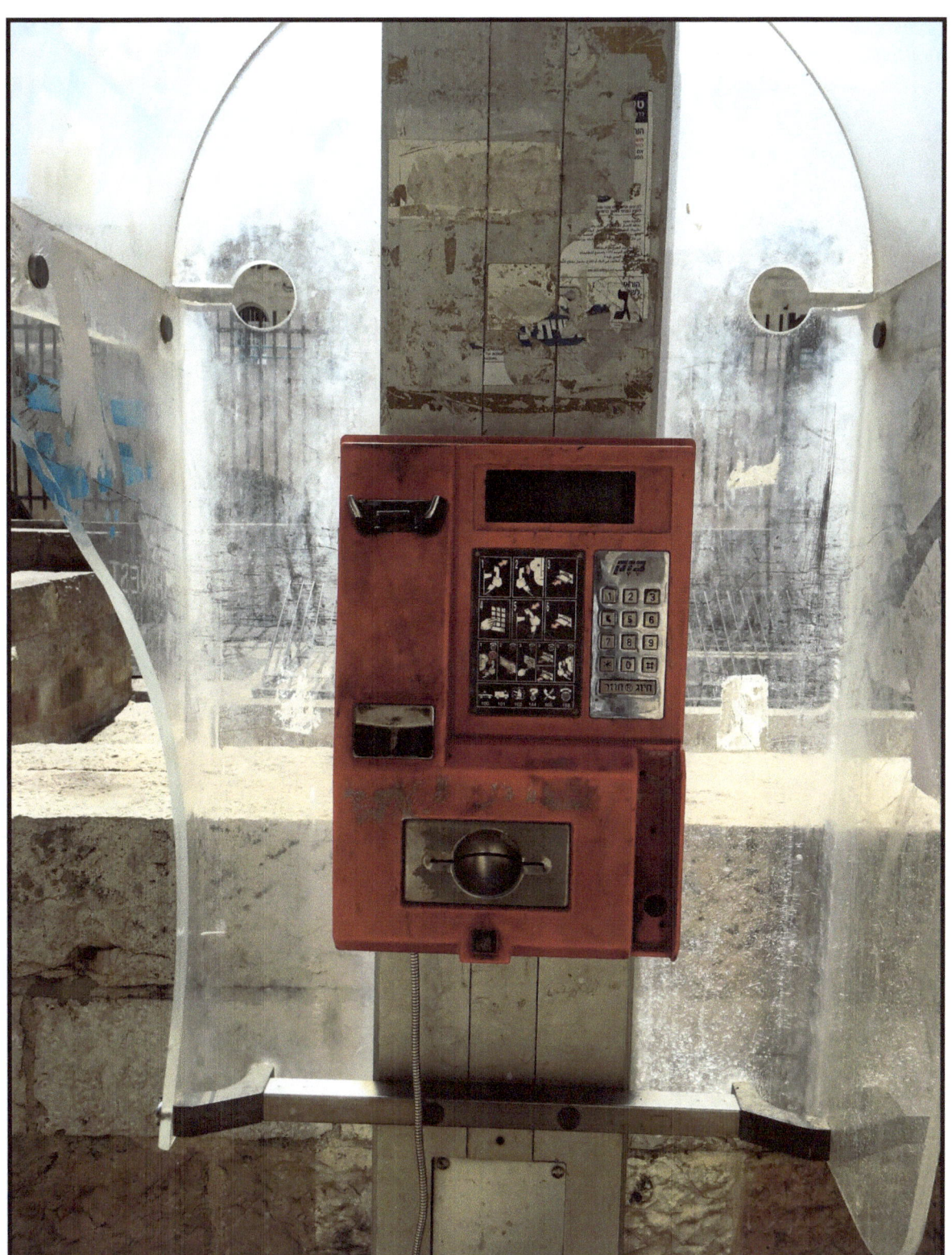

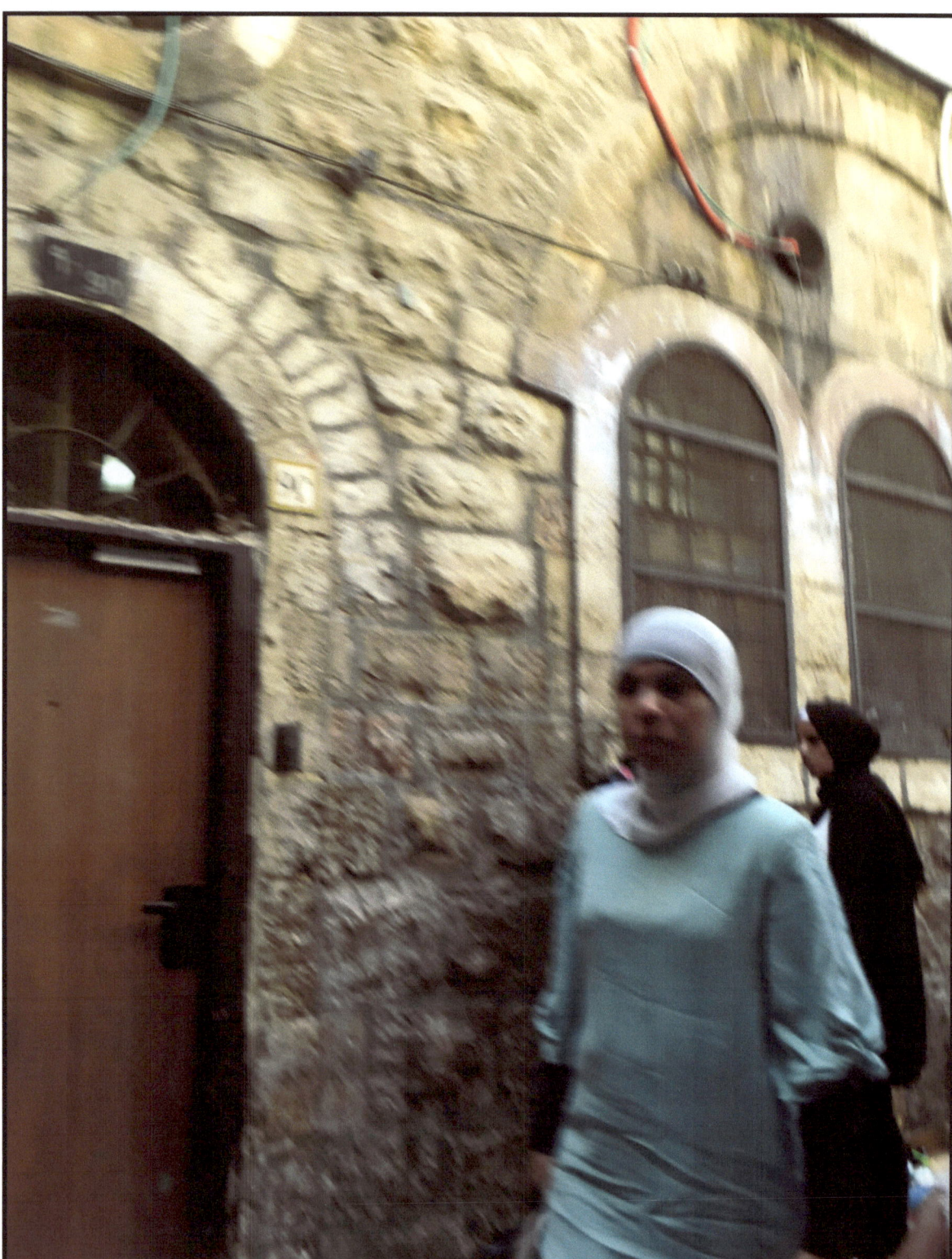

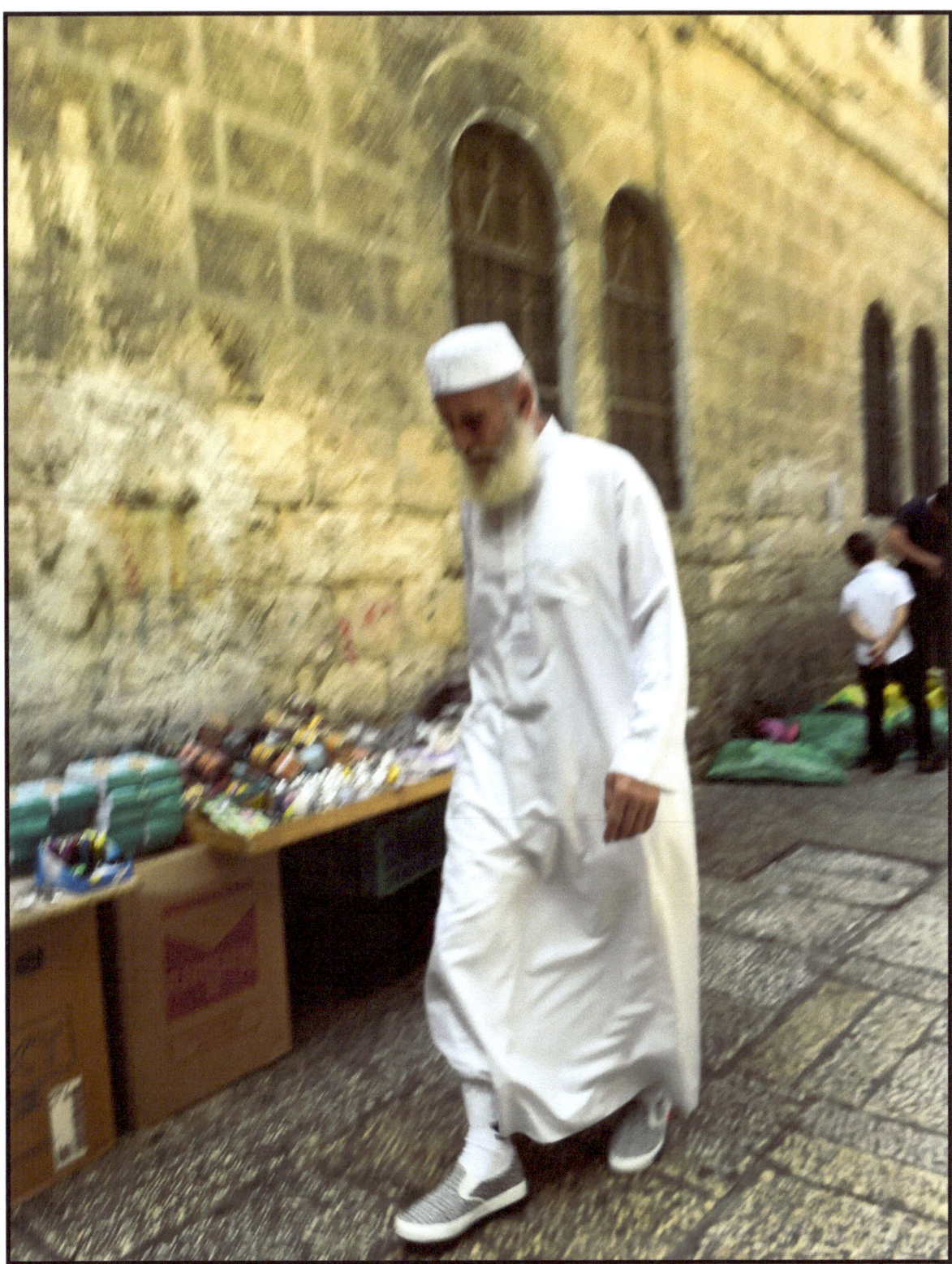

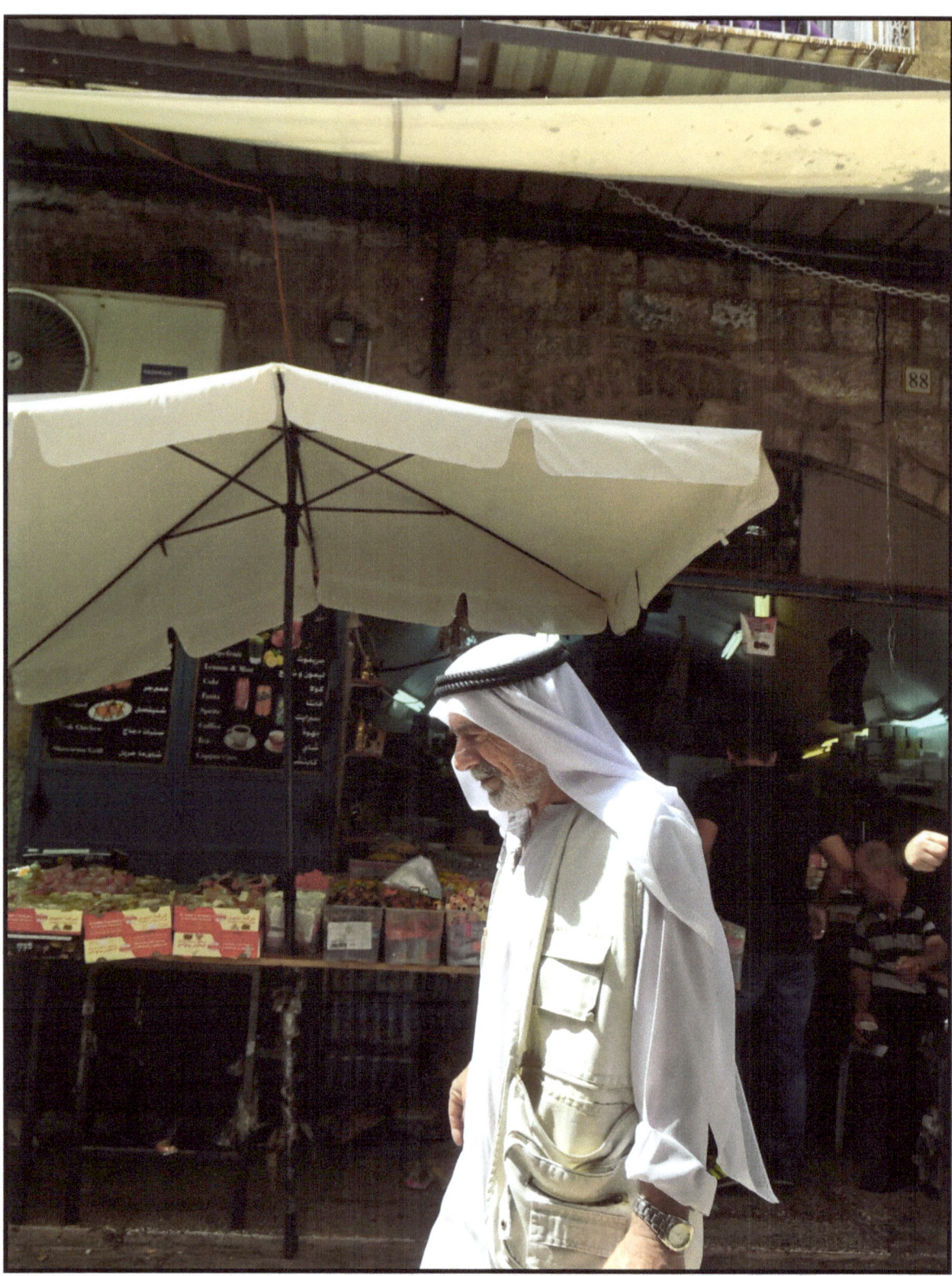

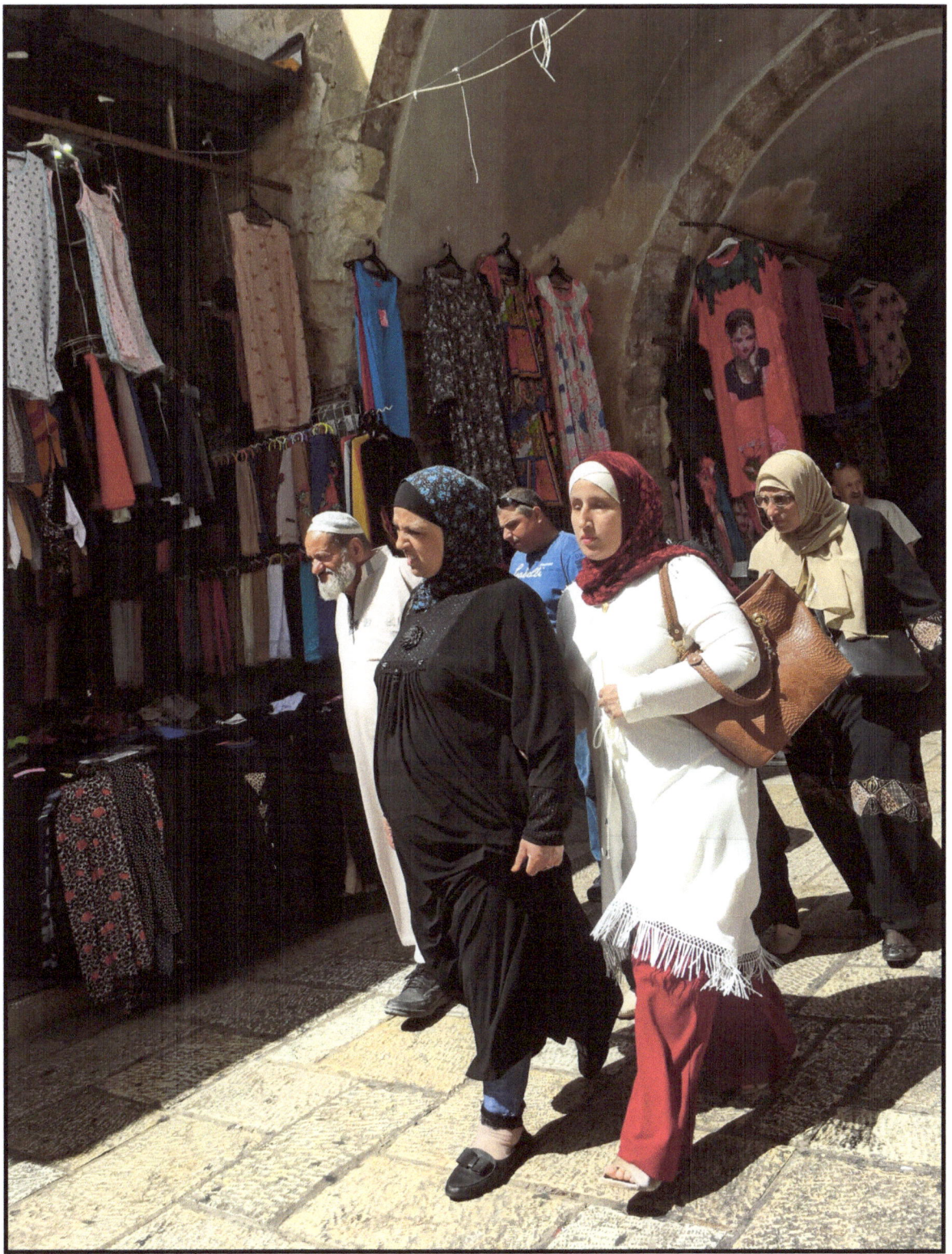

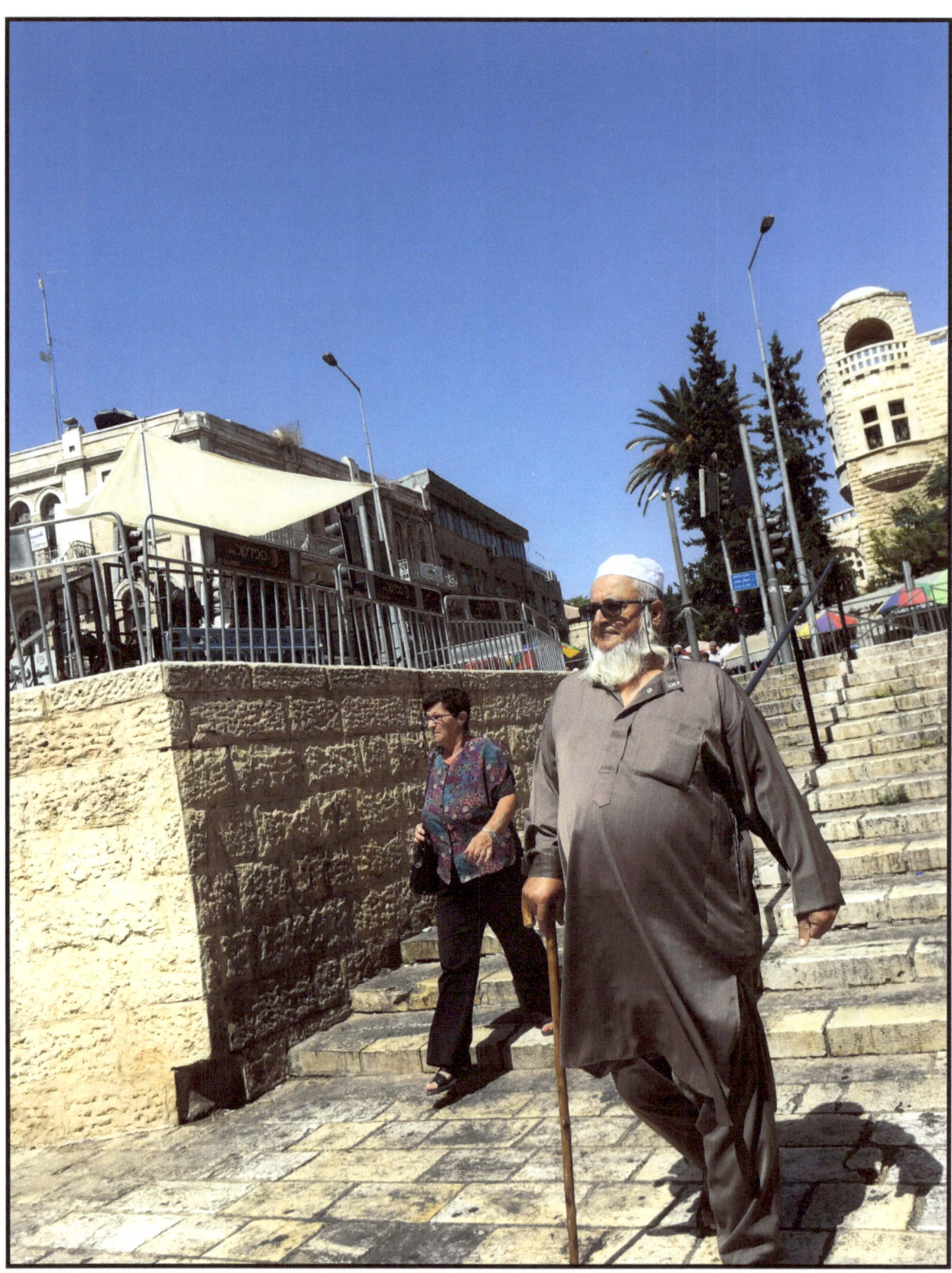

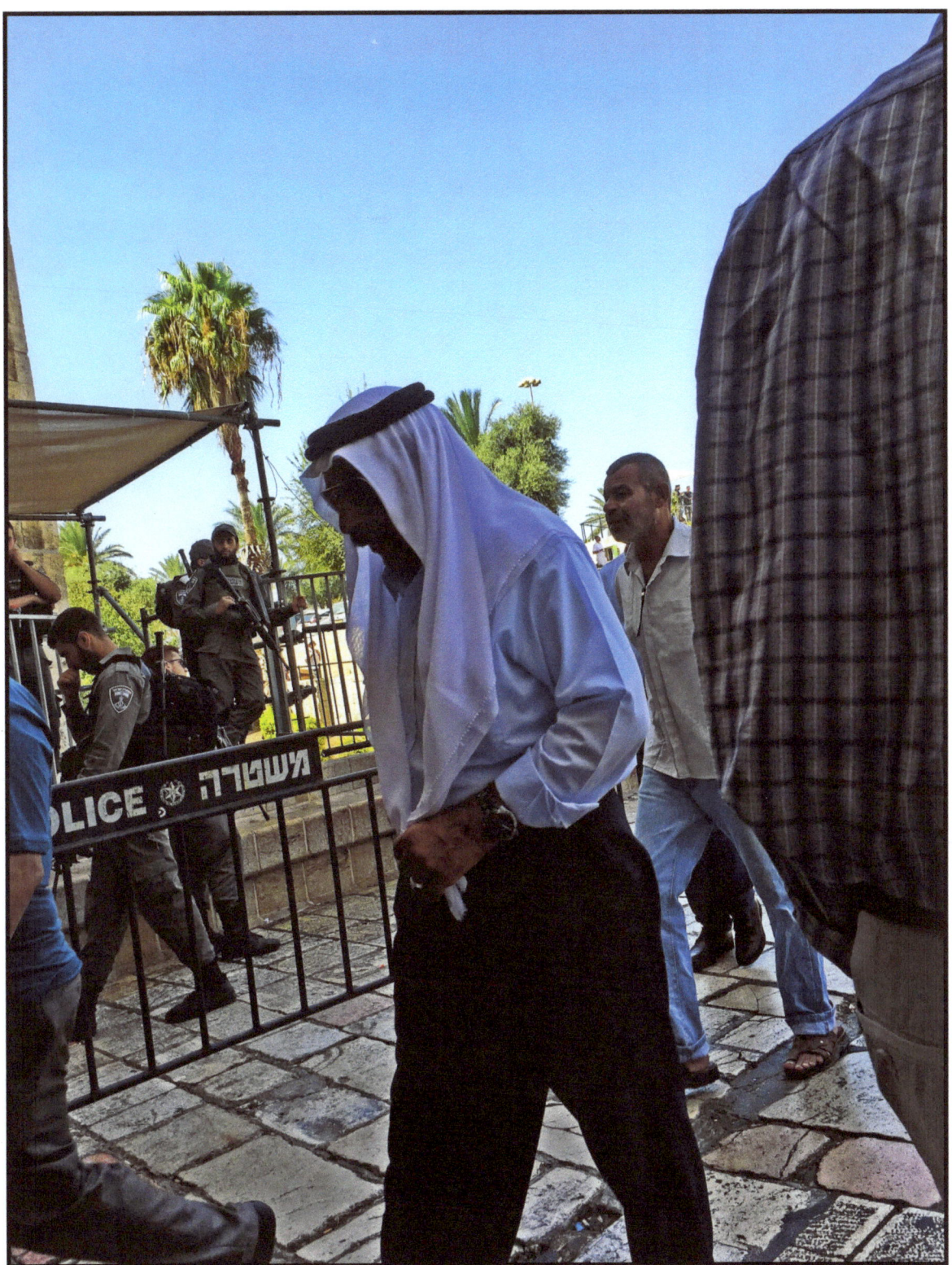

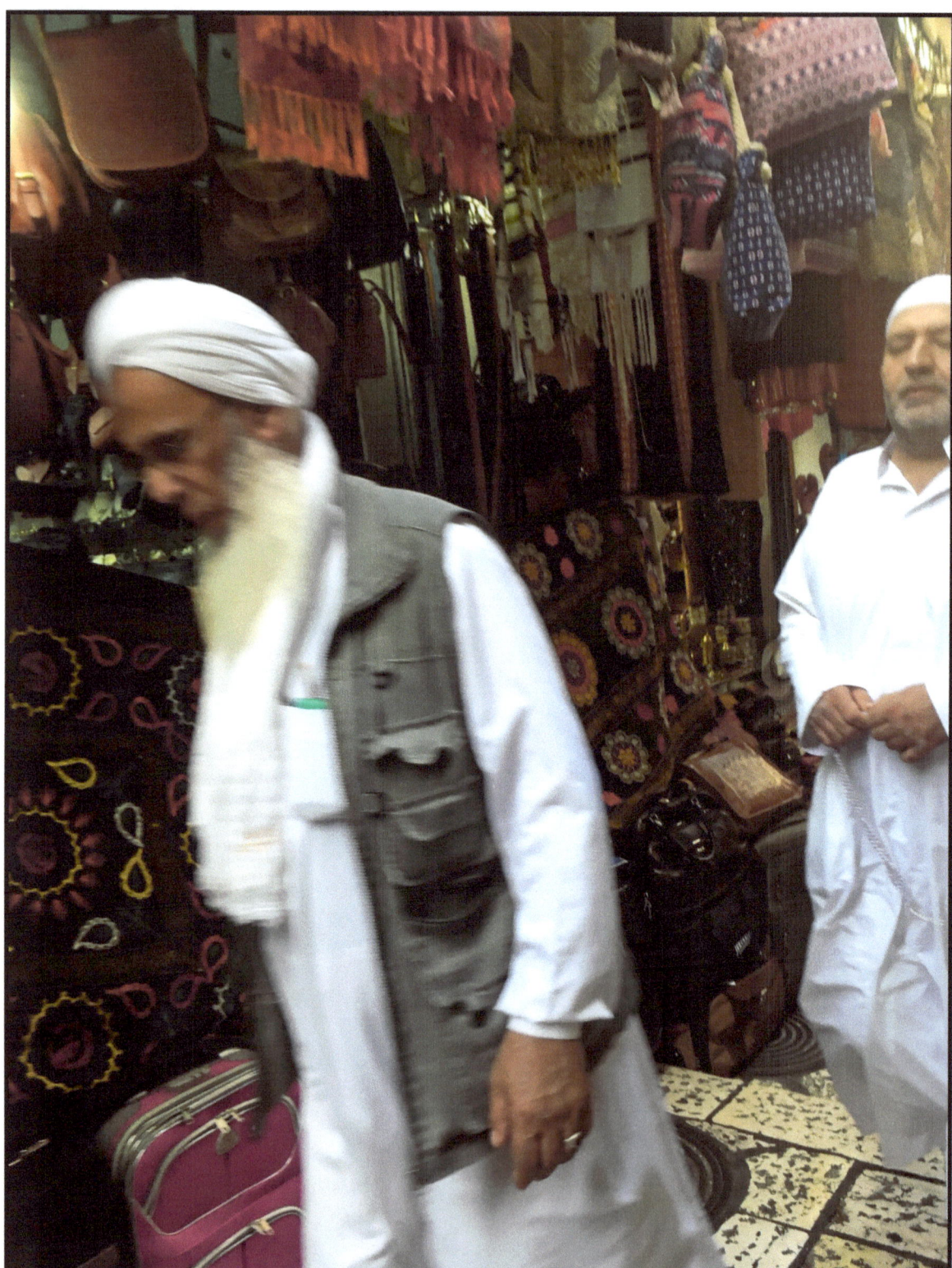

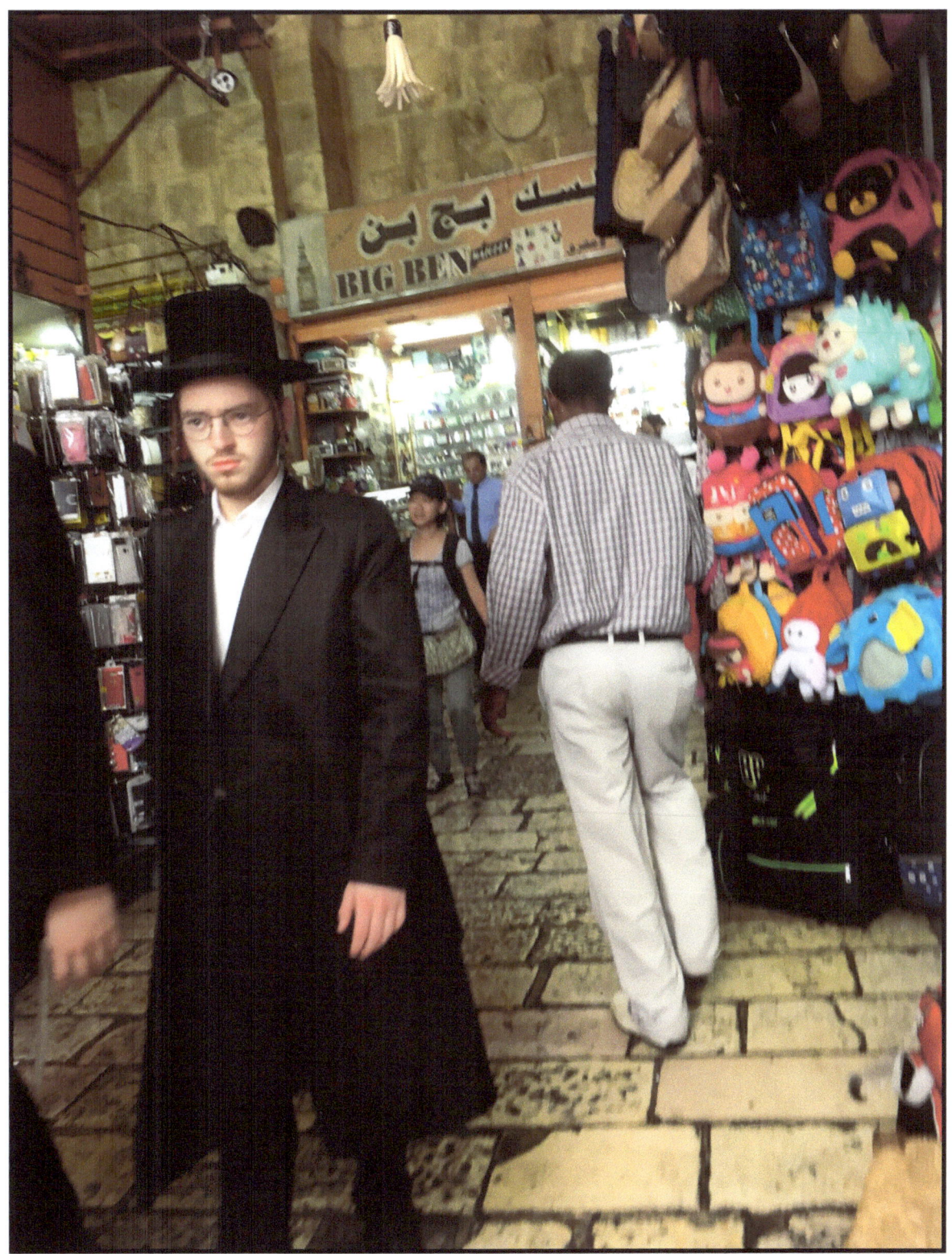

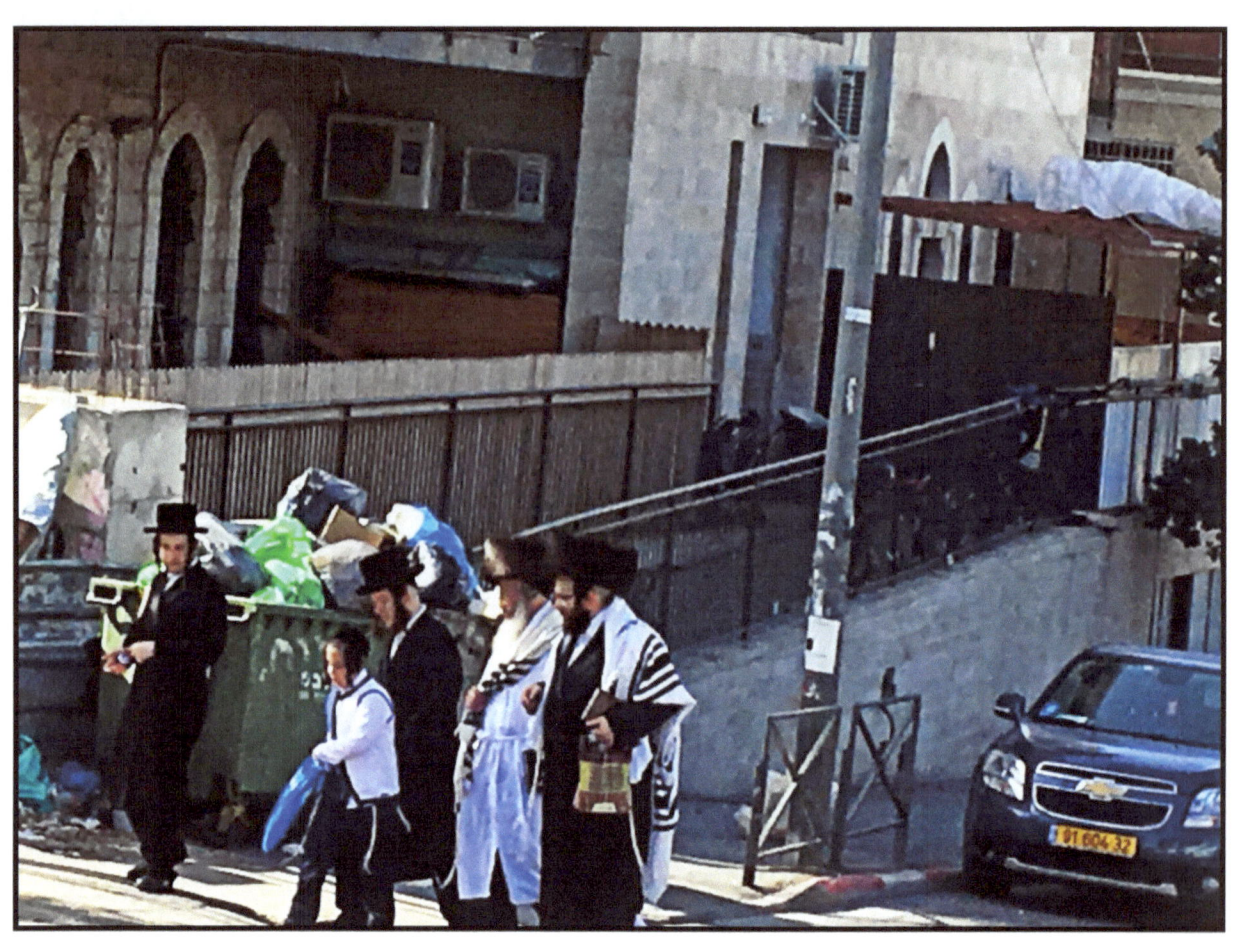

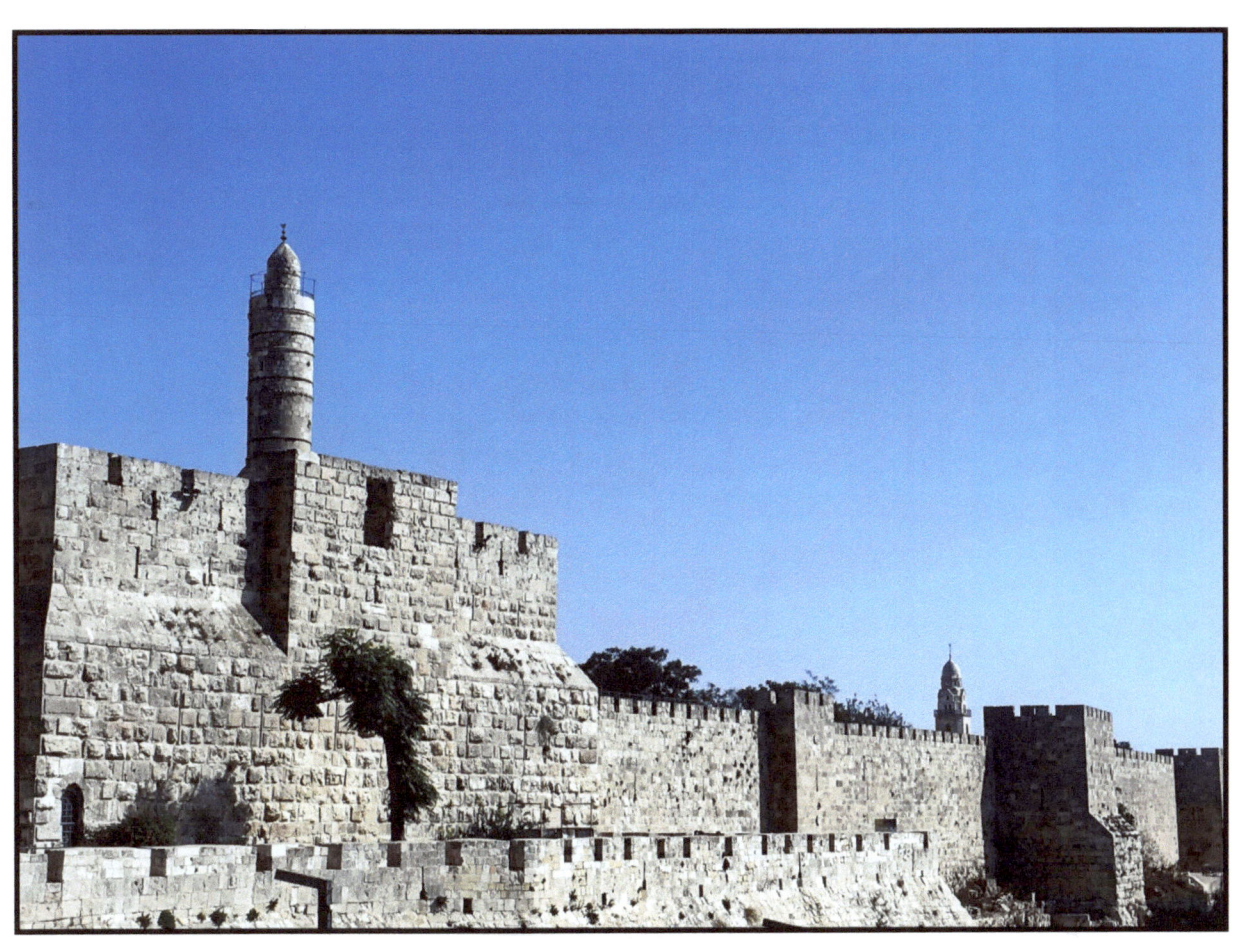

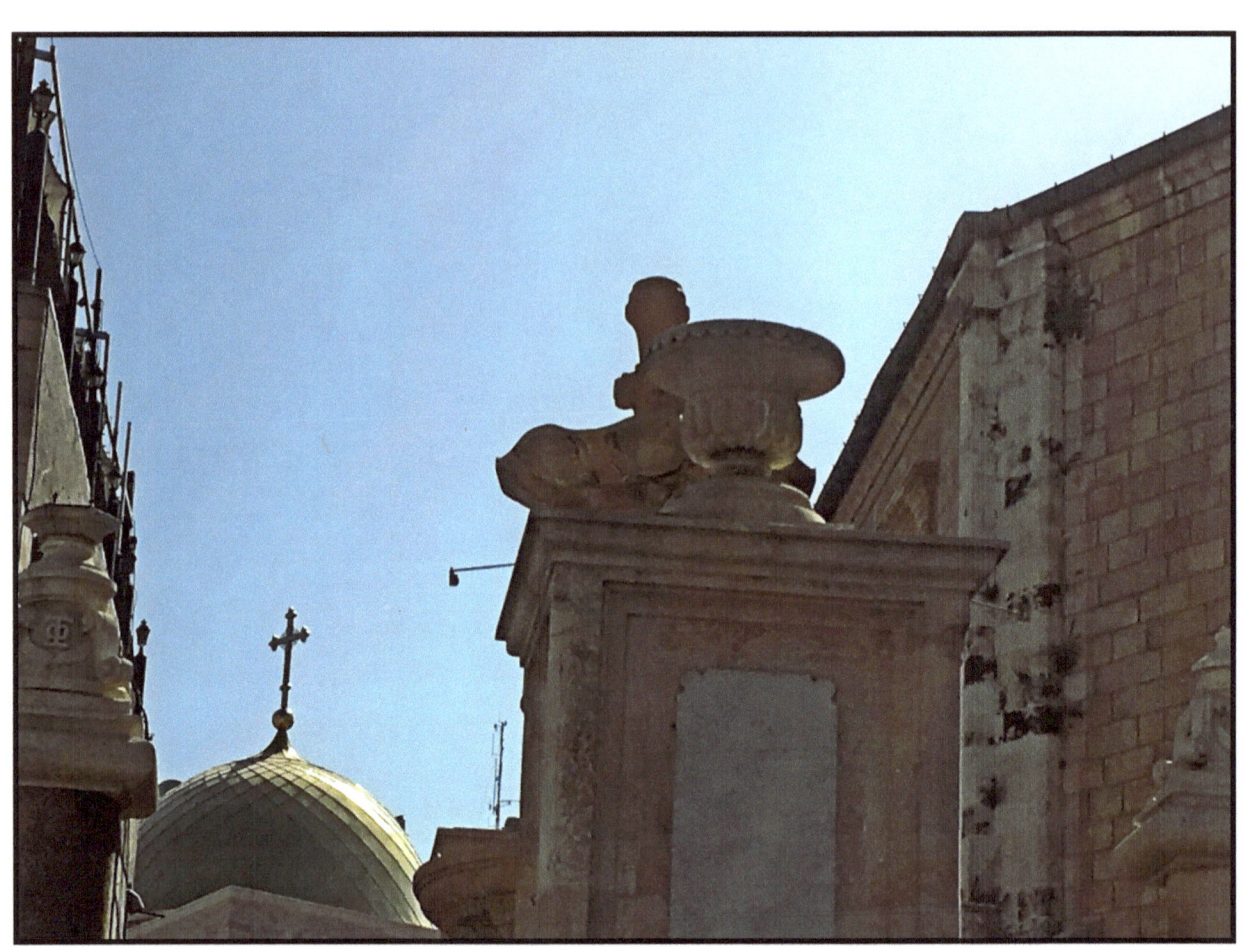

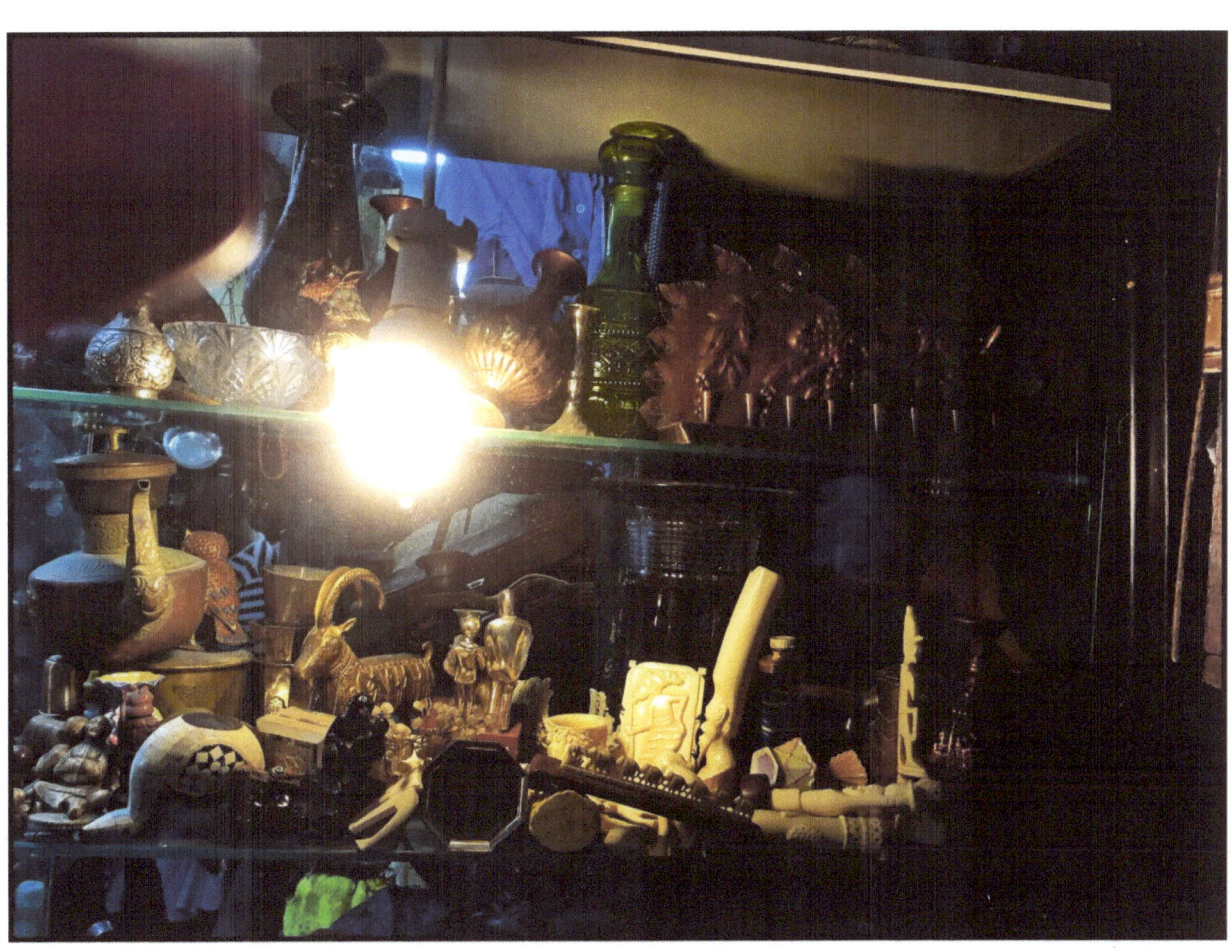

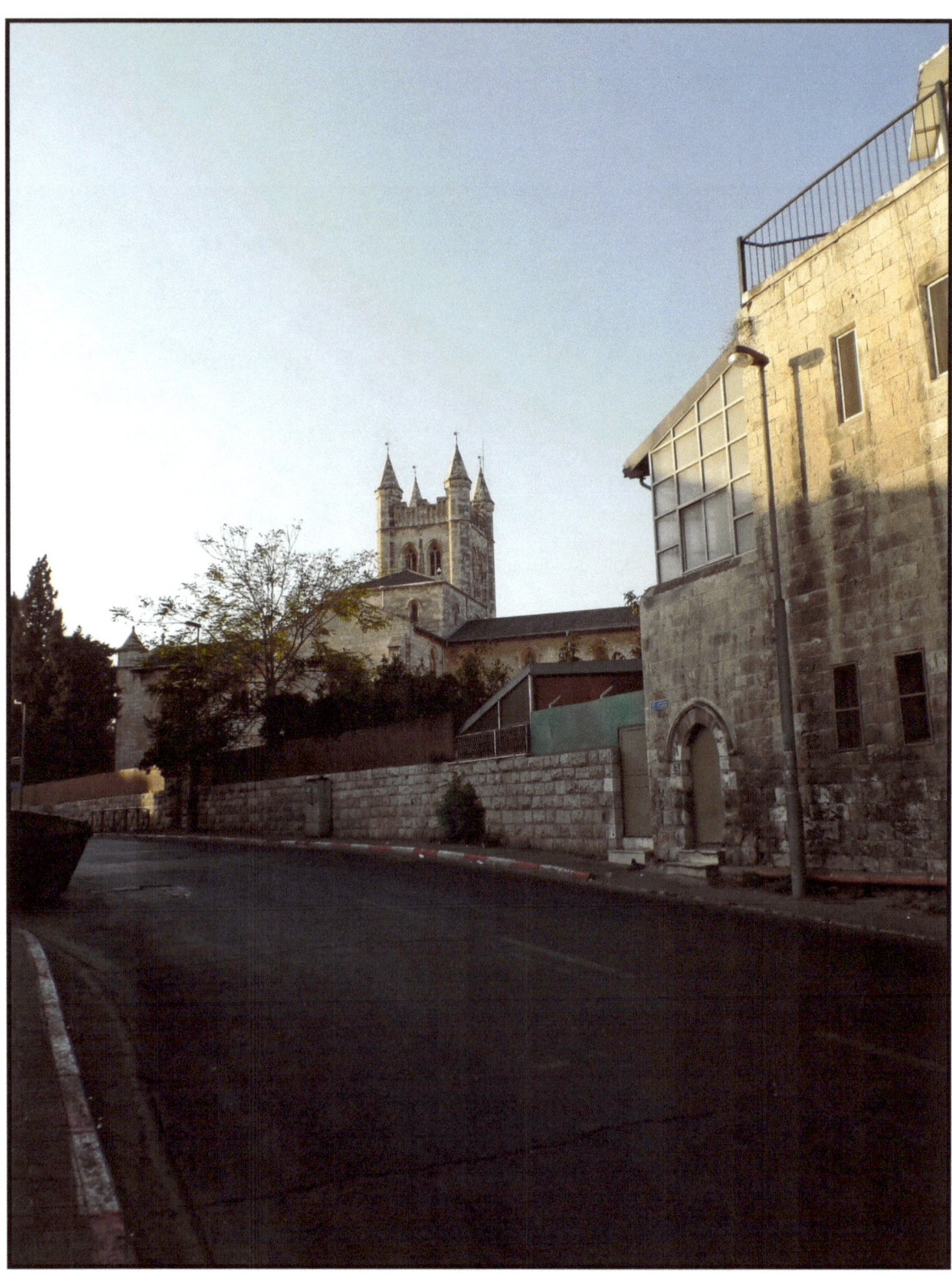

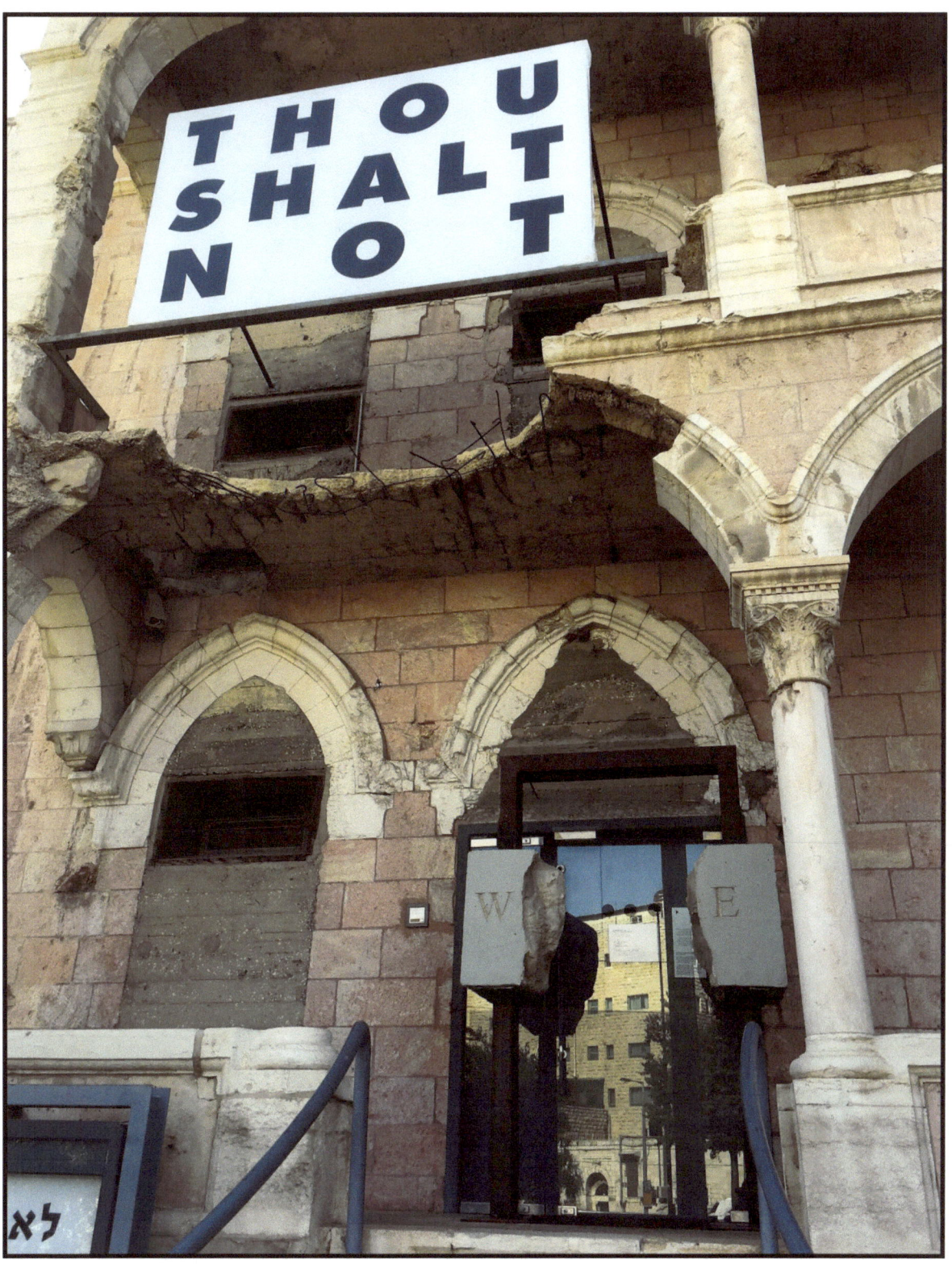

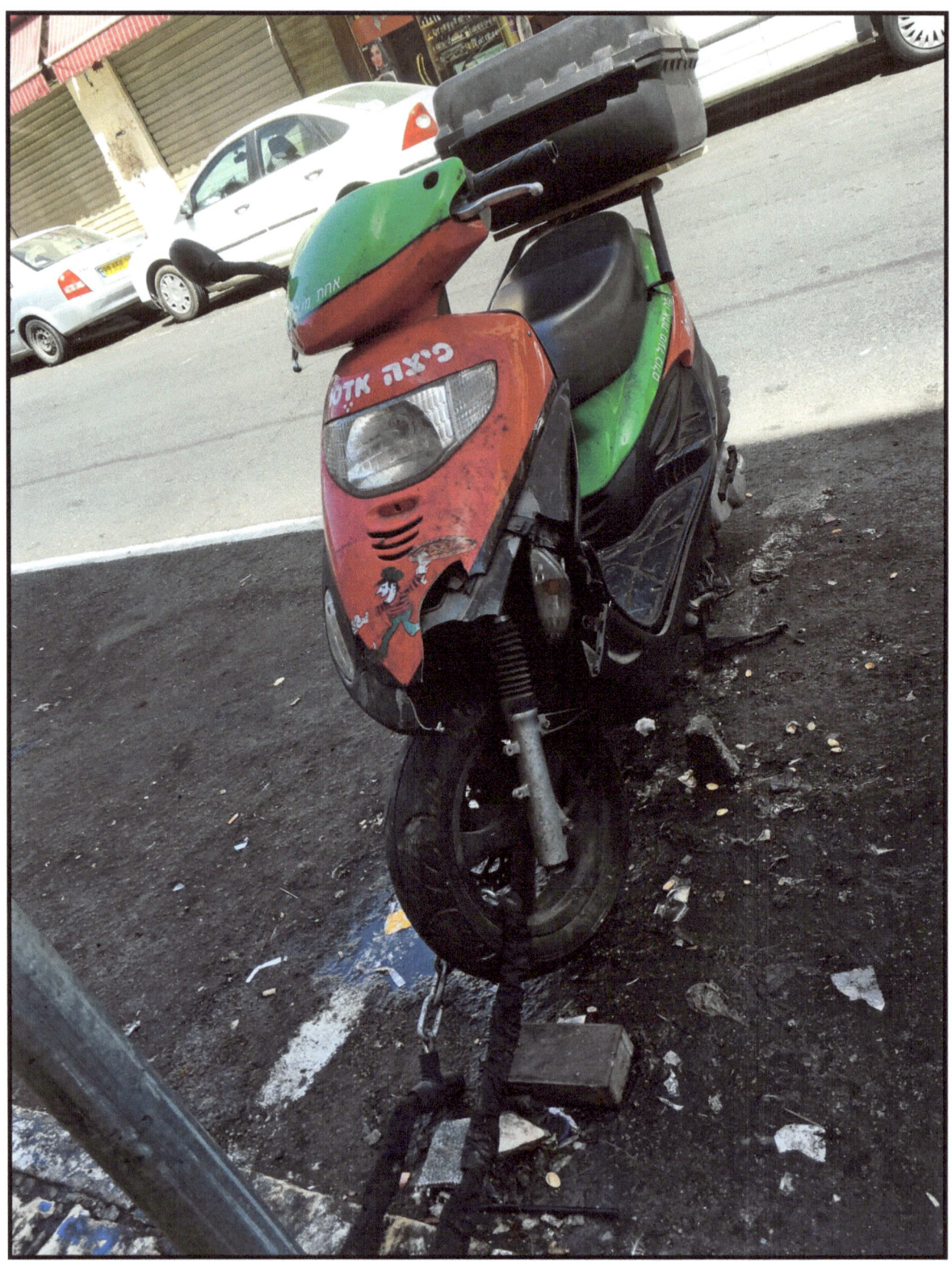

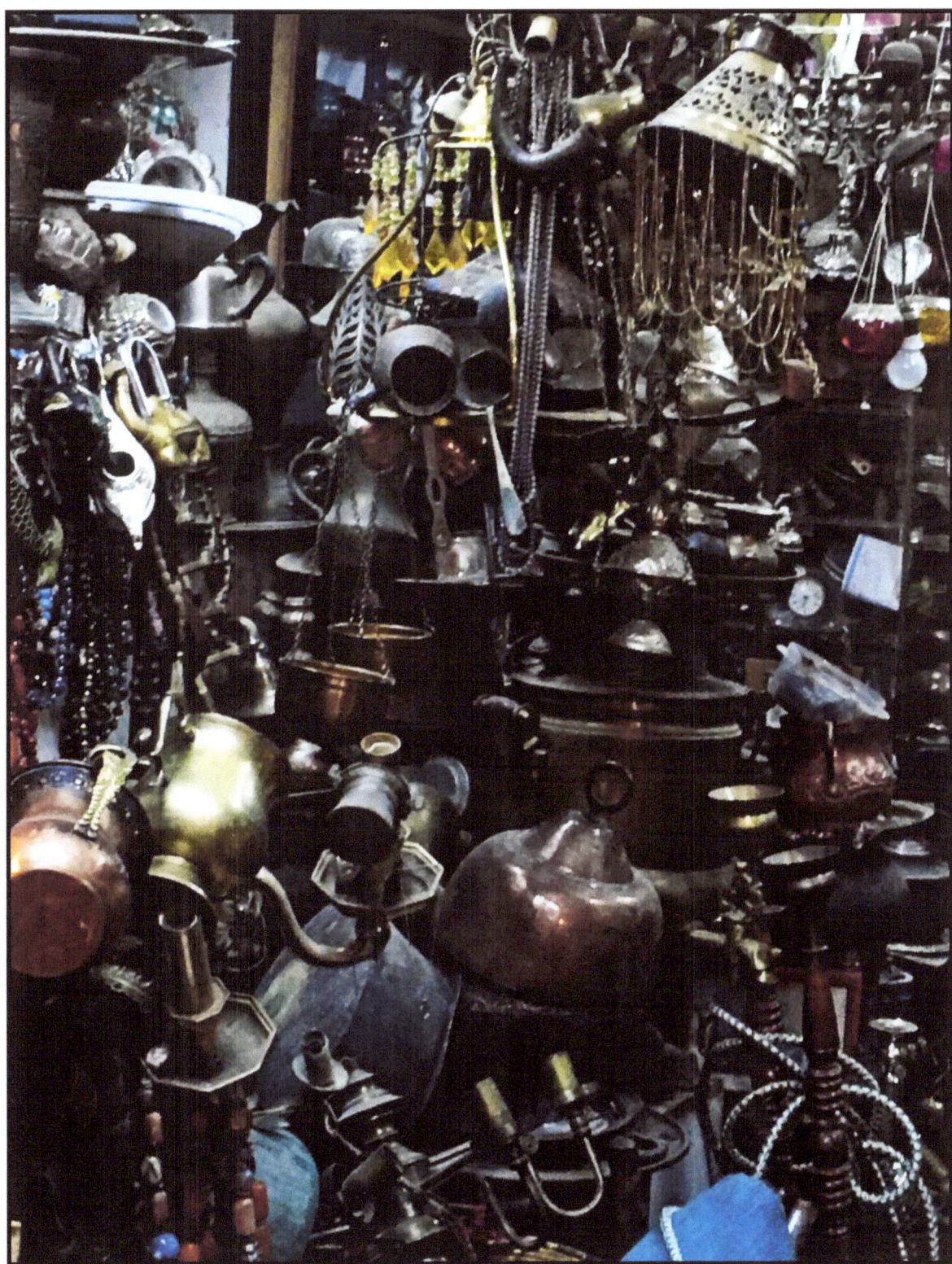

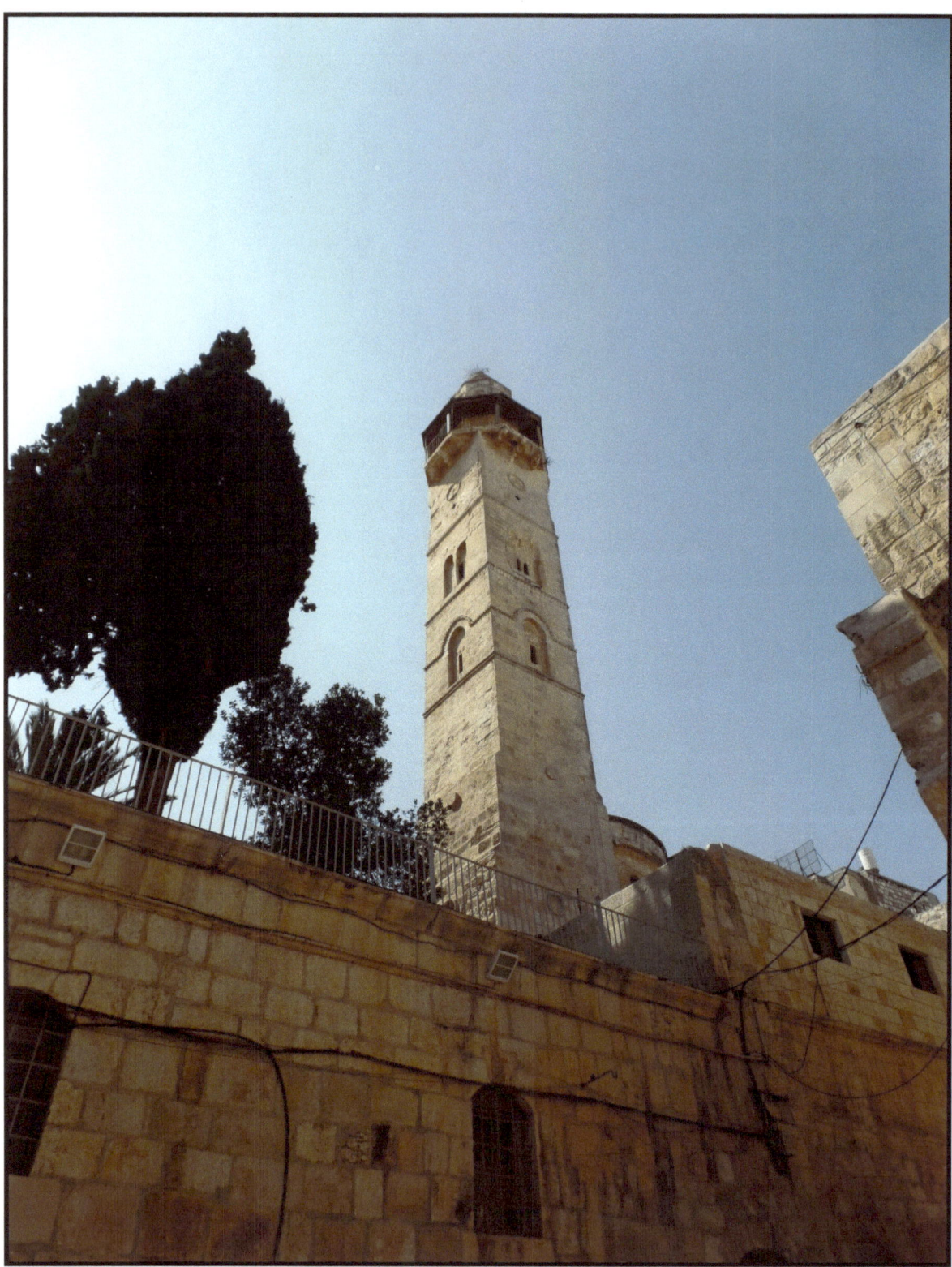

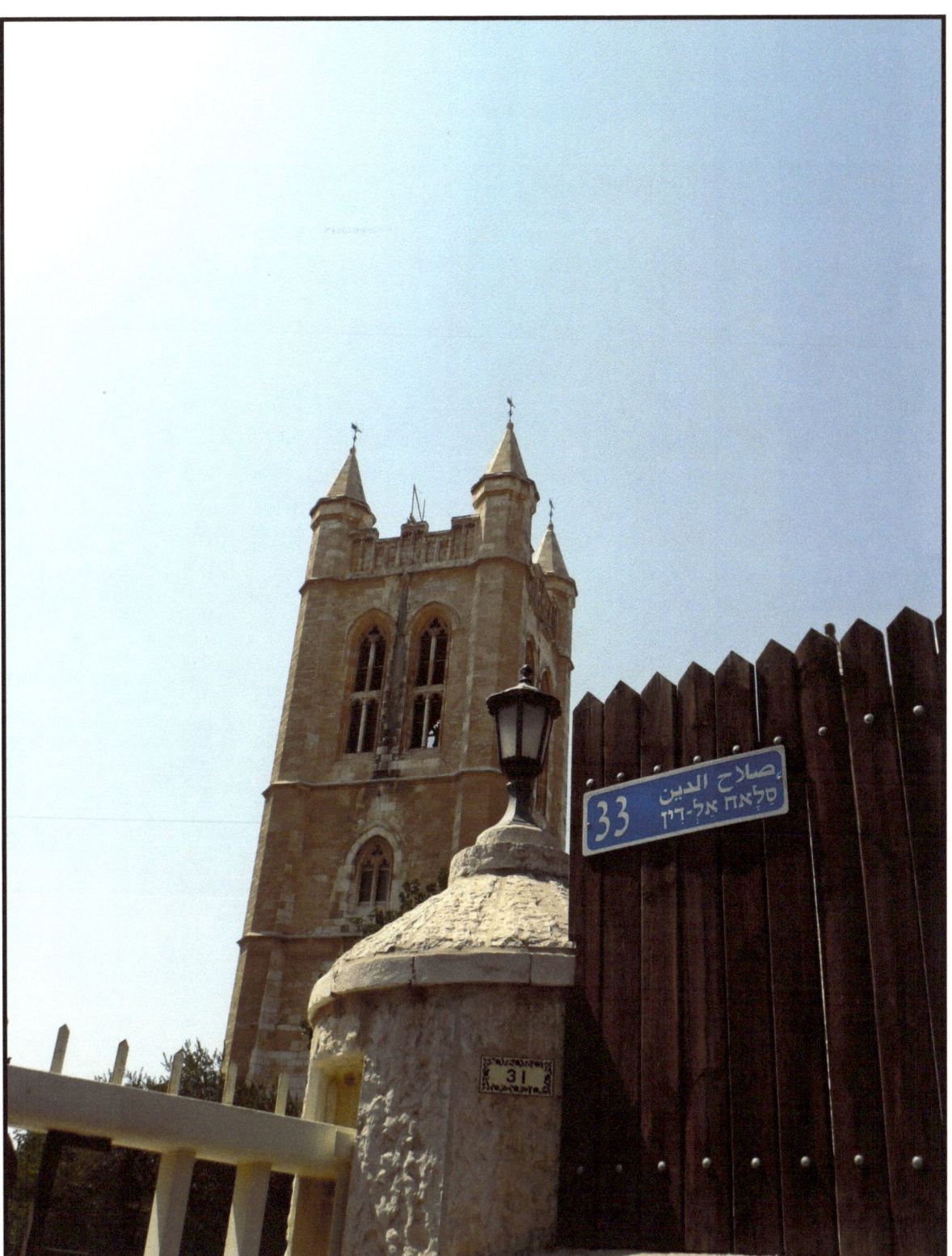

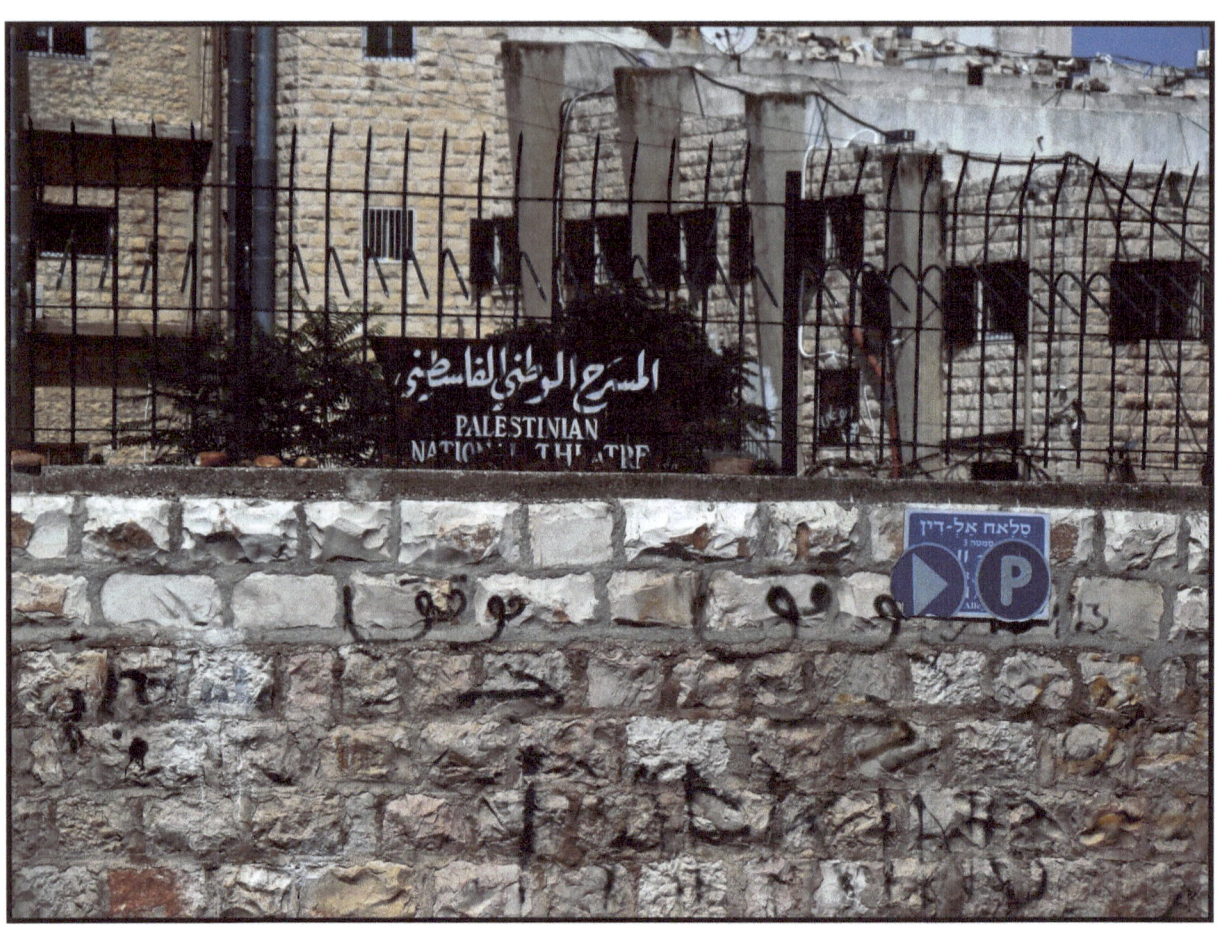

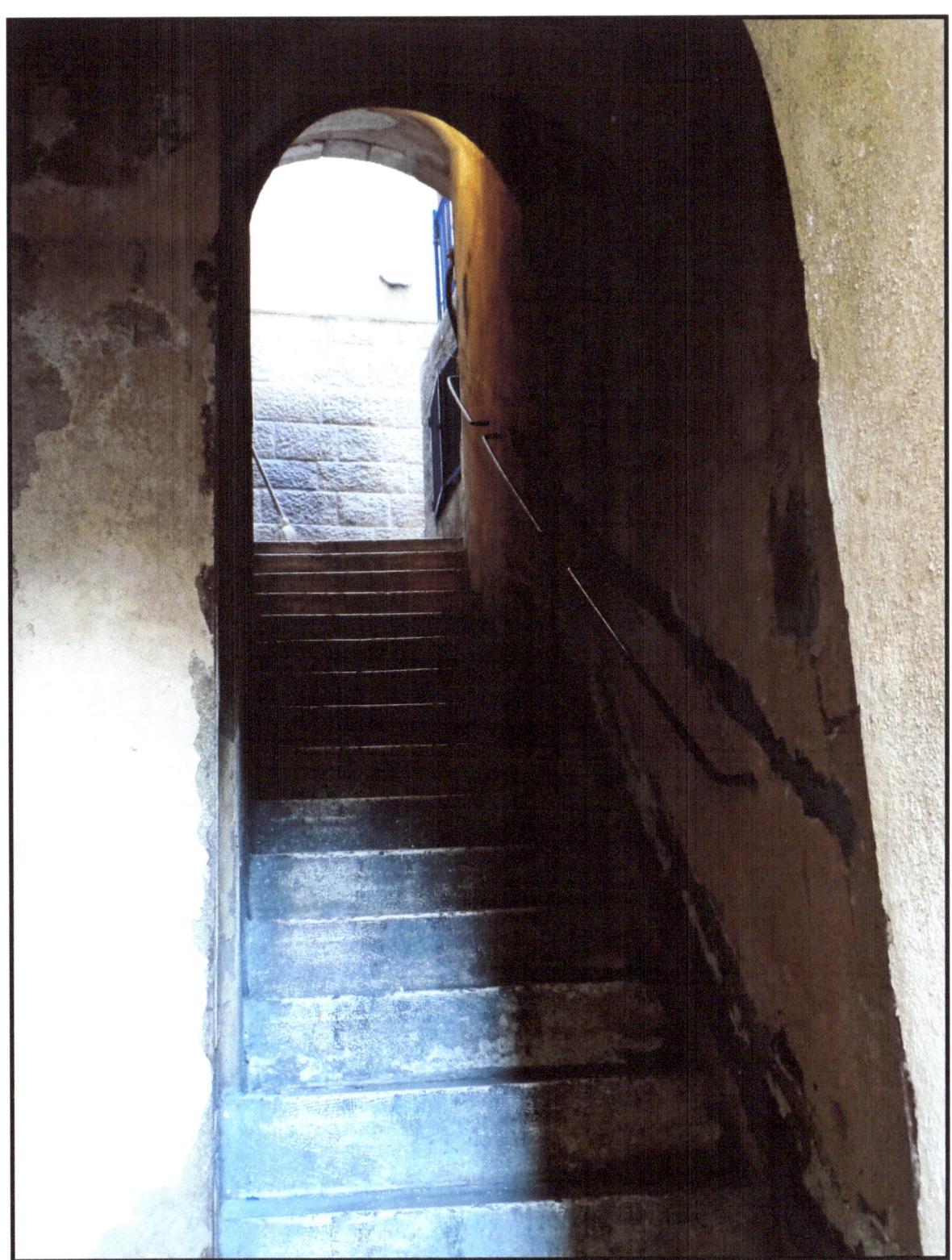

TEL AVIV

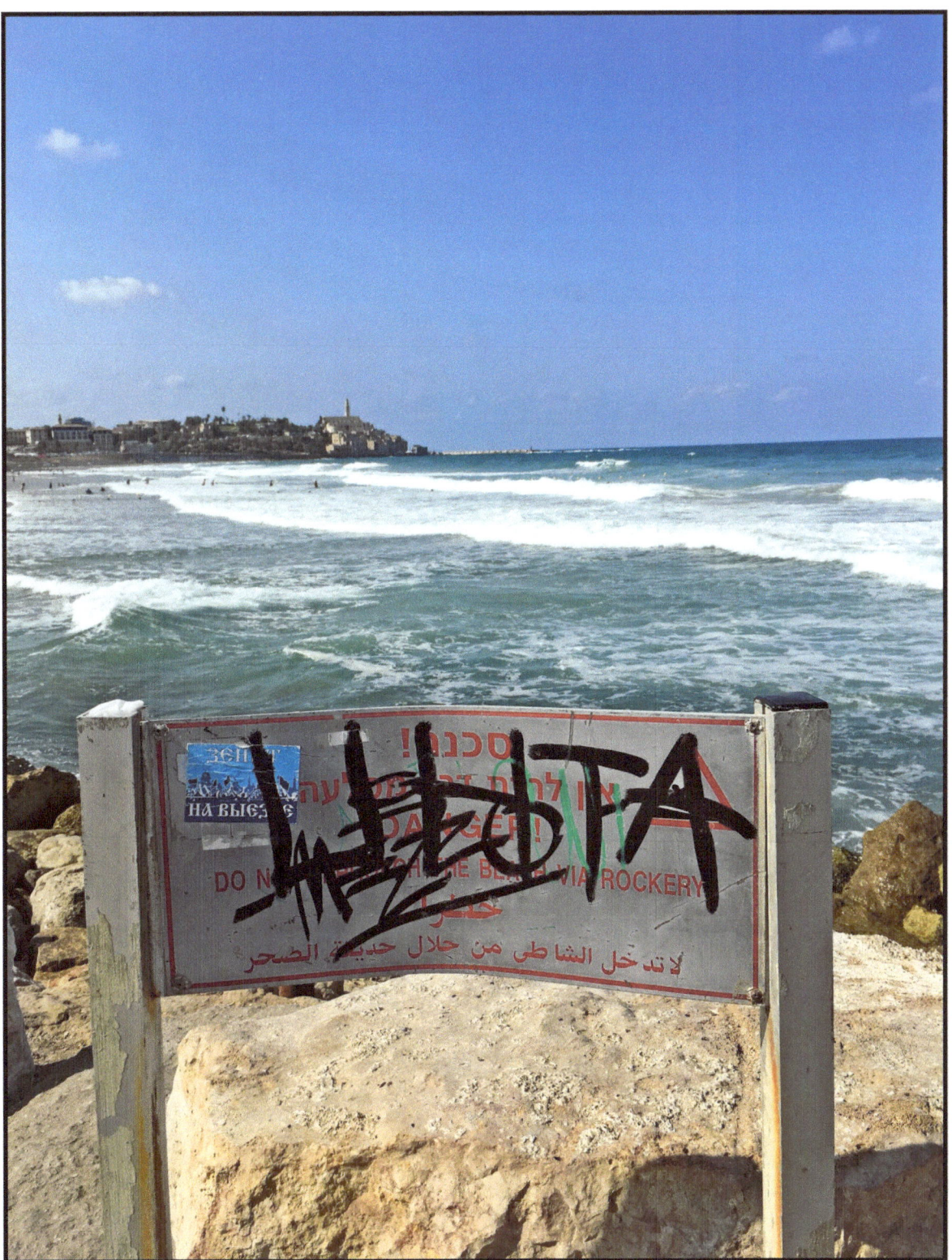

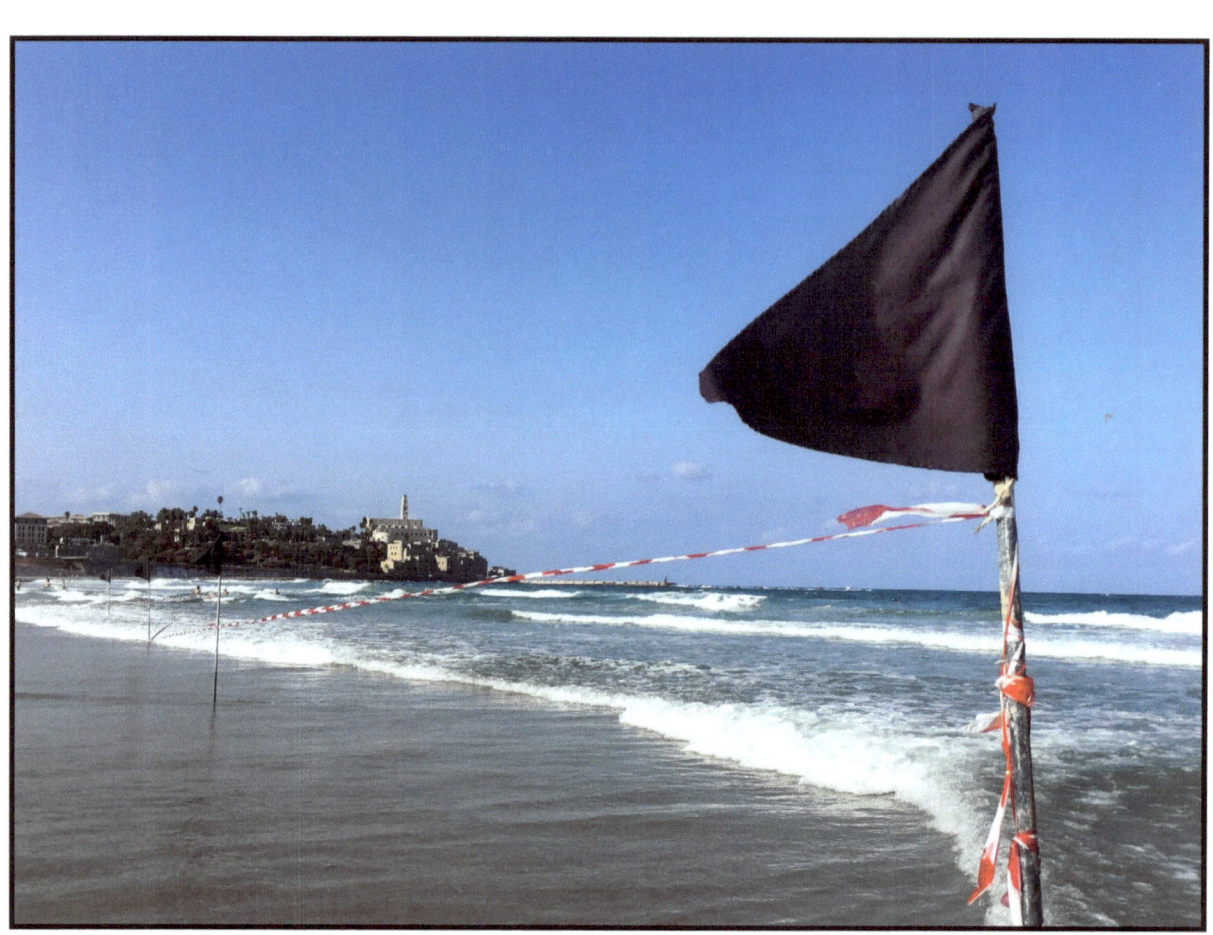

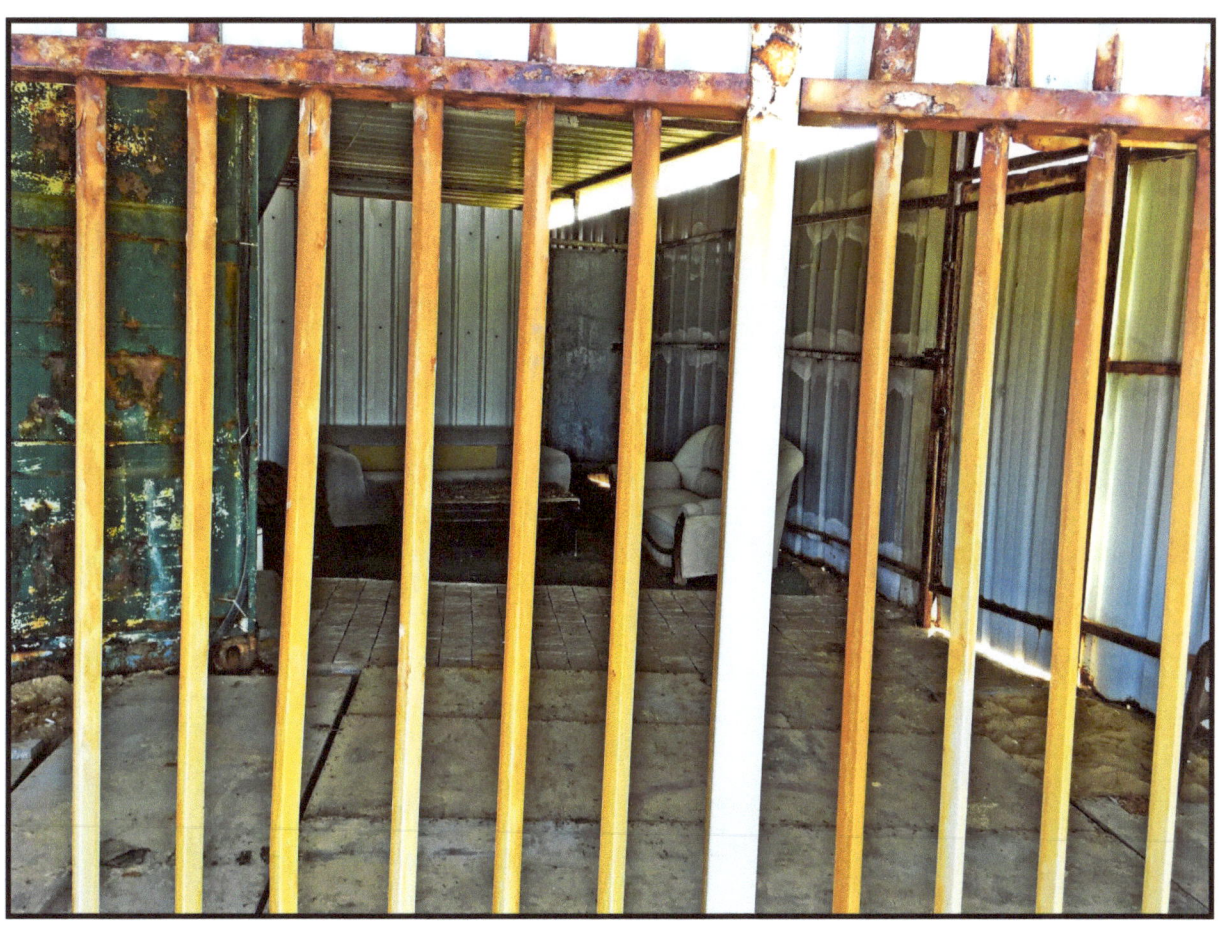

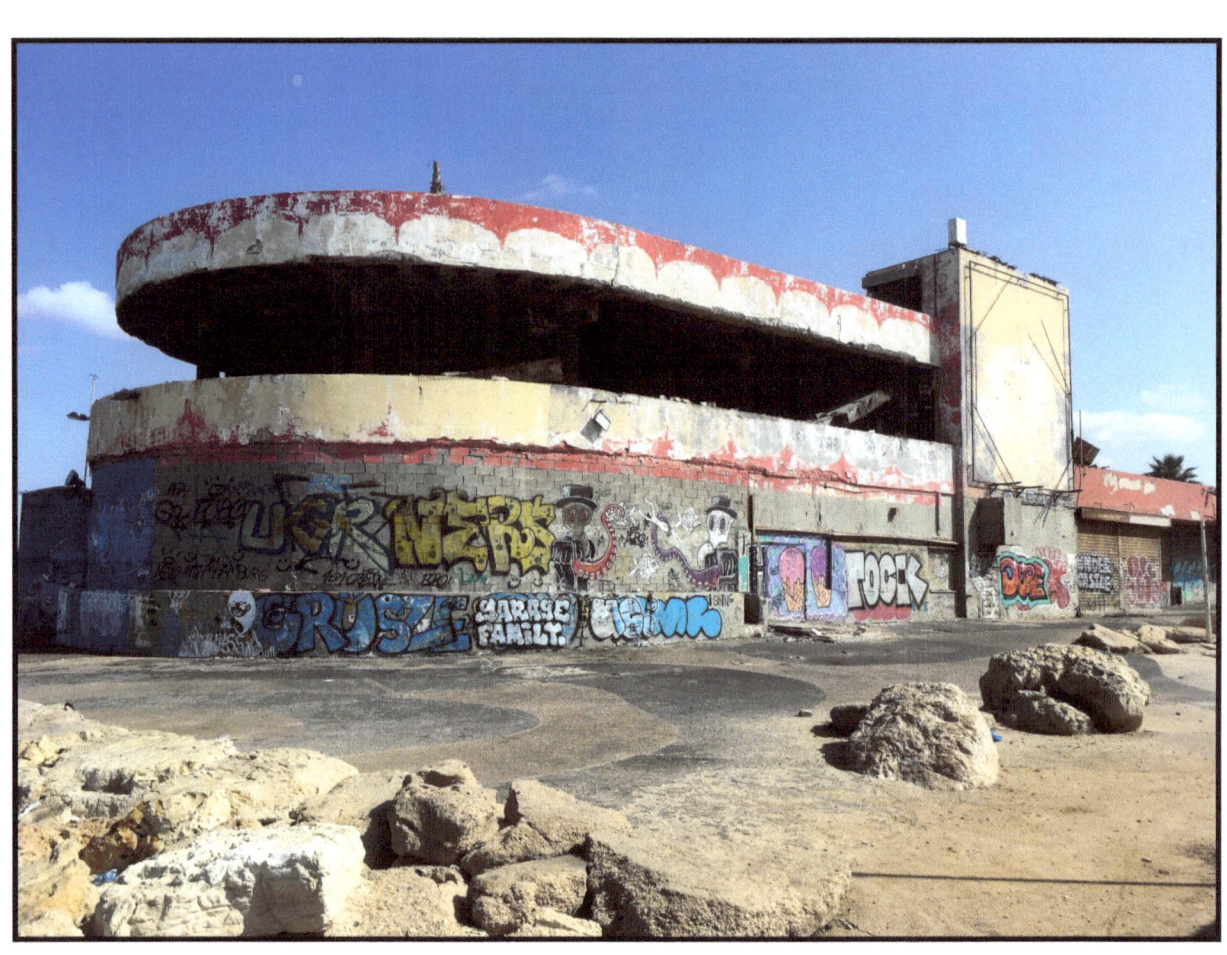

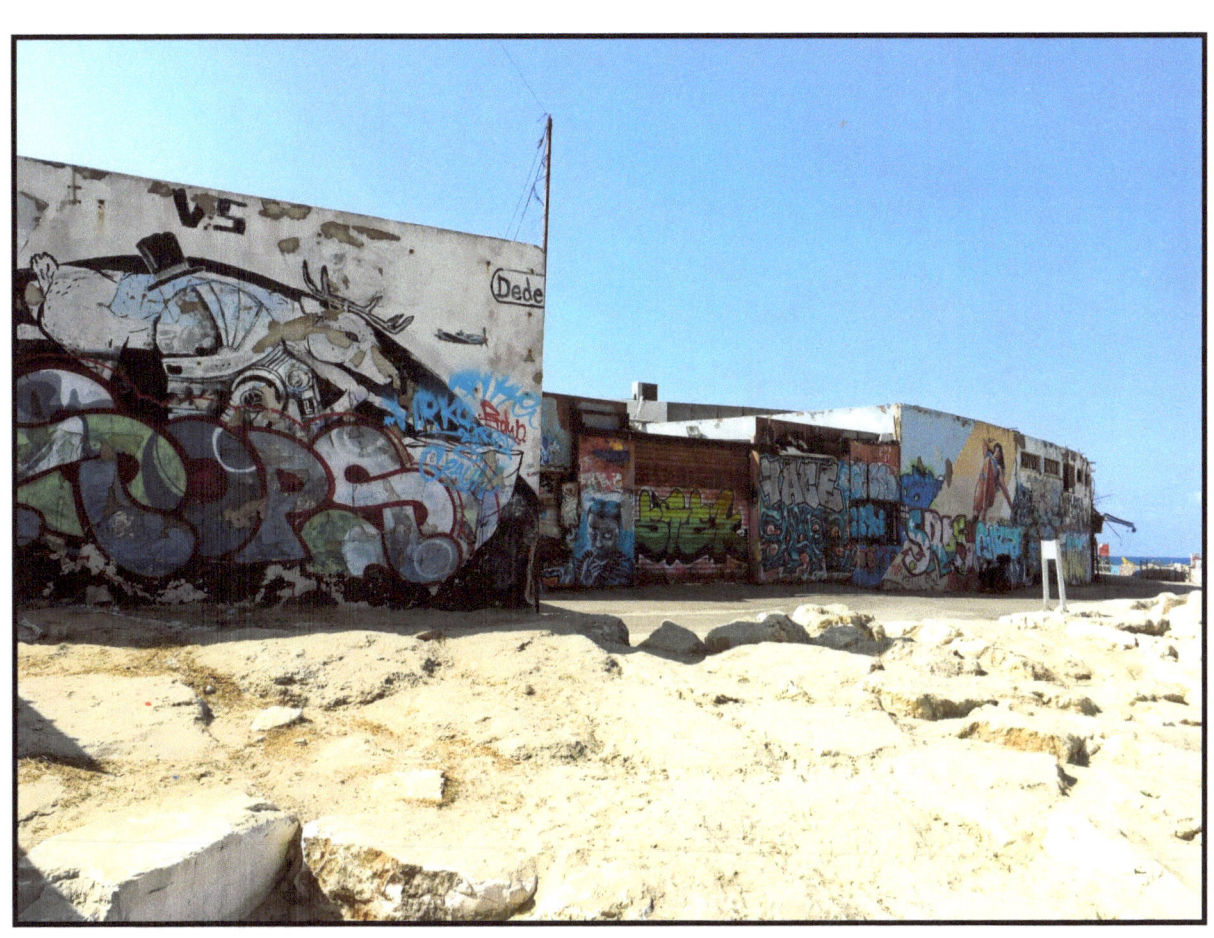

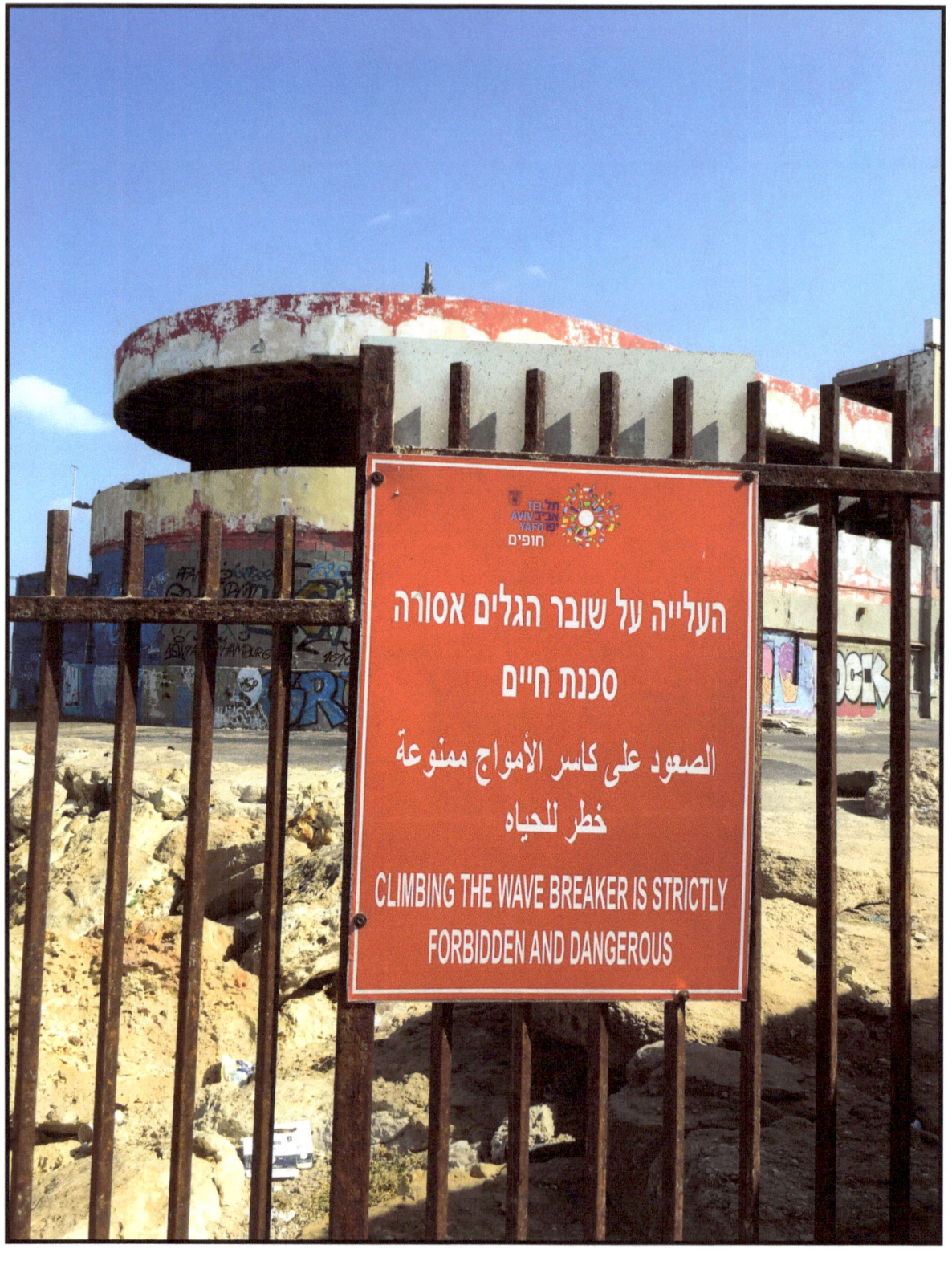

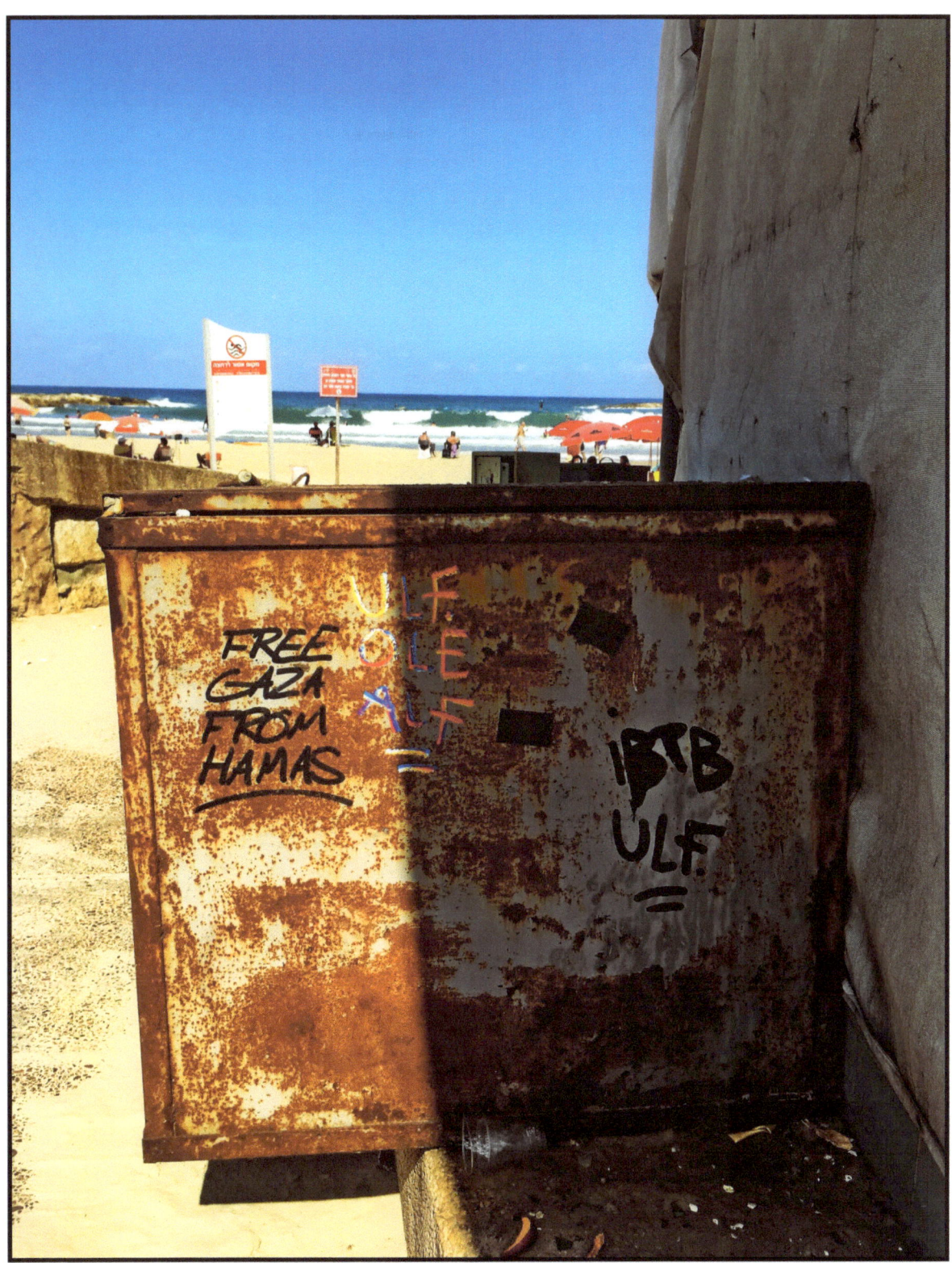

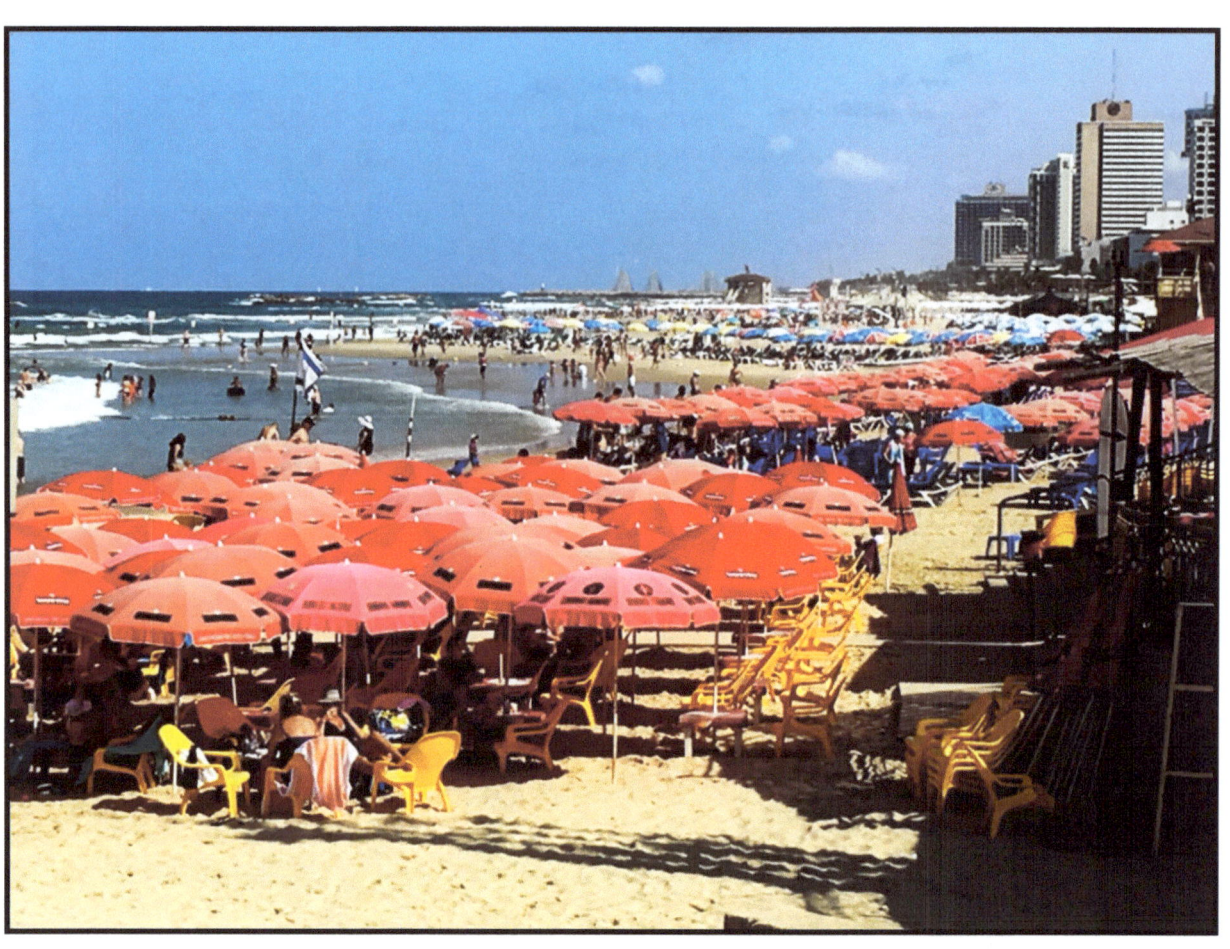

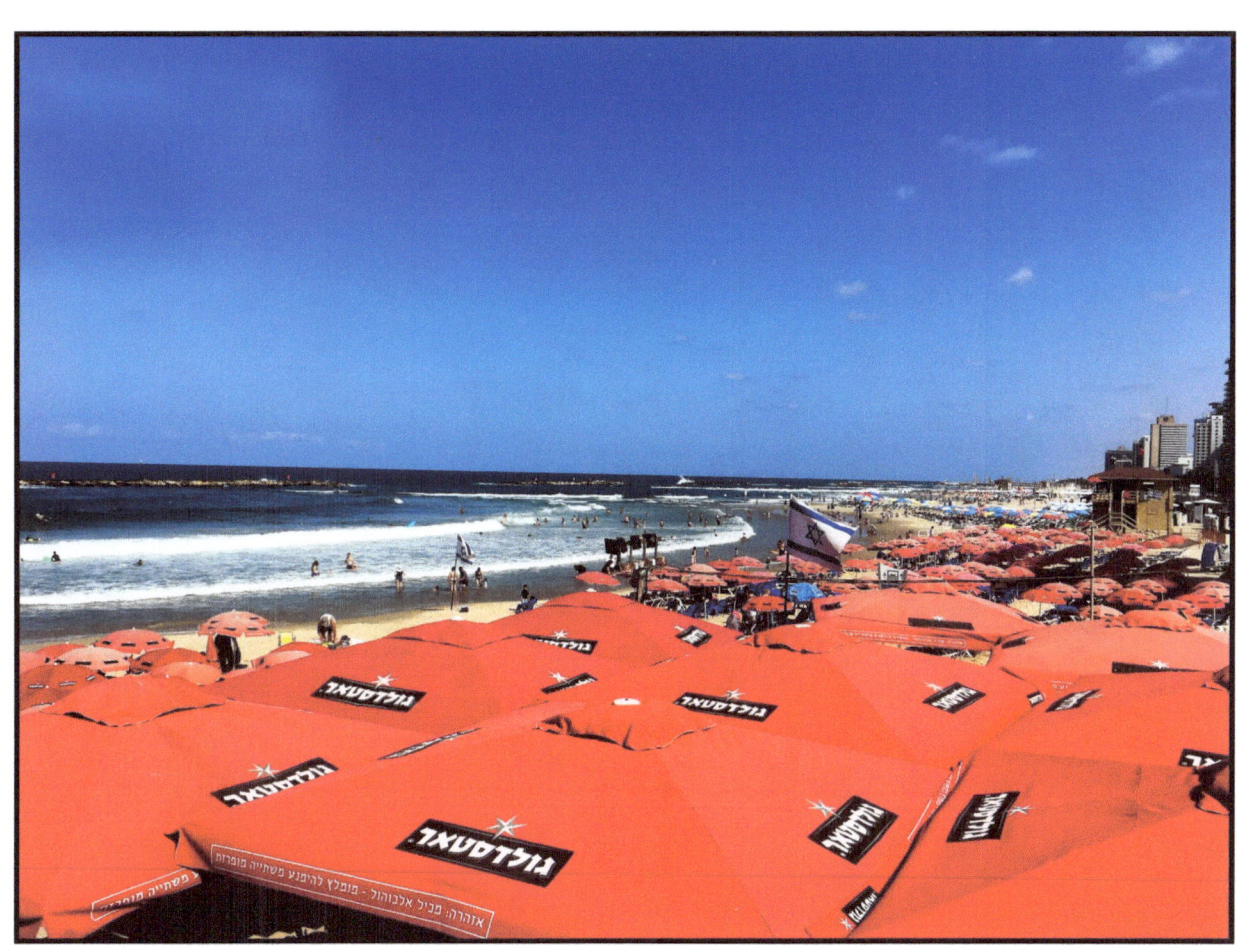

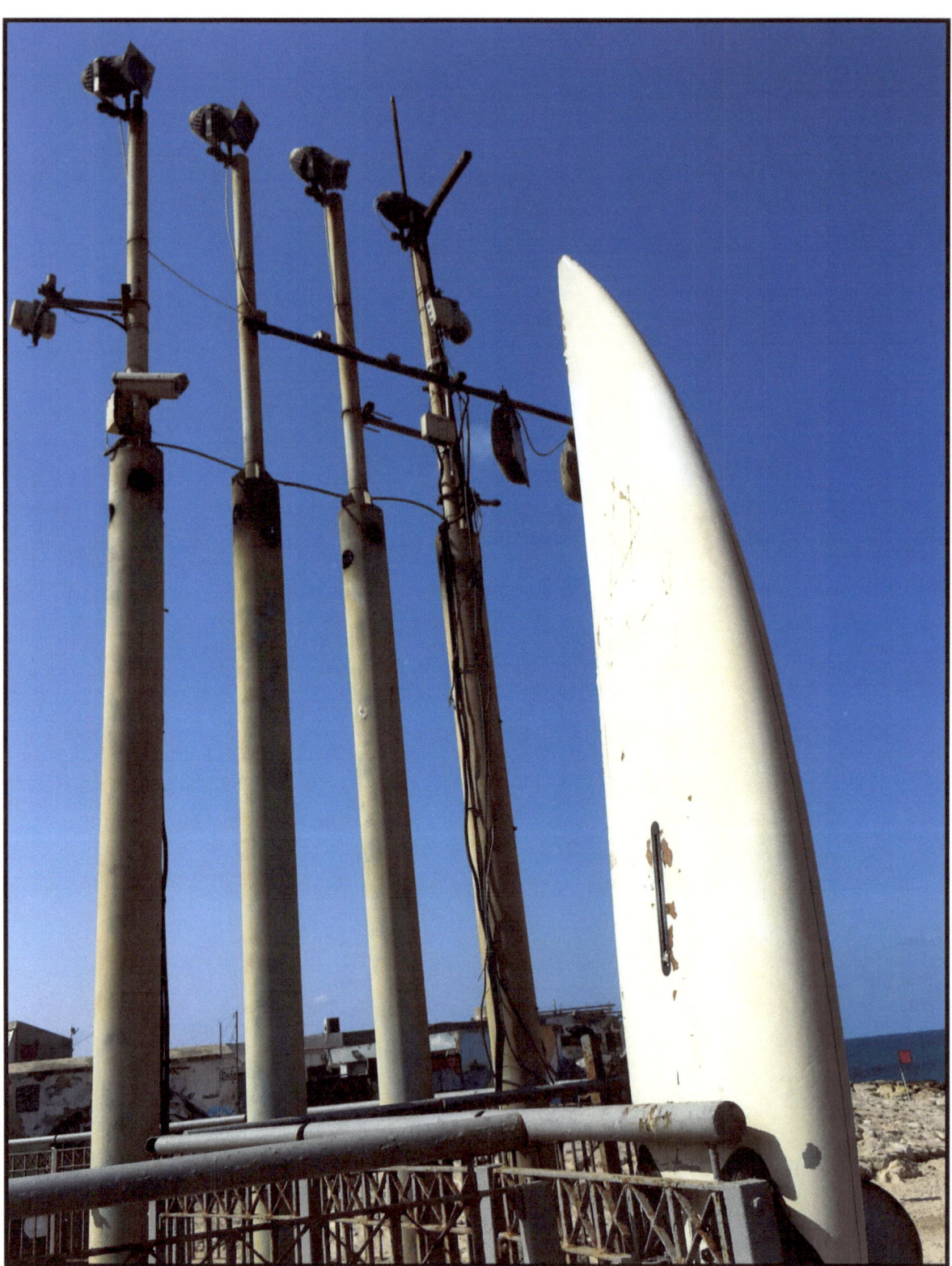

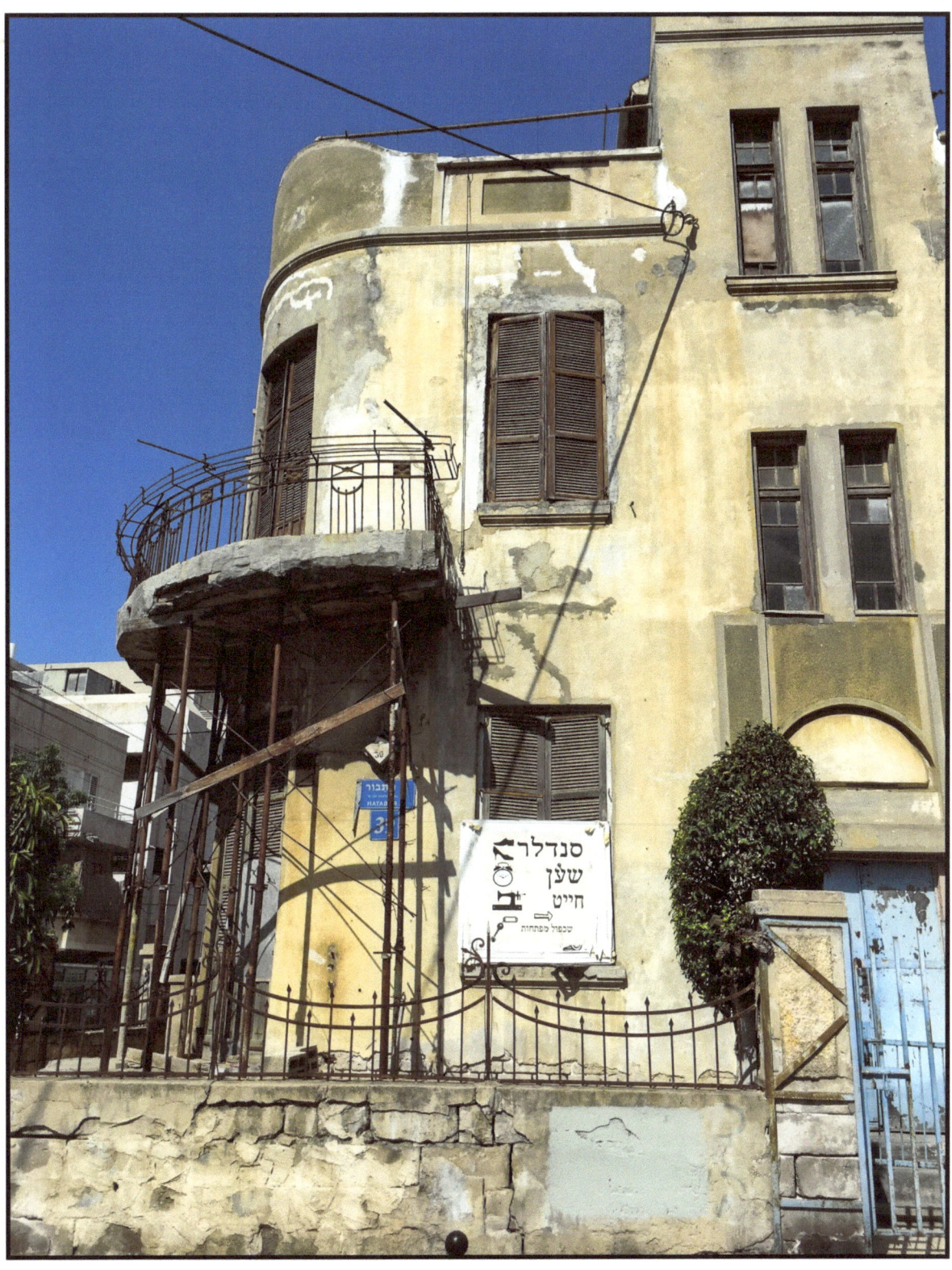

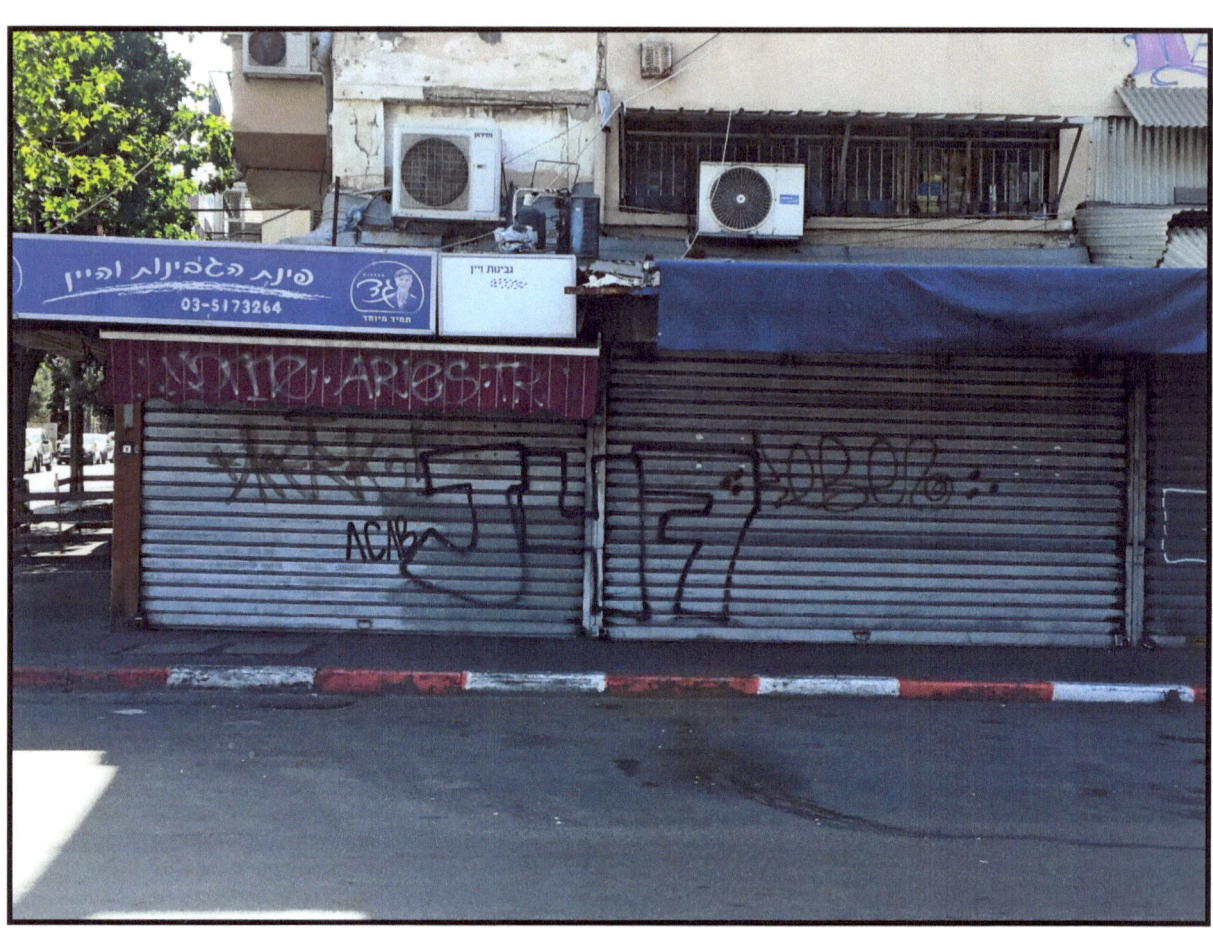

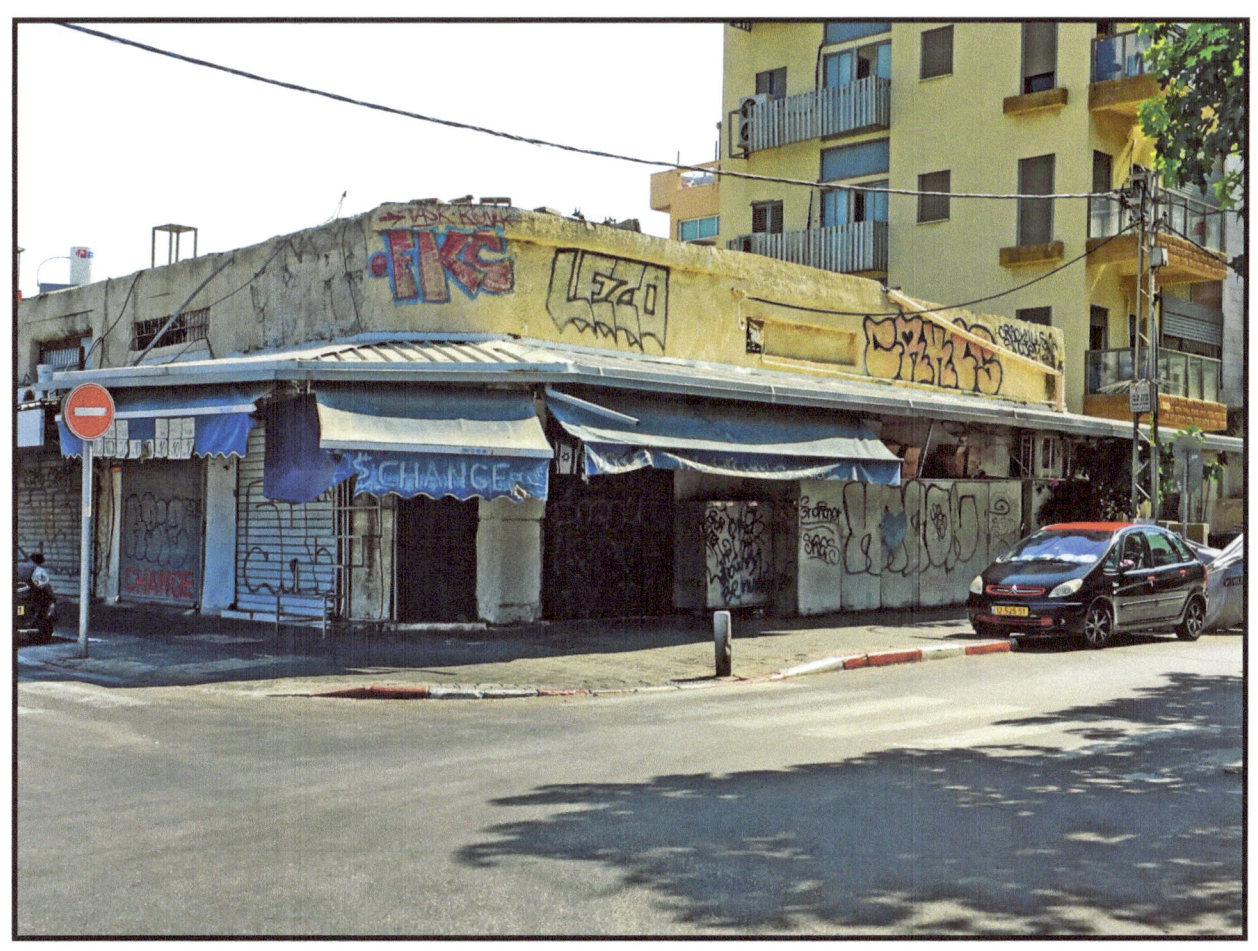

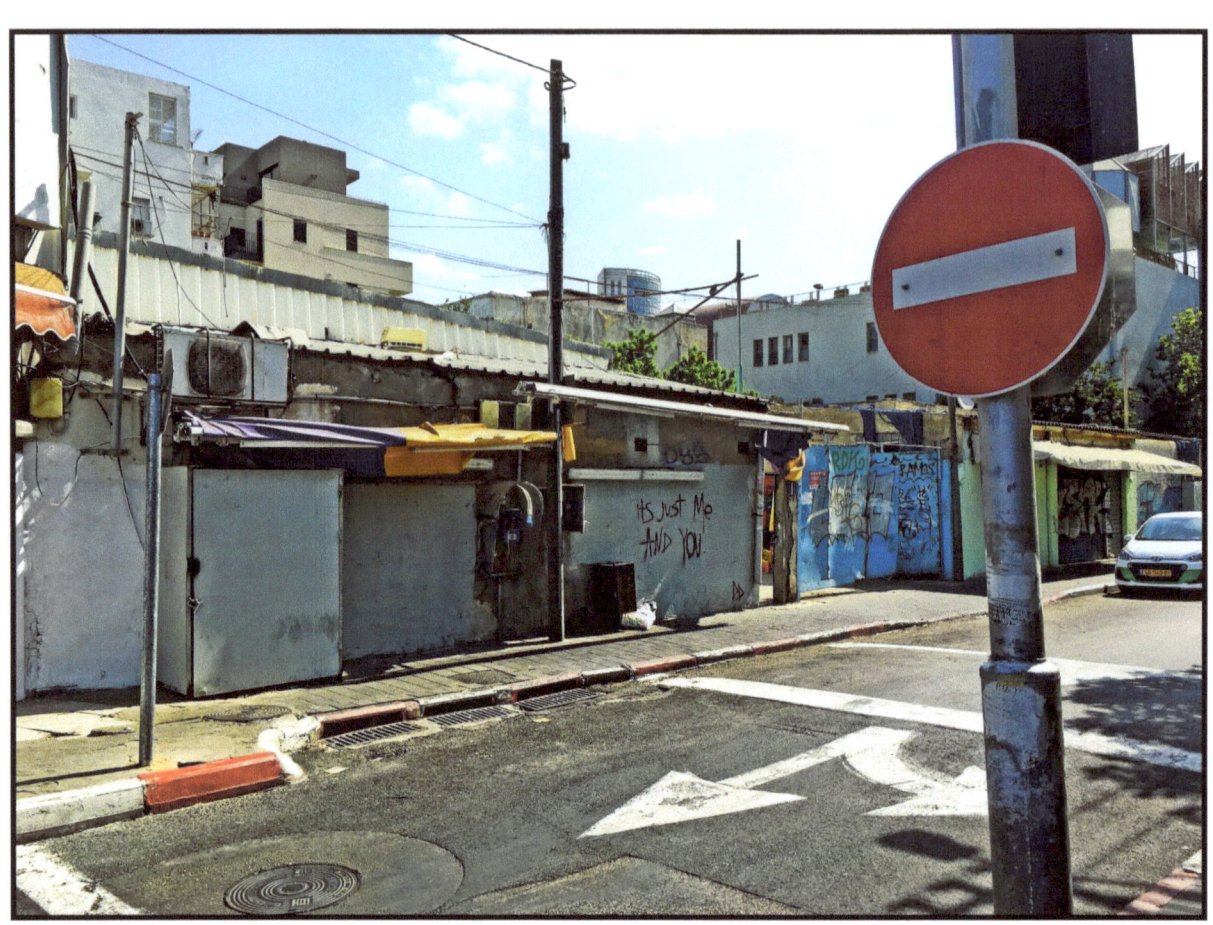

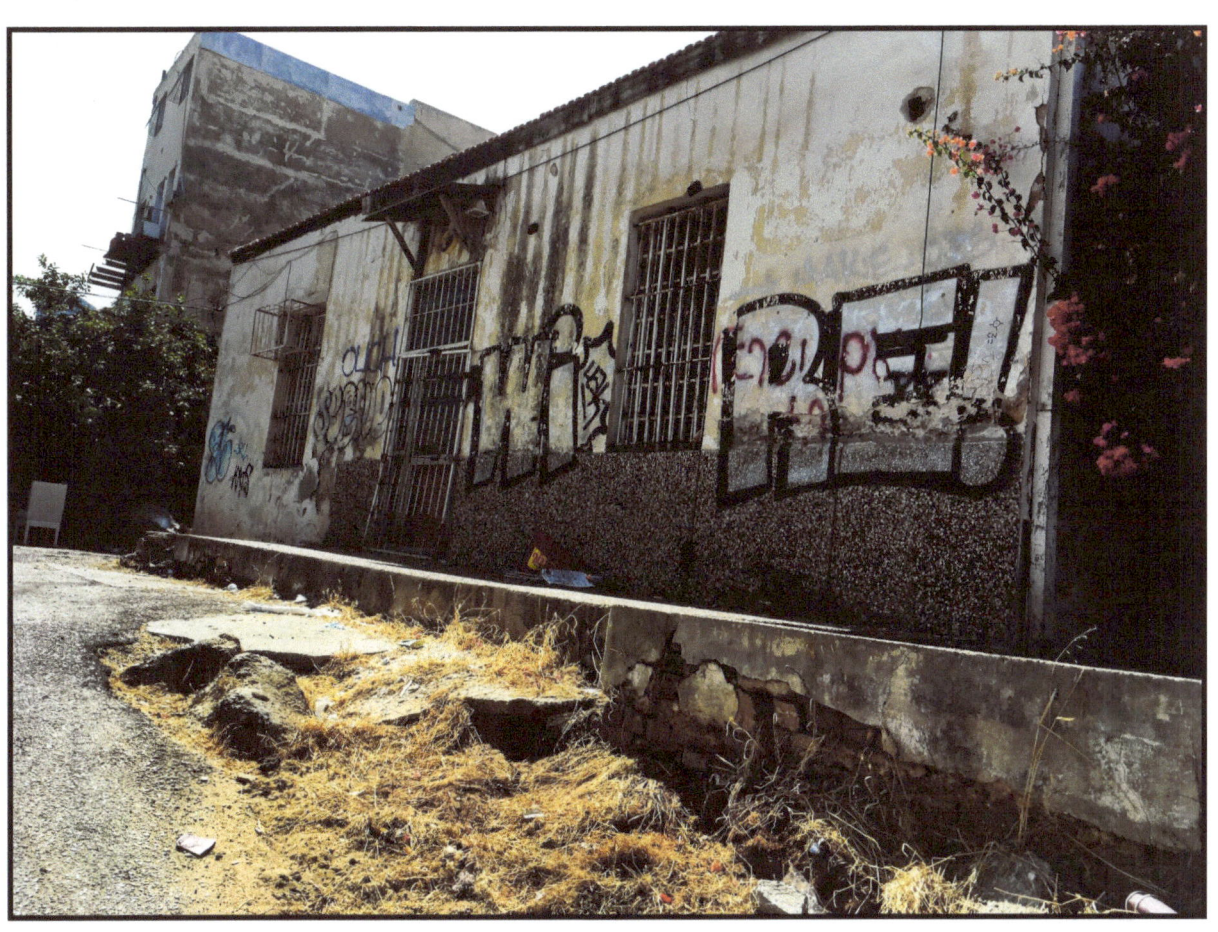

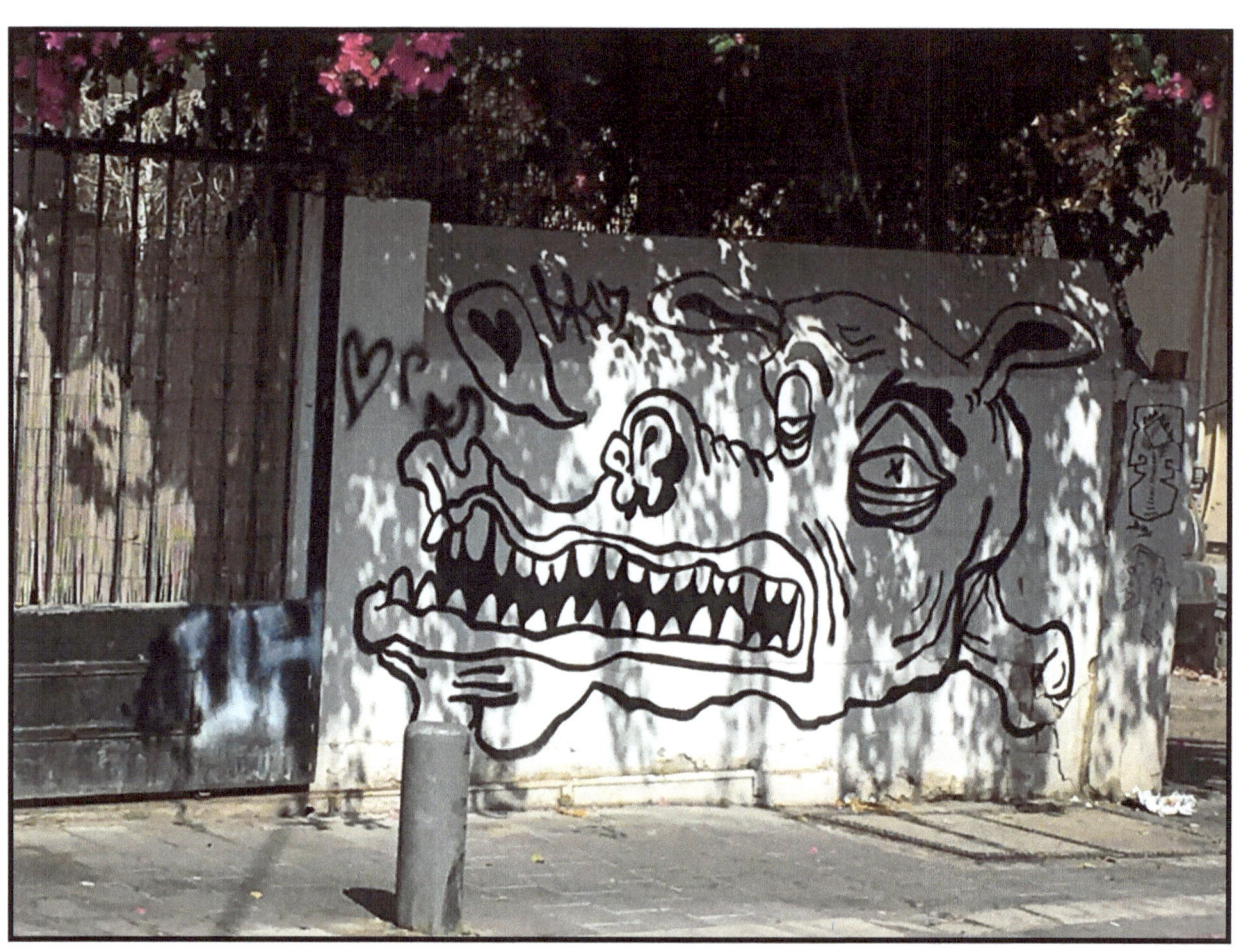

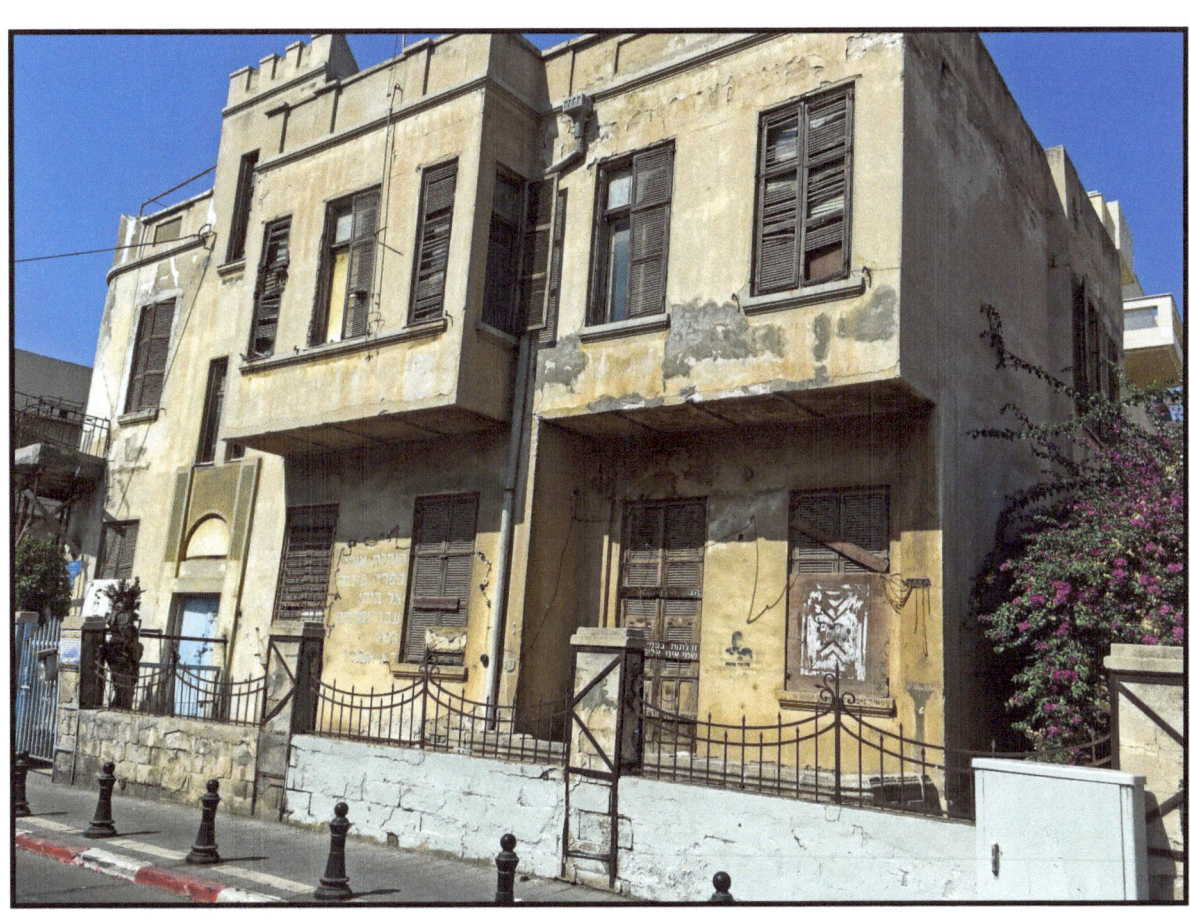

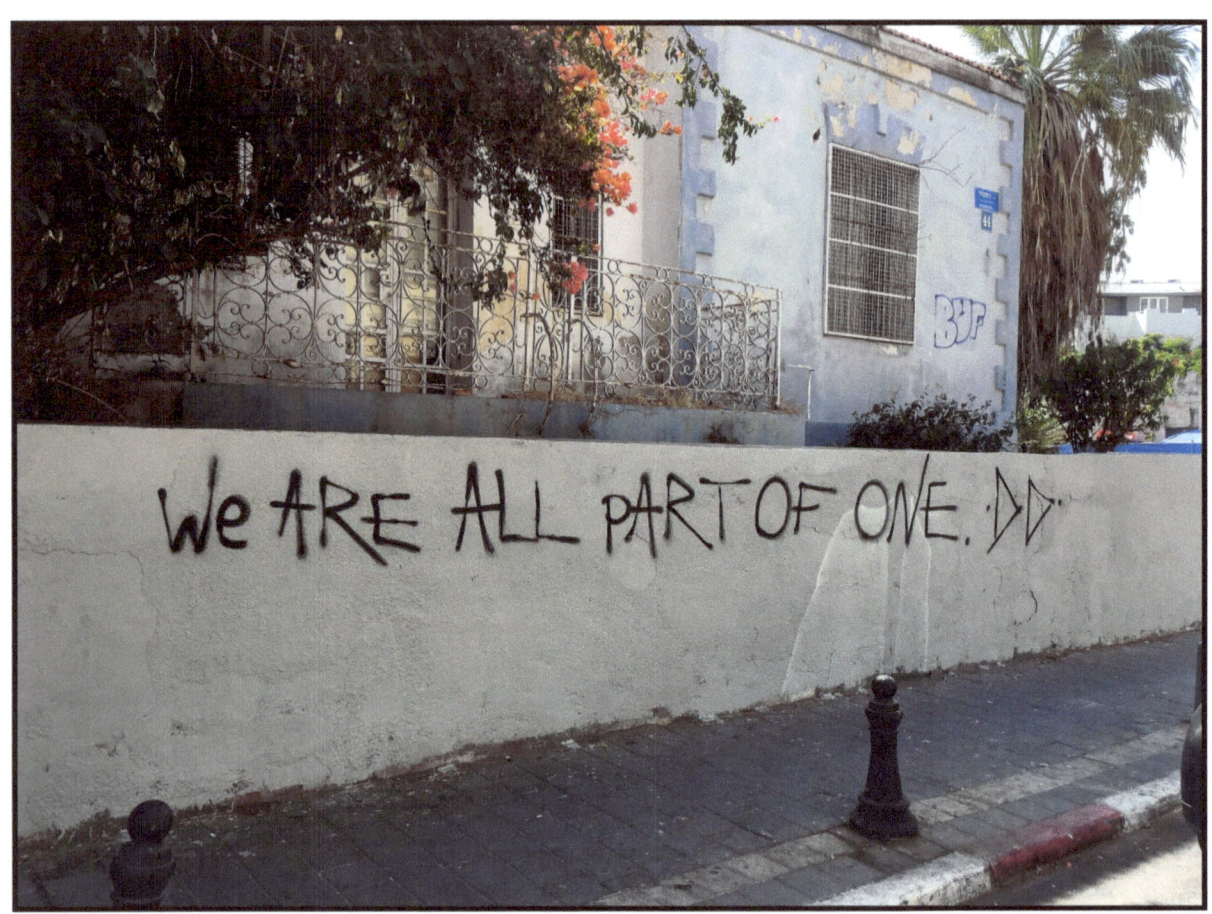

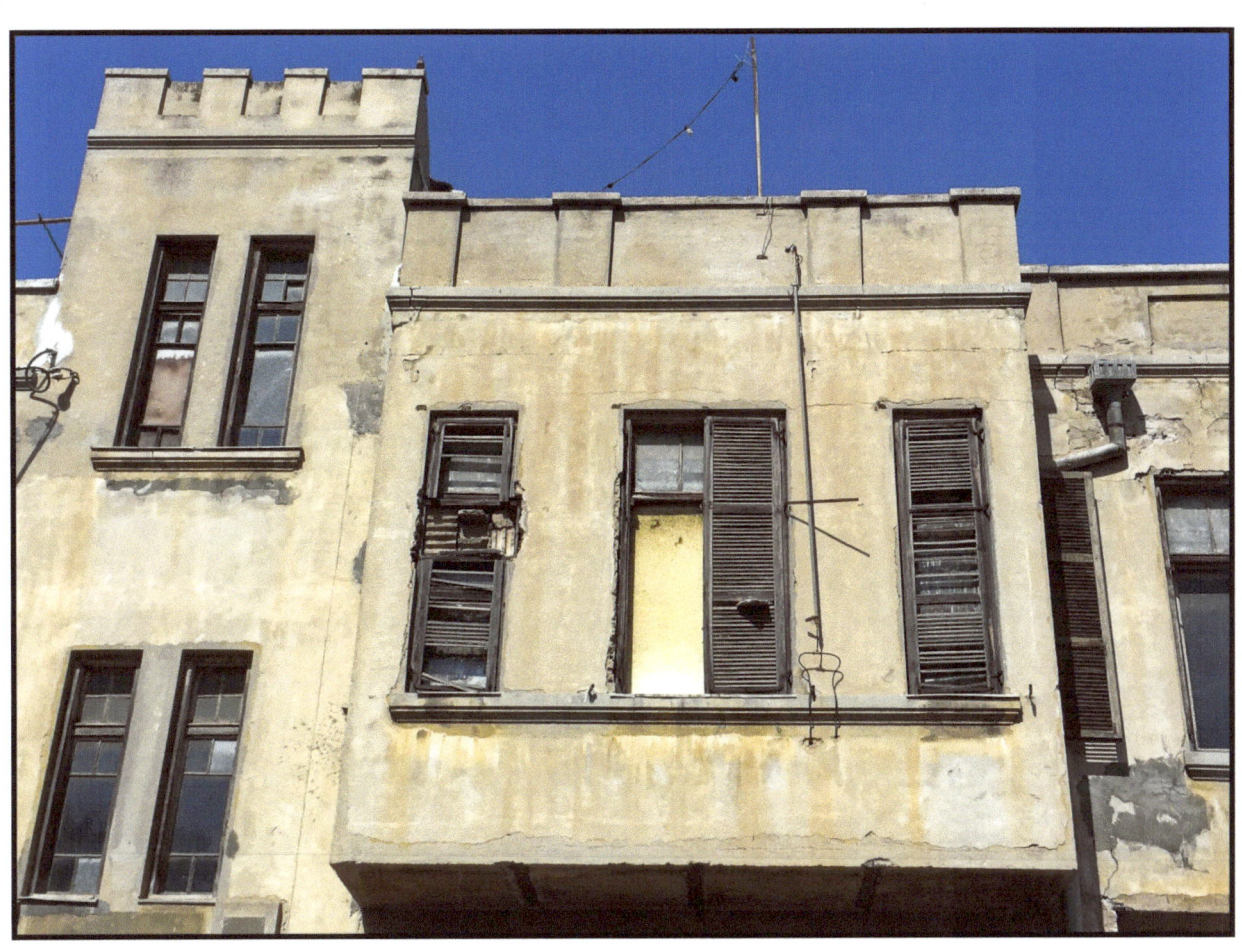

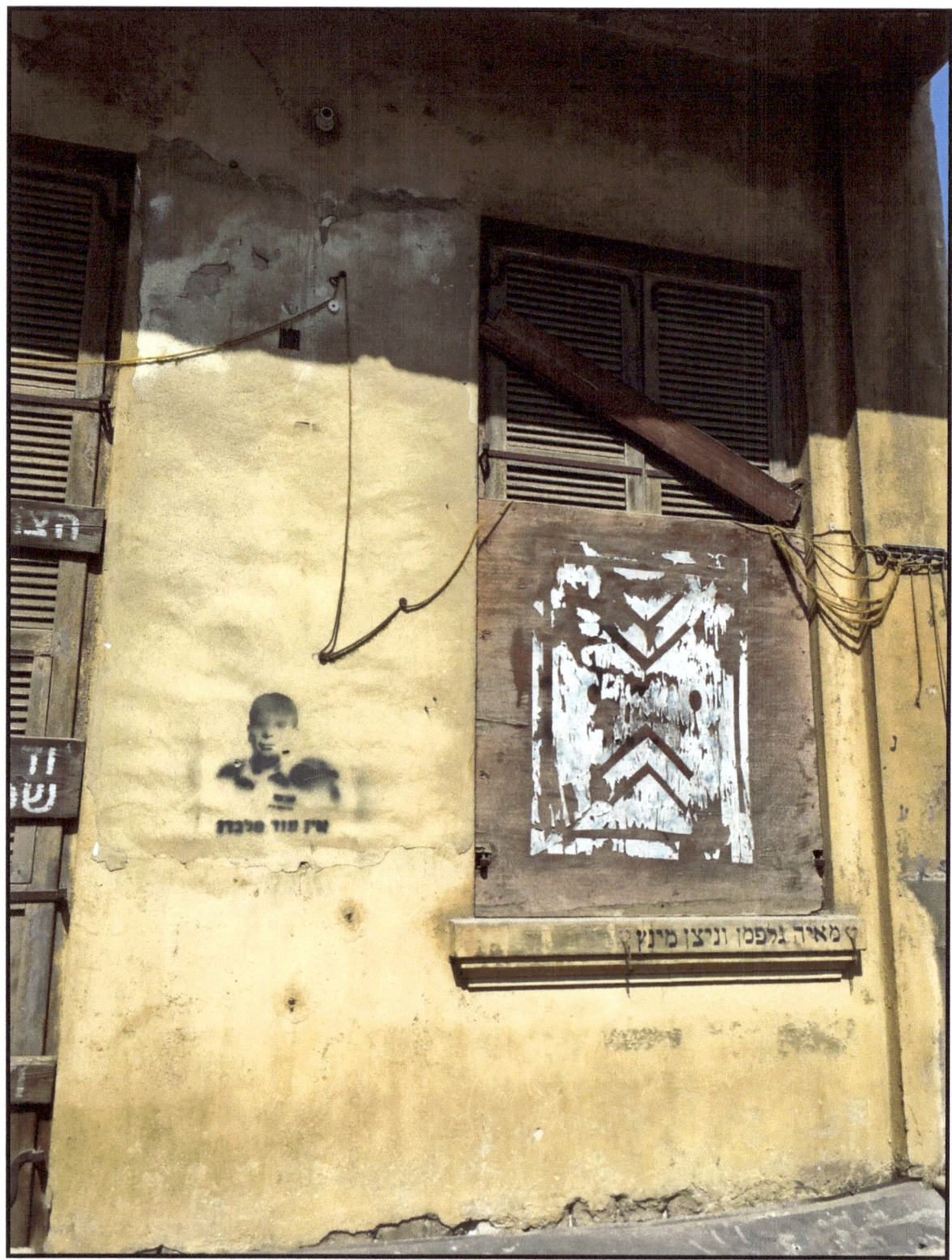

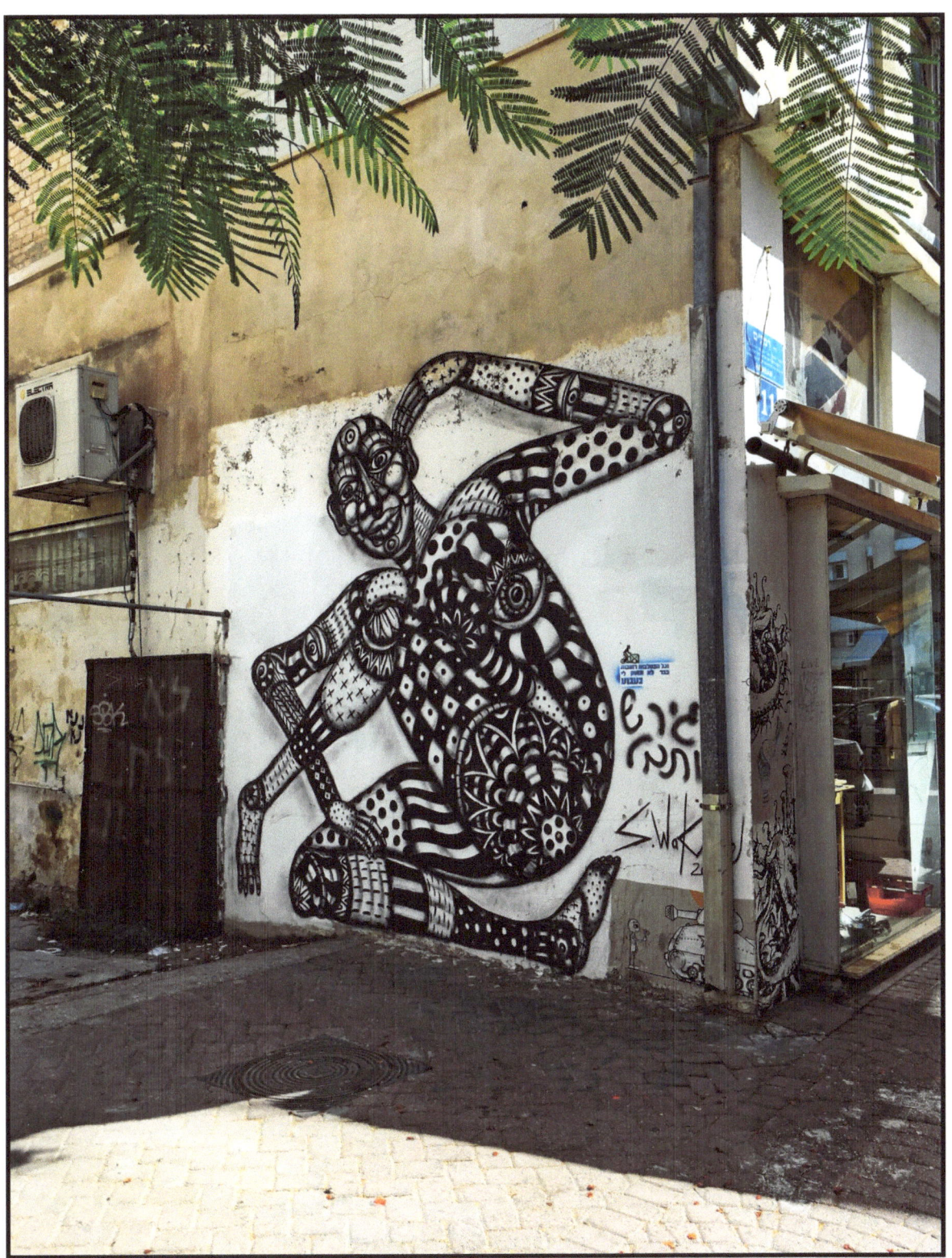

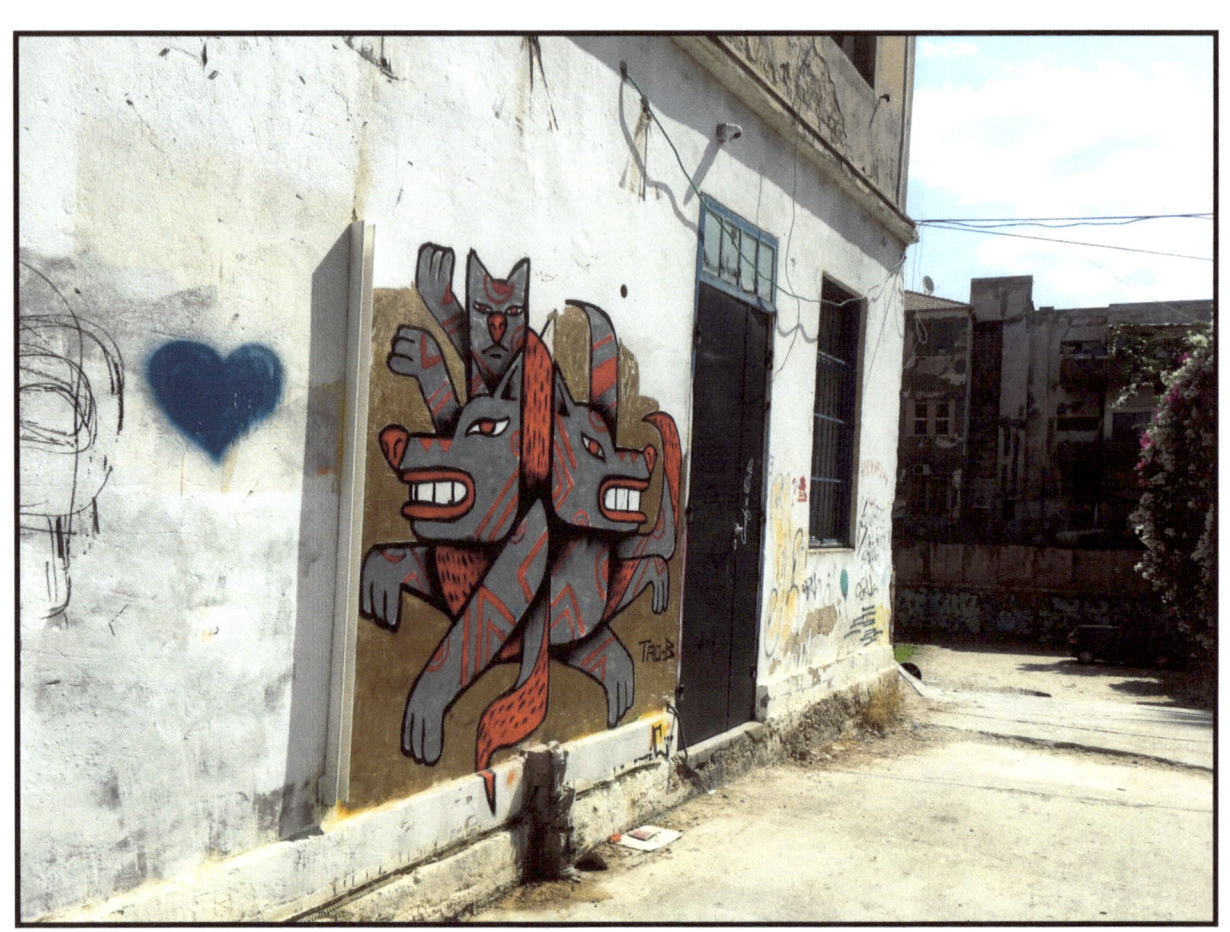

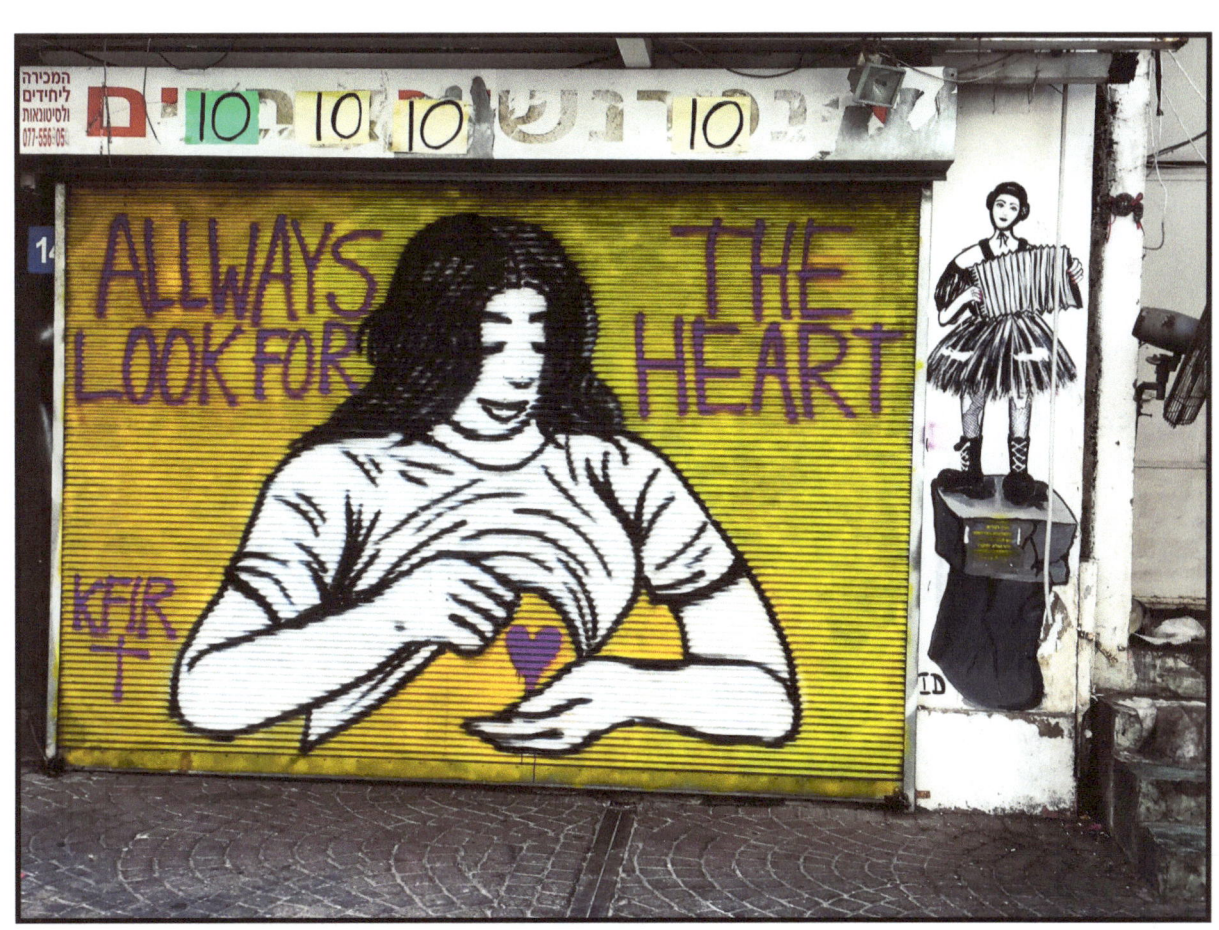

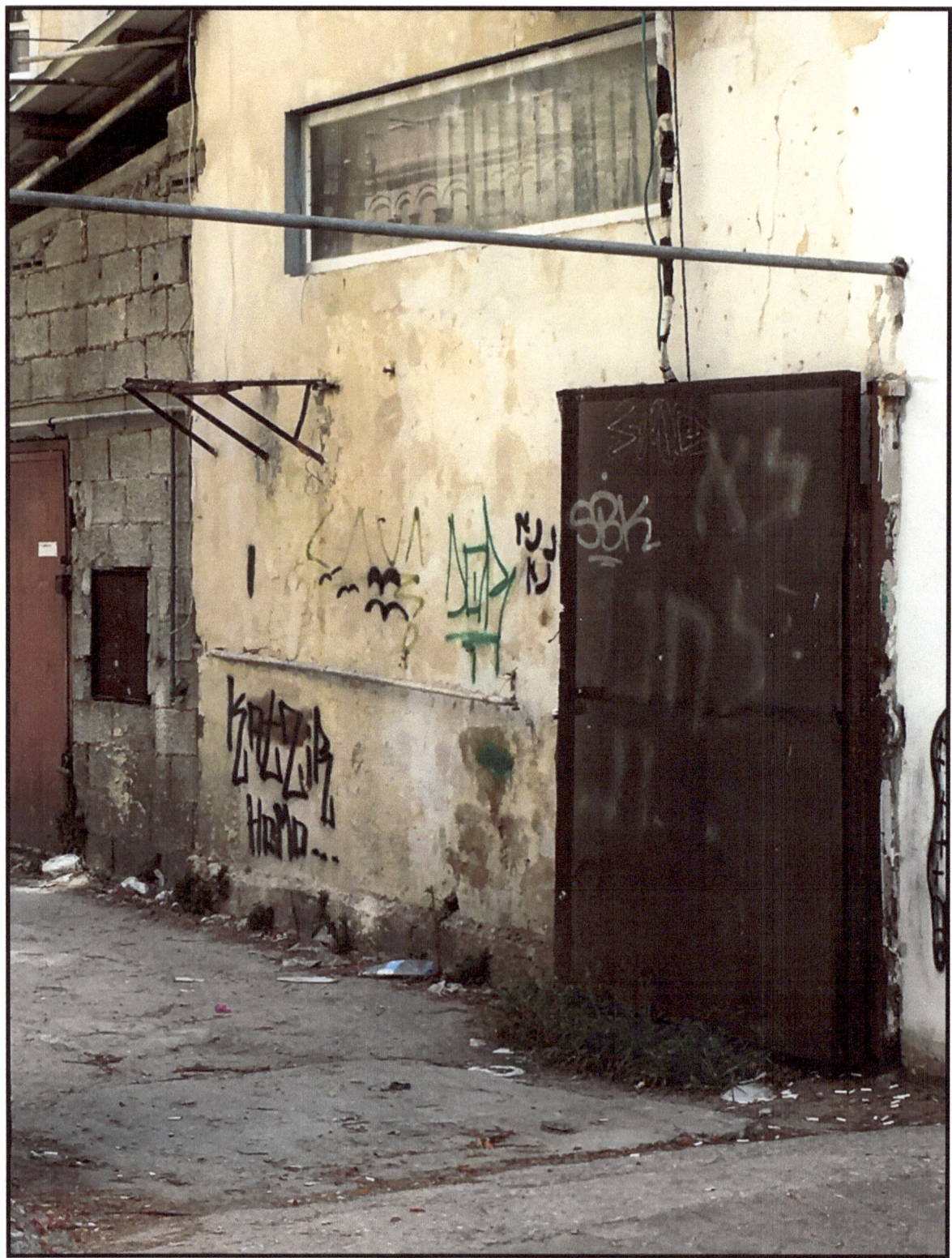

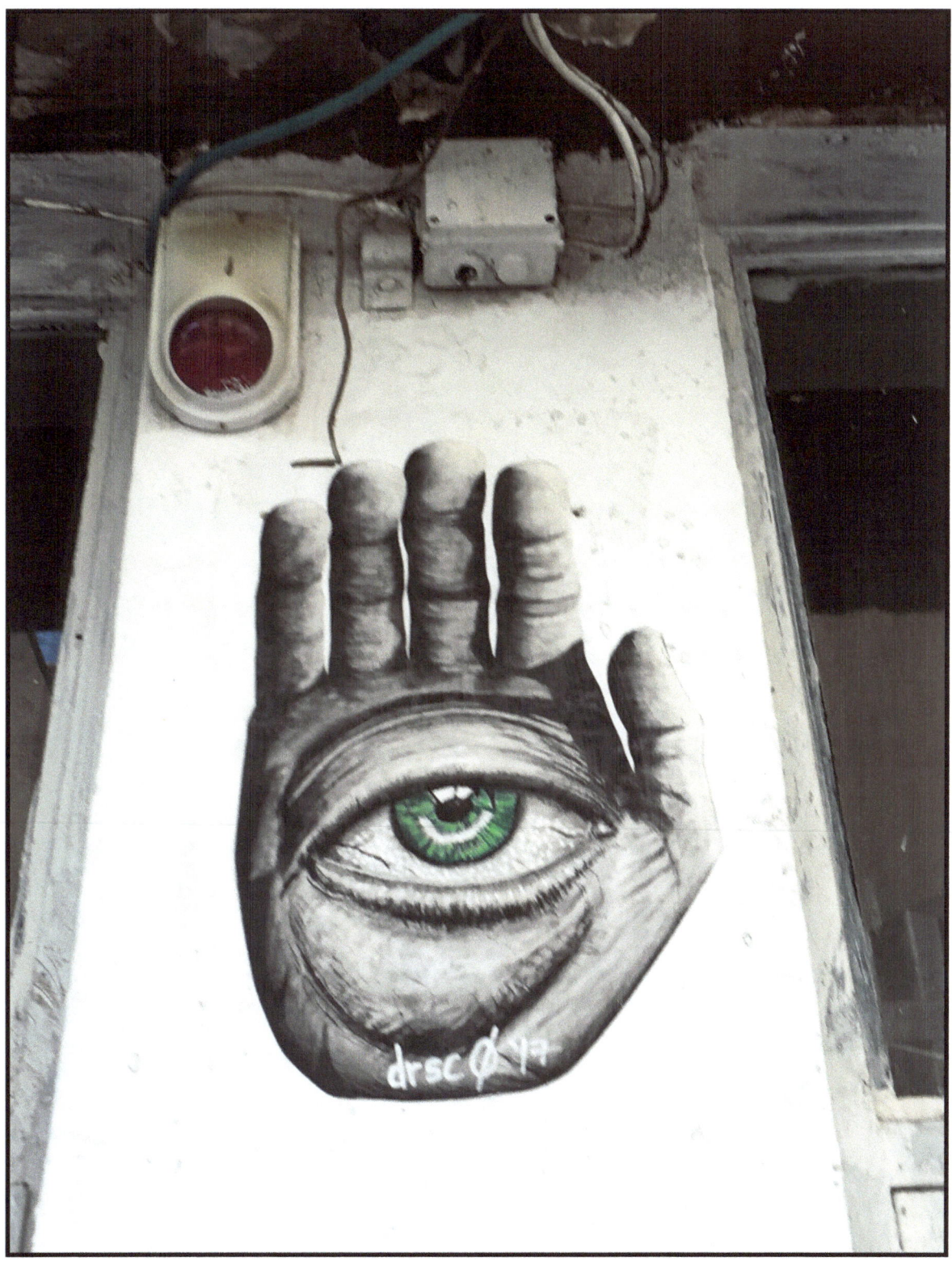

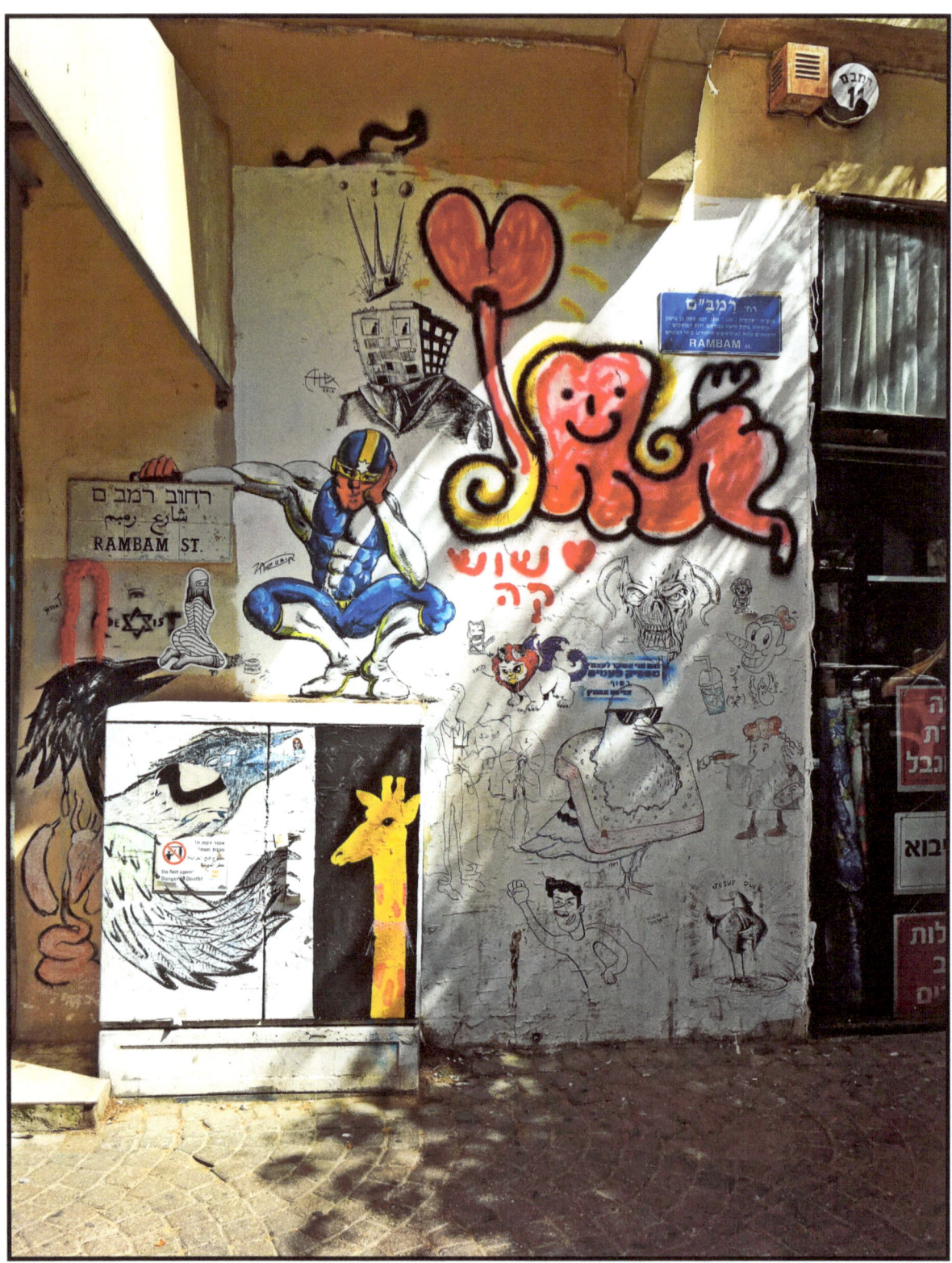

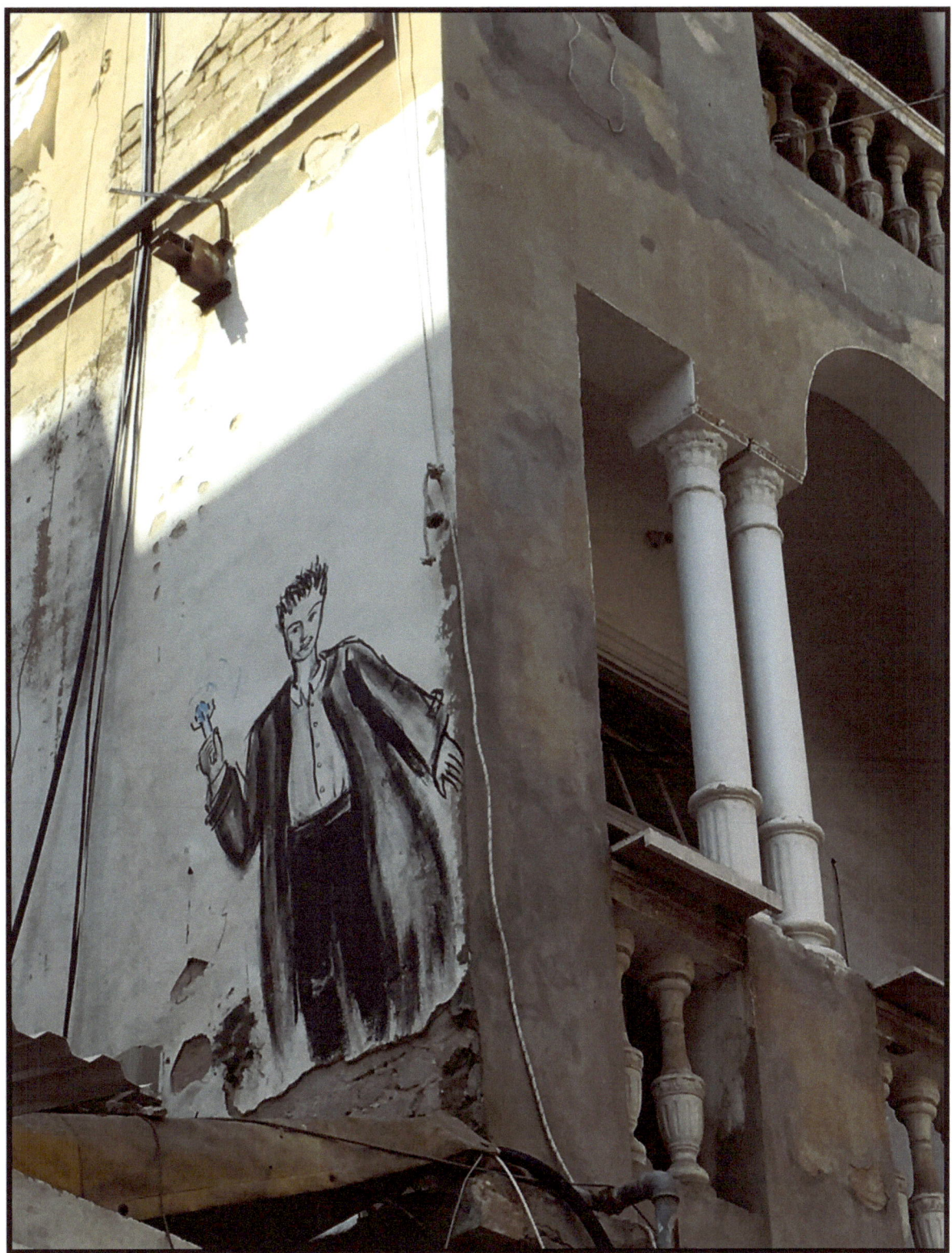

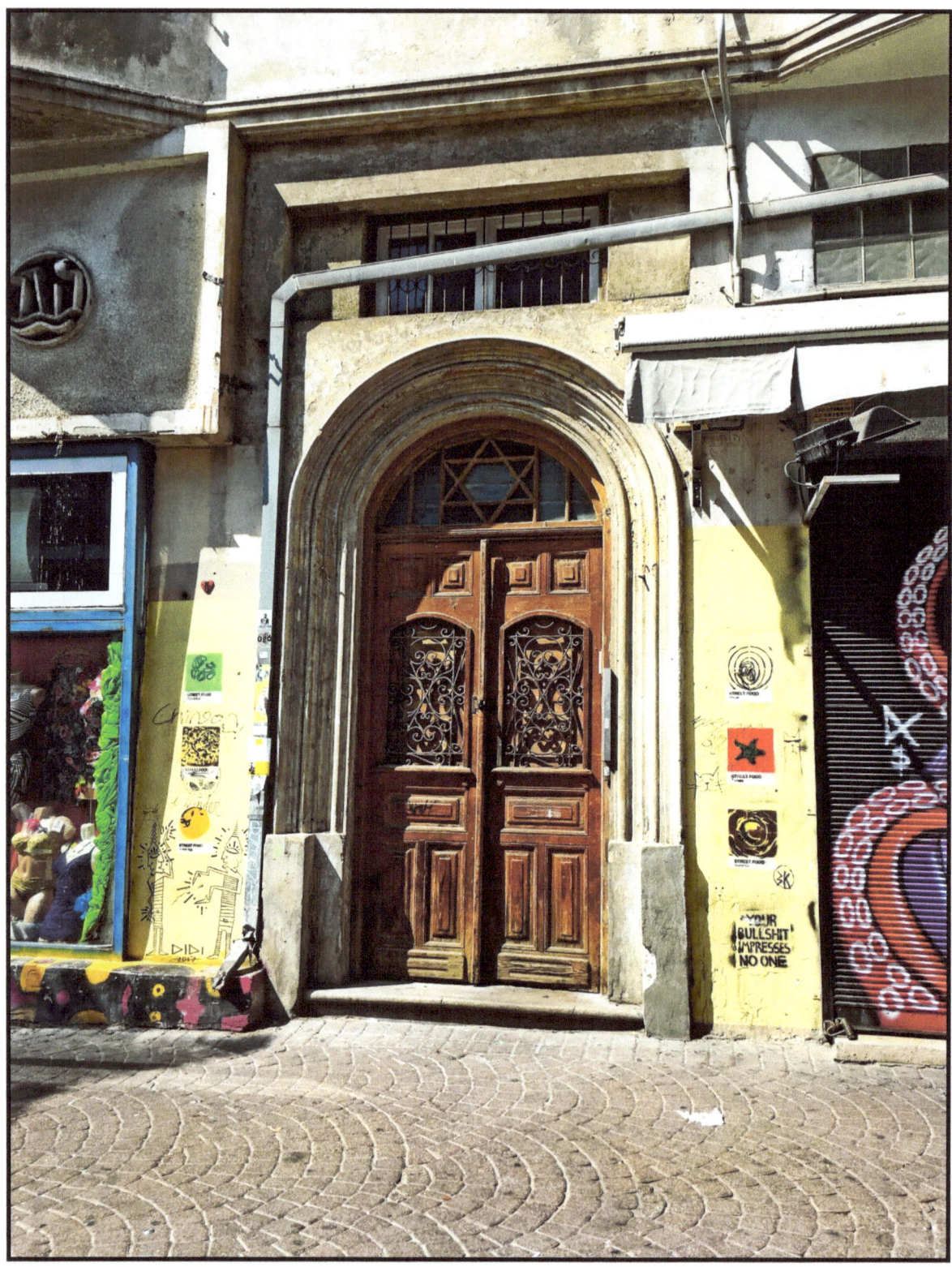

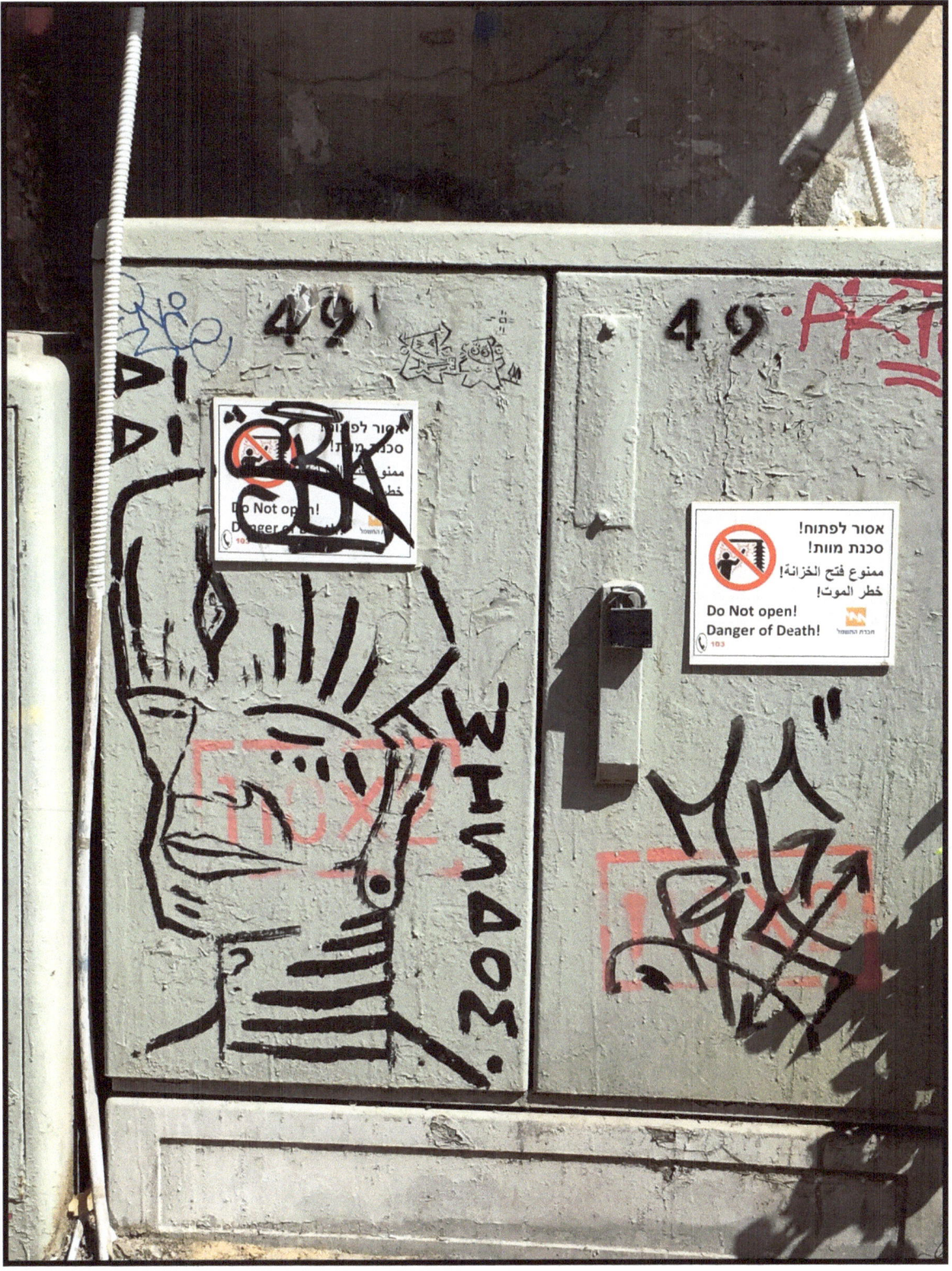

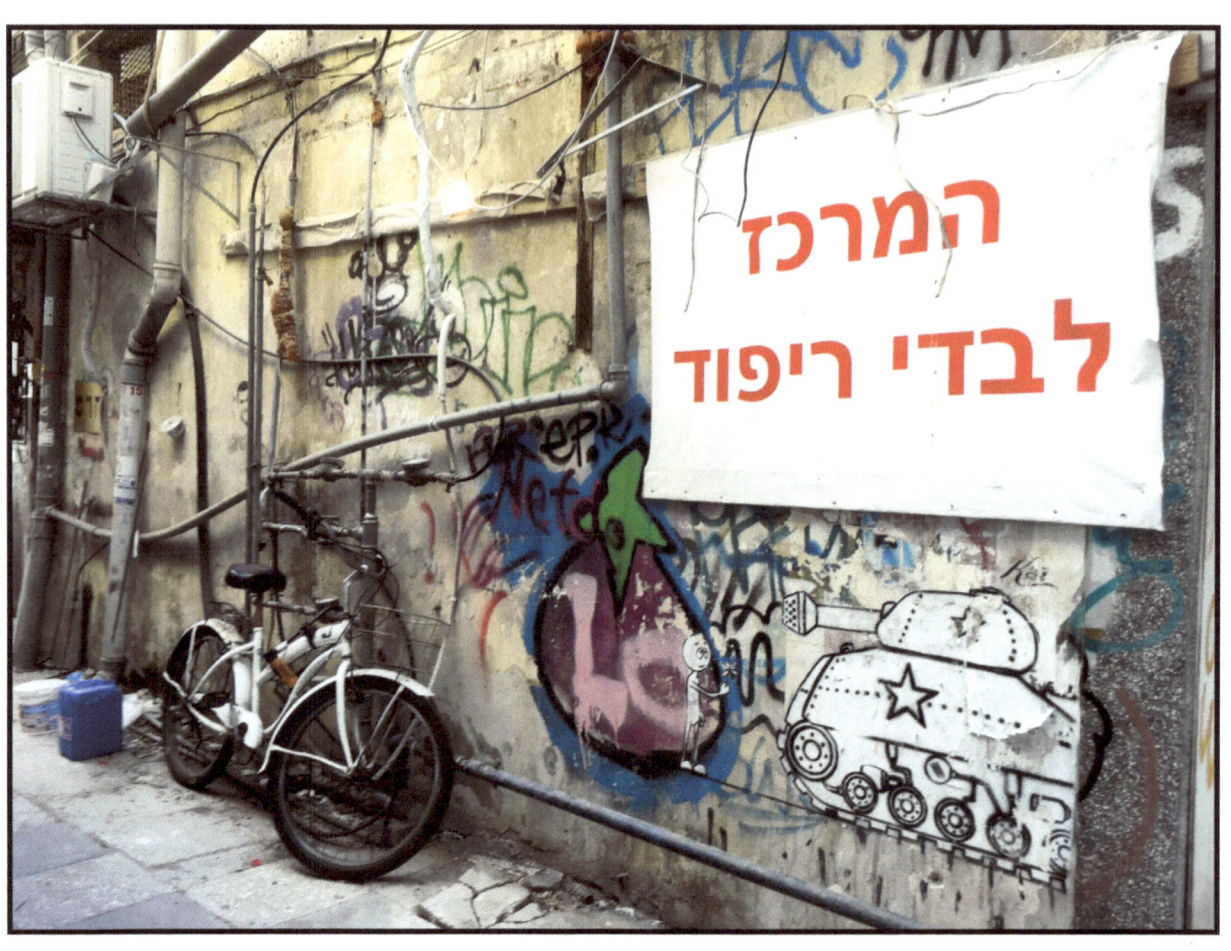

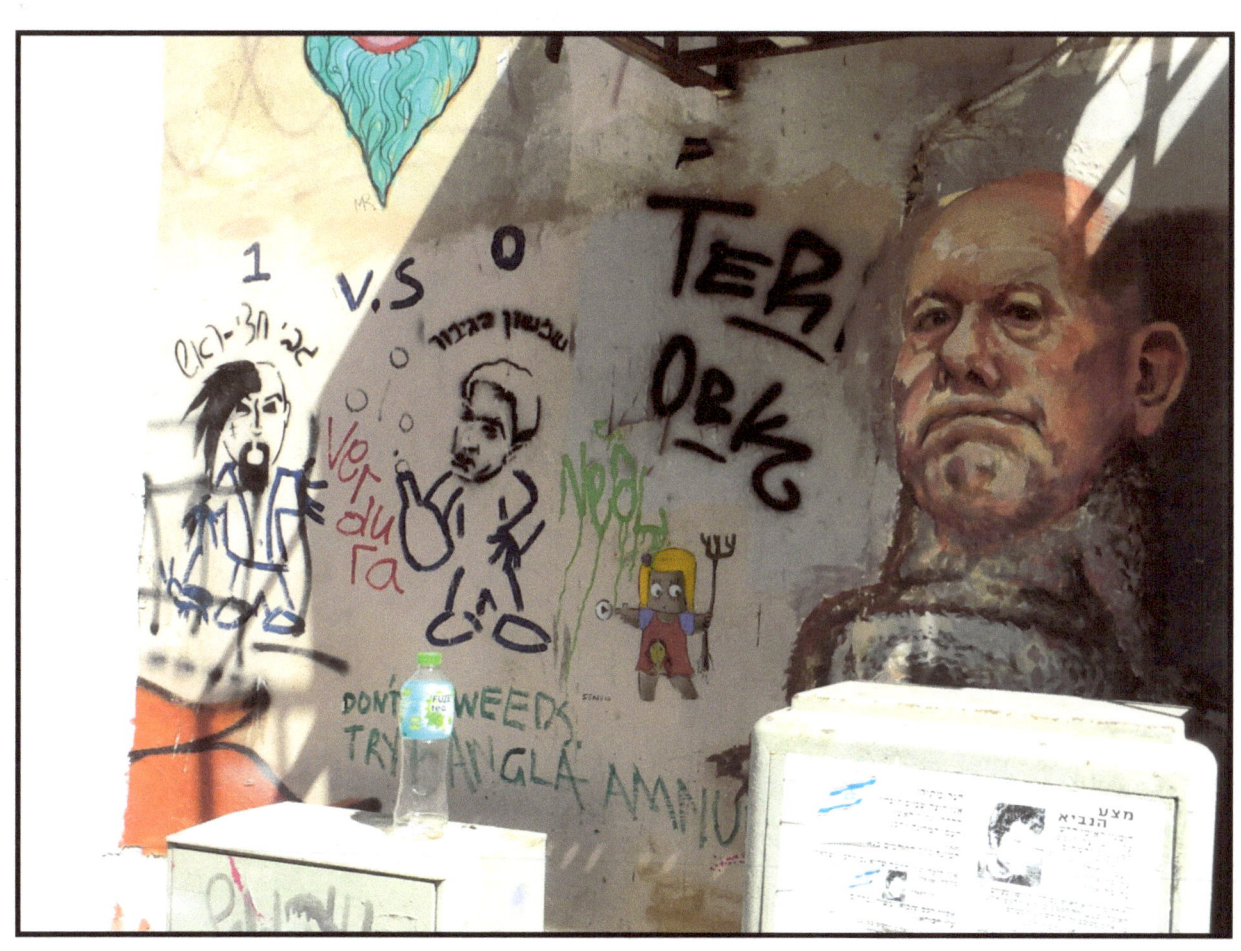

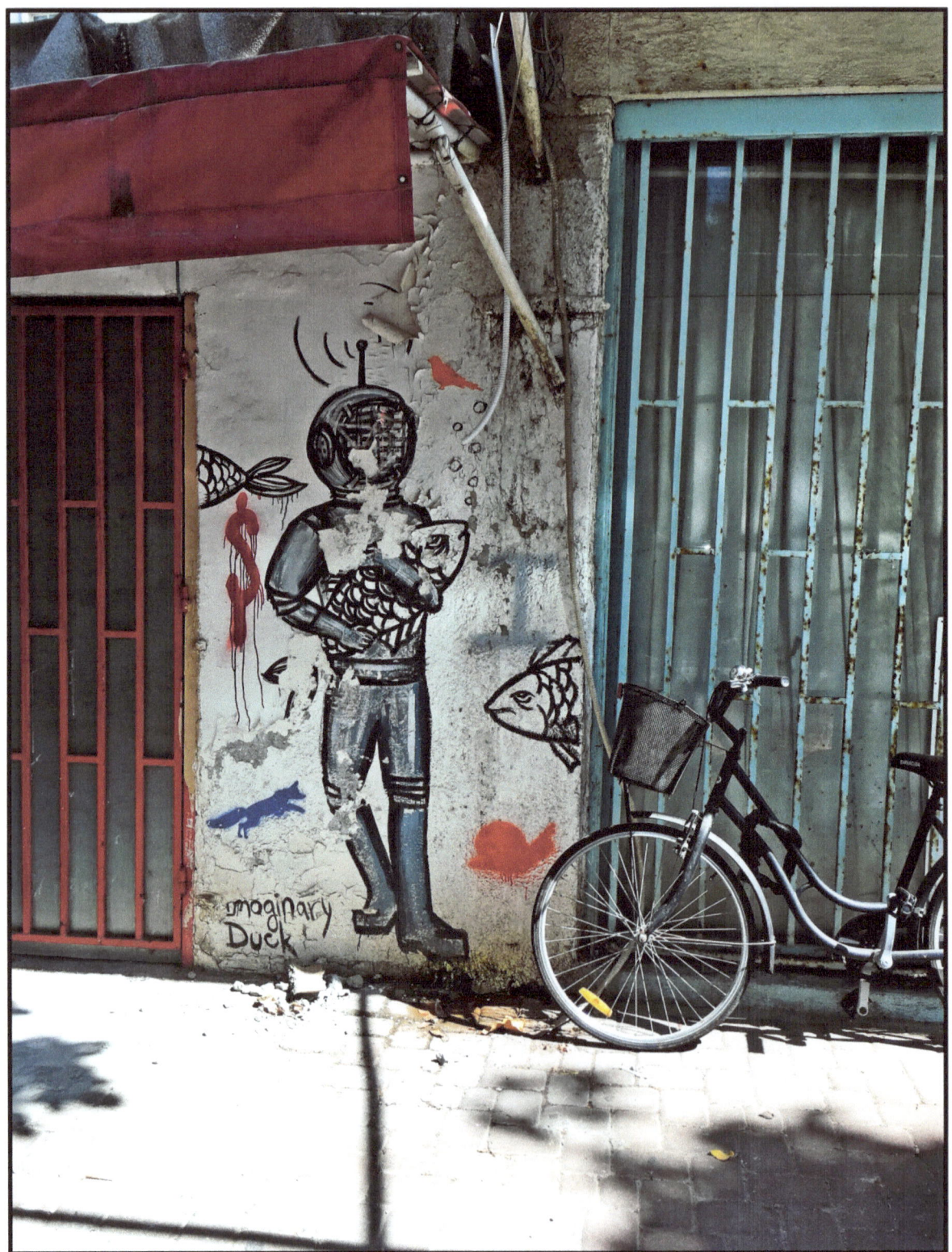

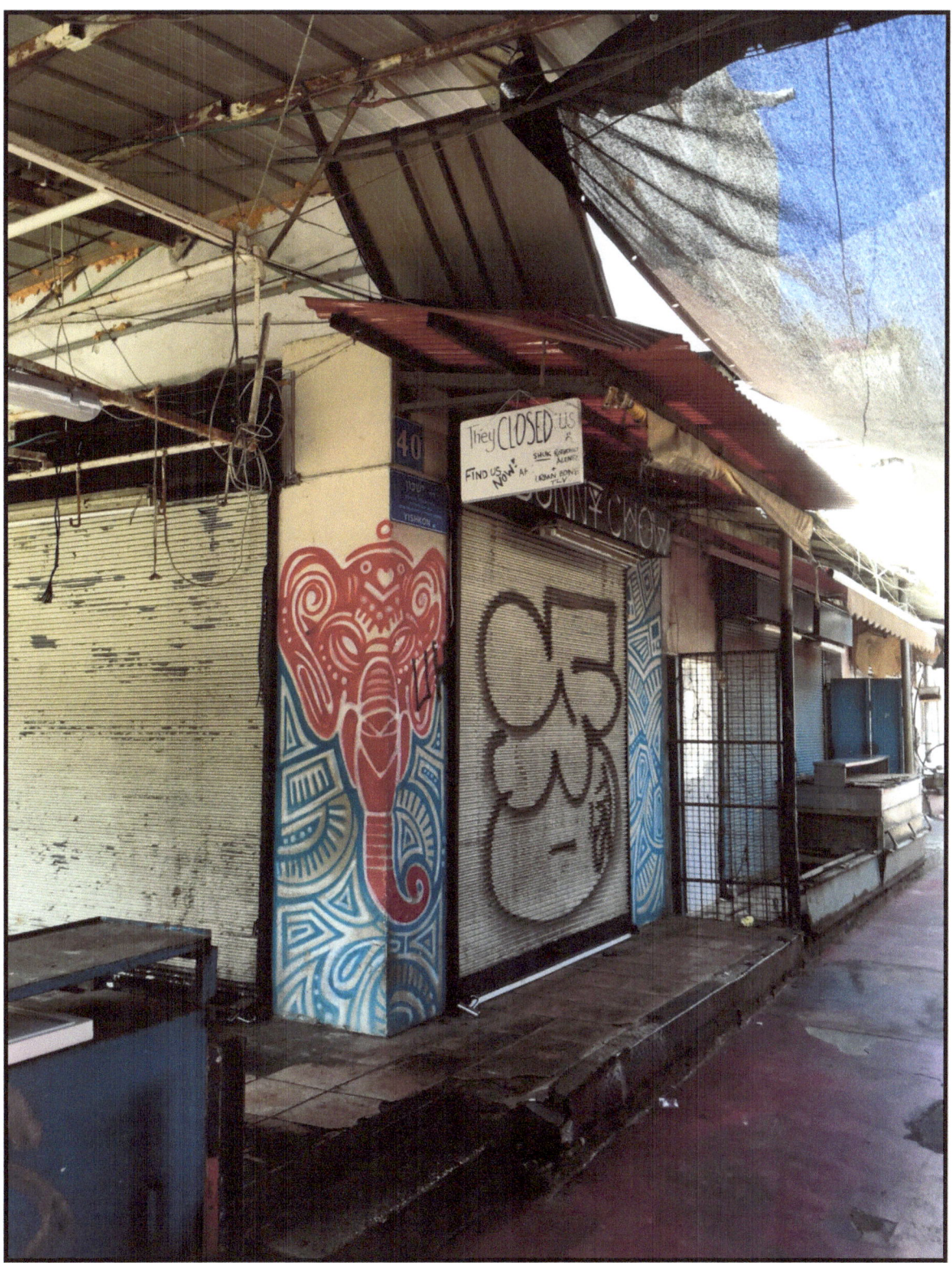

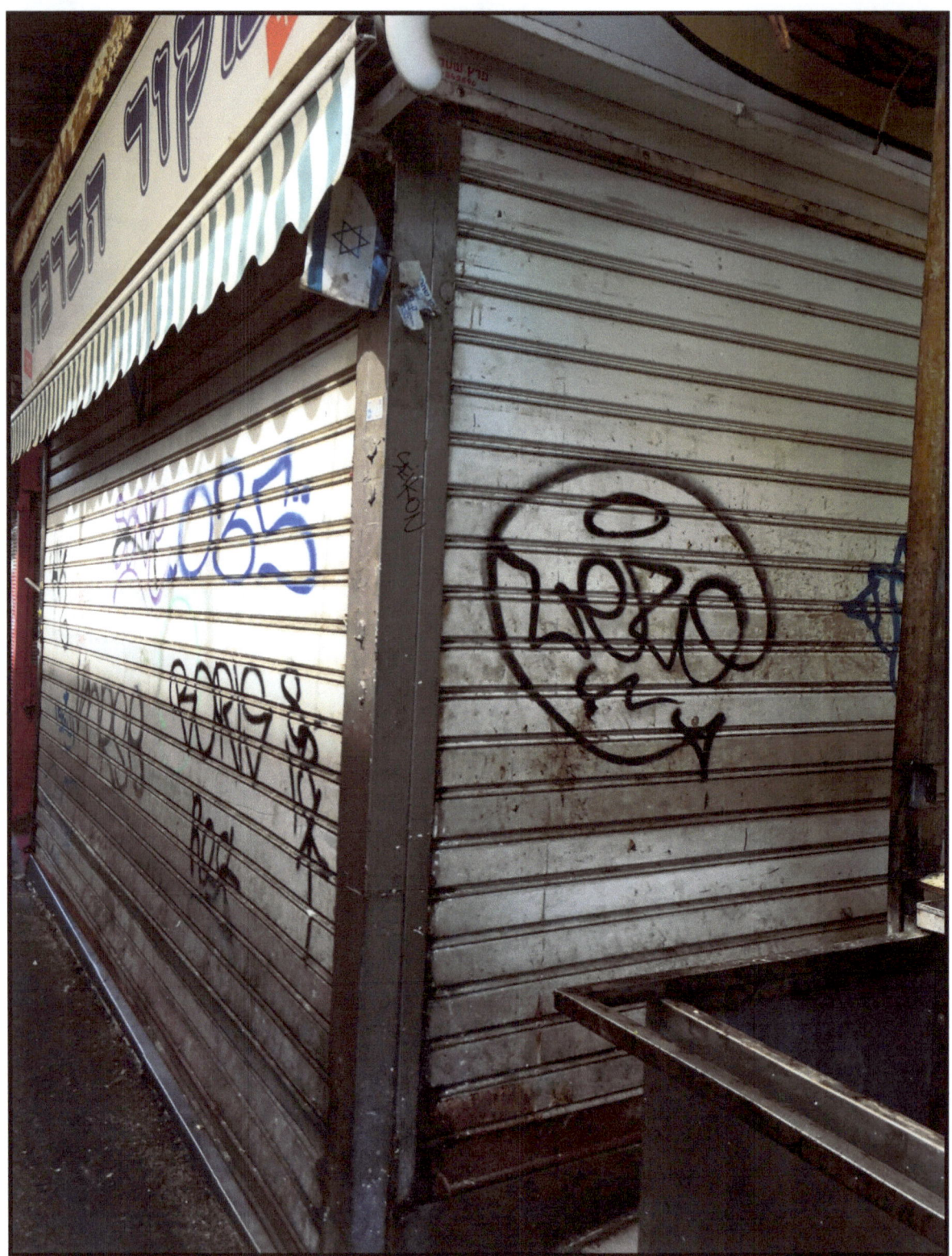

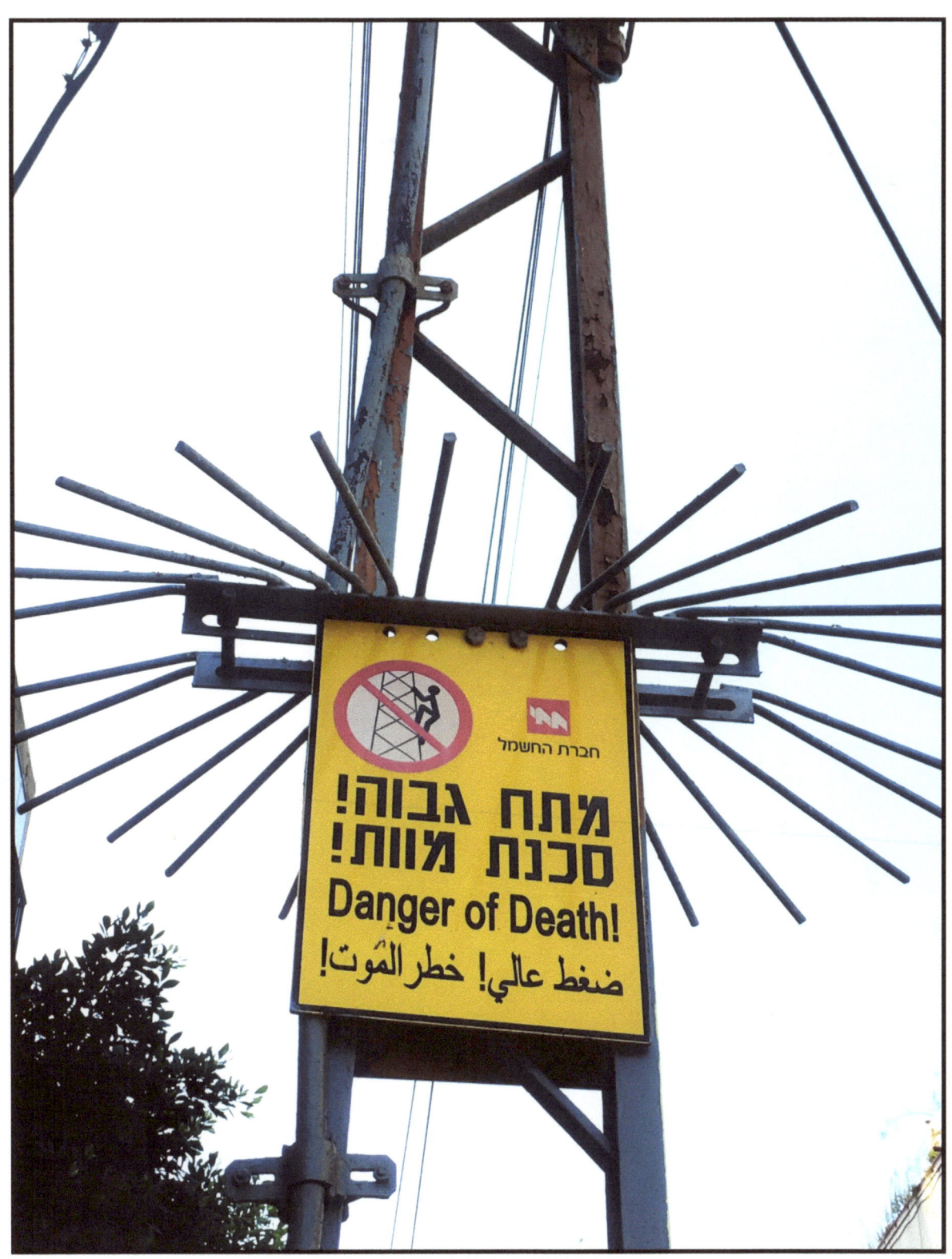

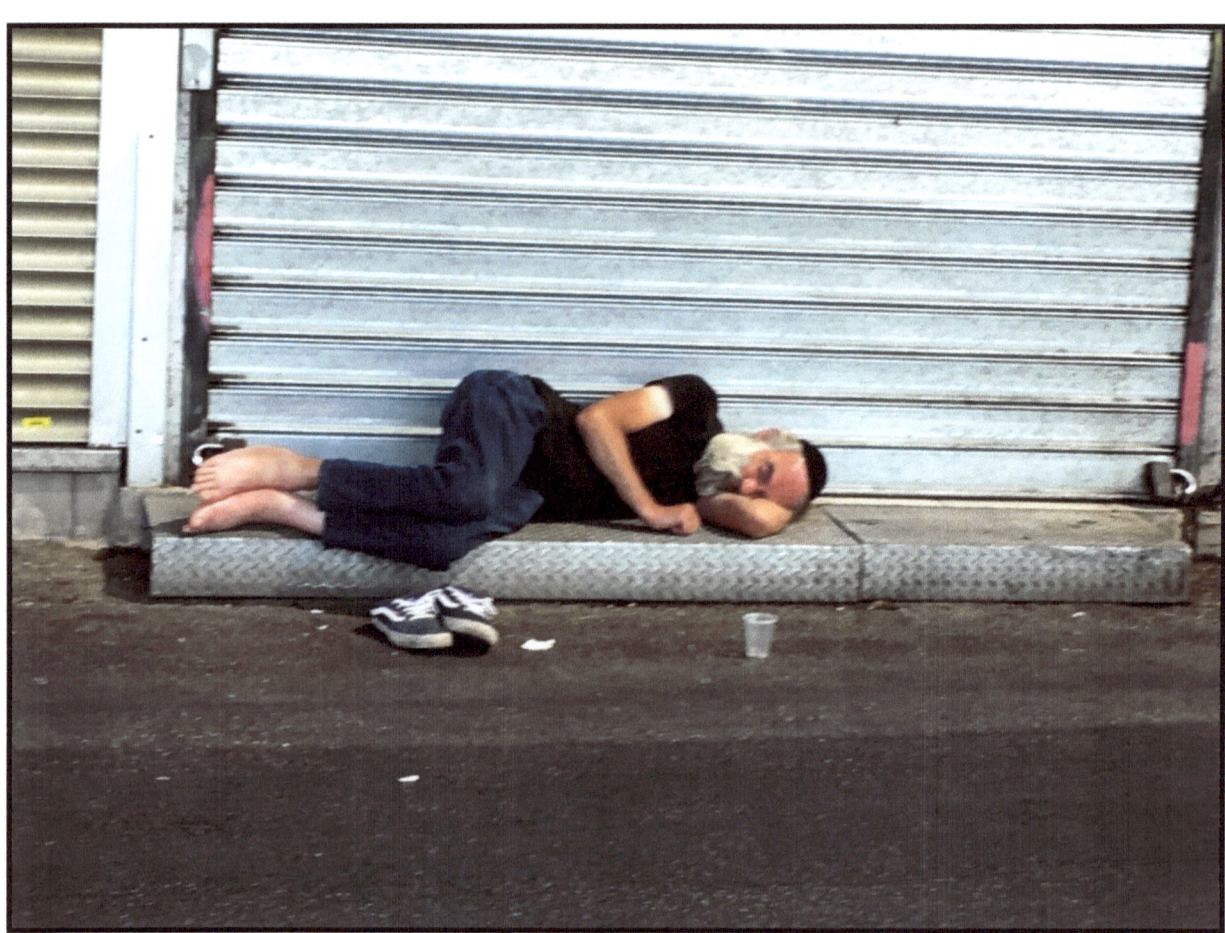

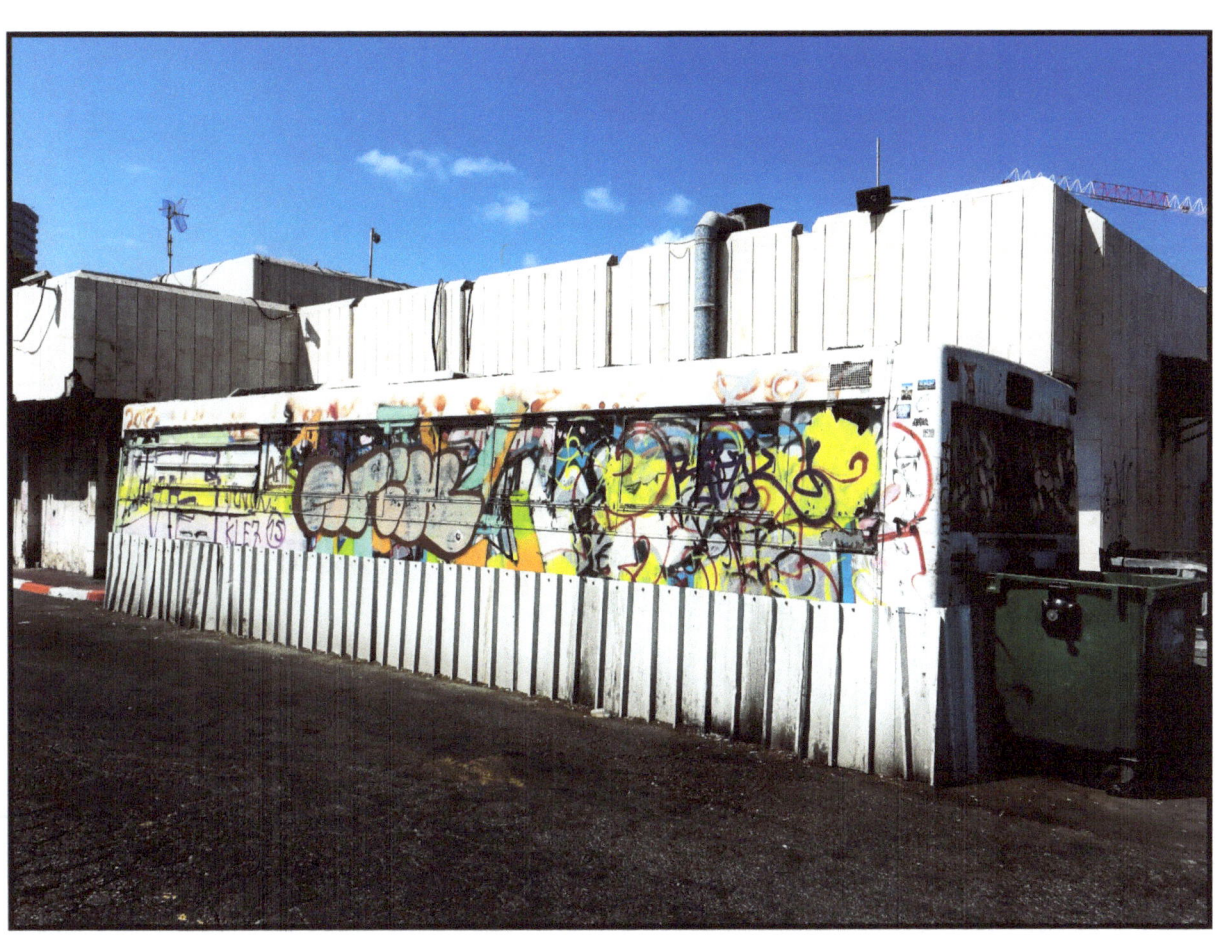

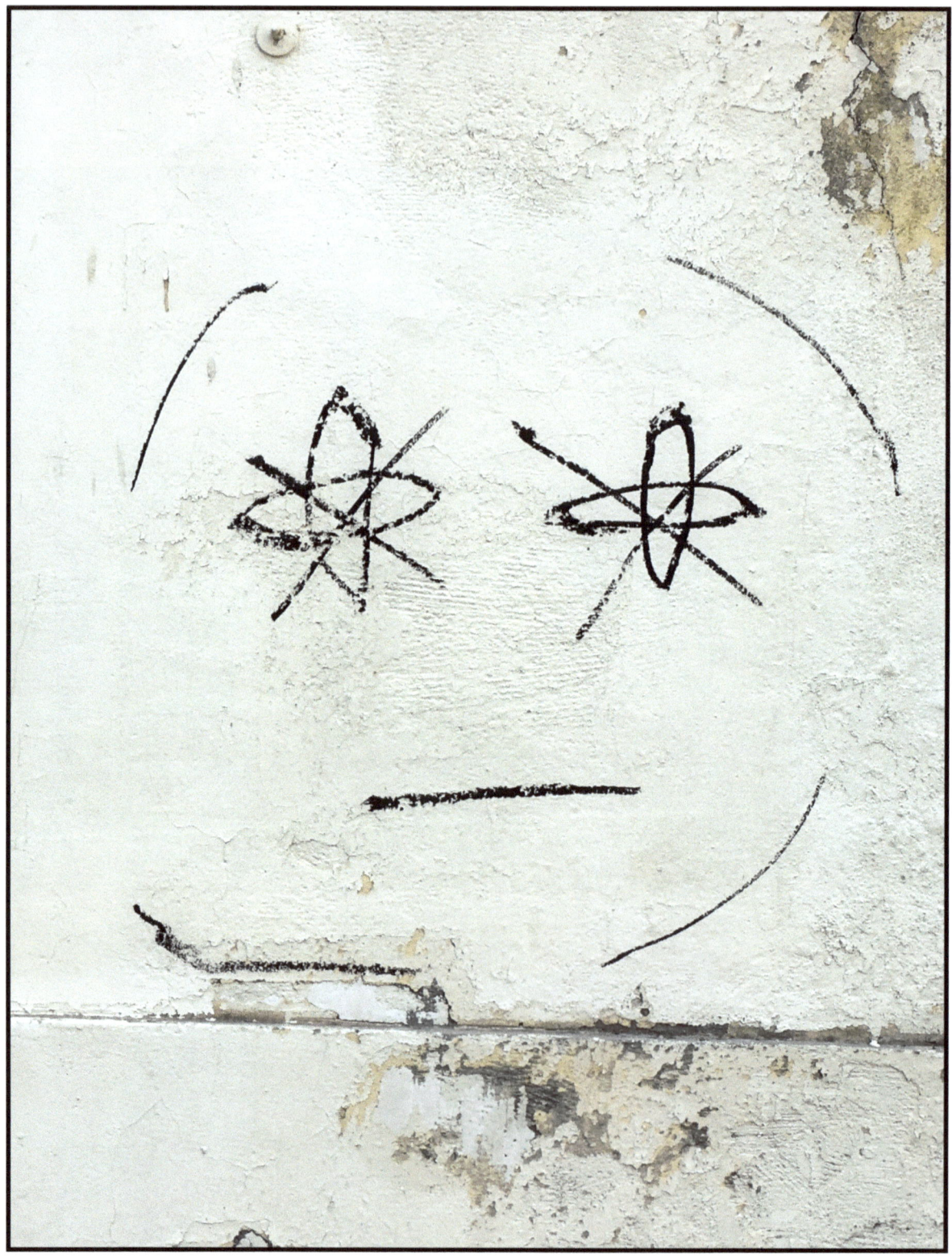

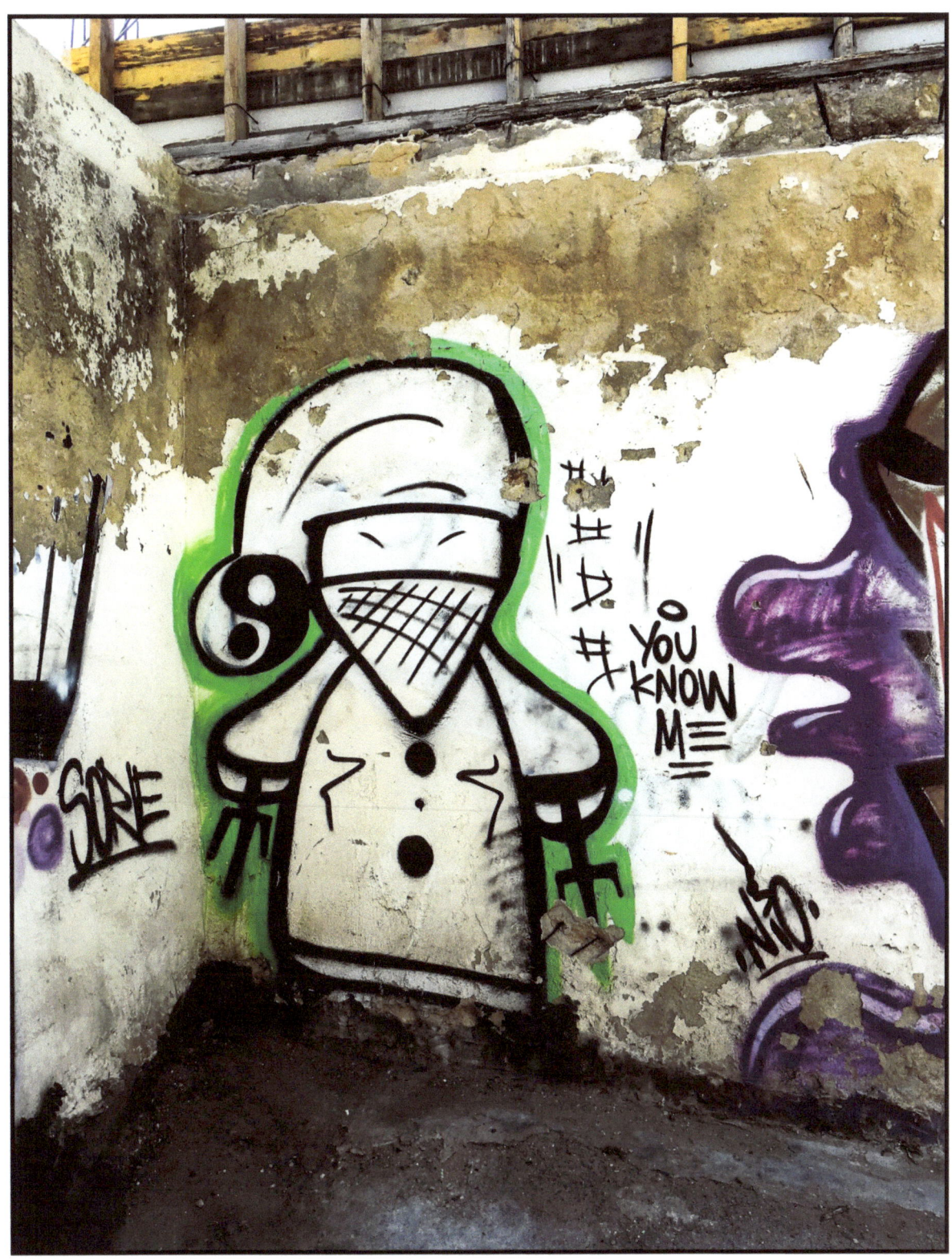

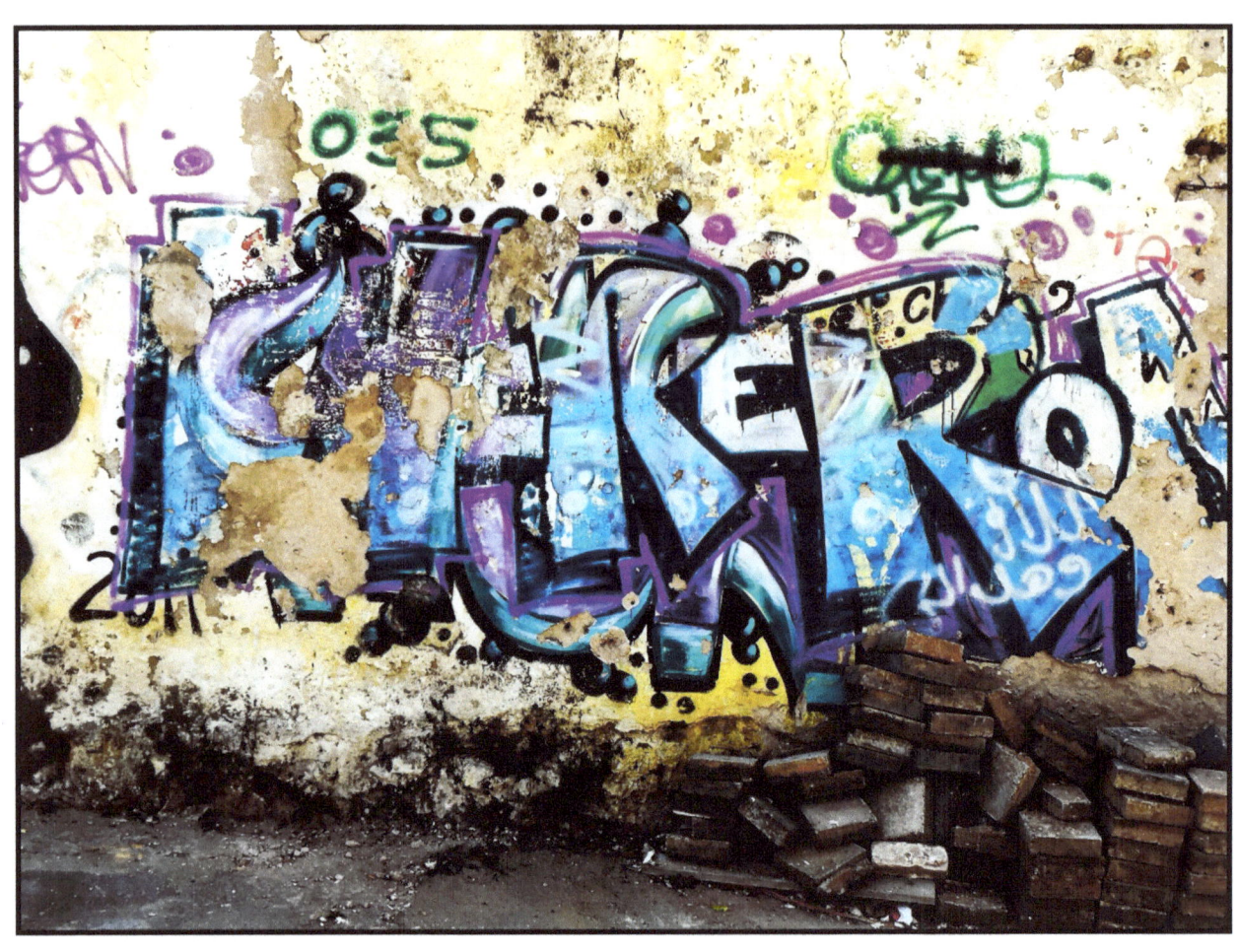

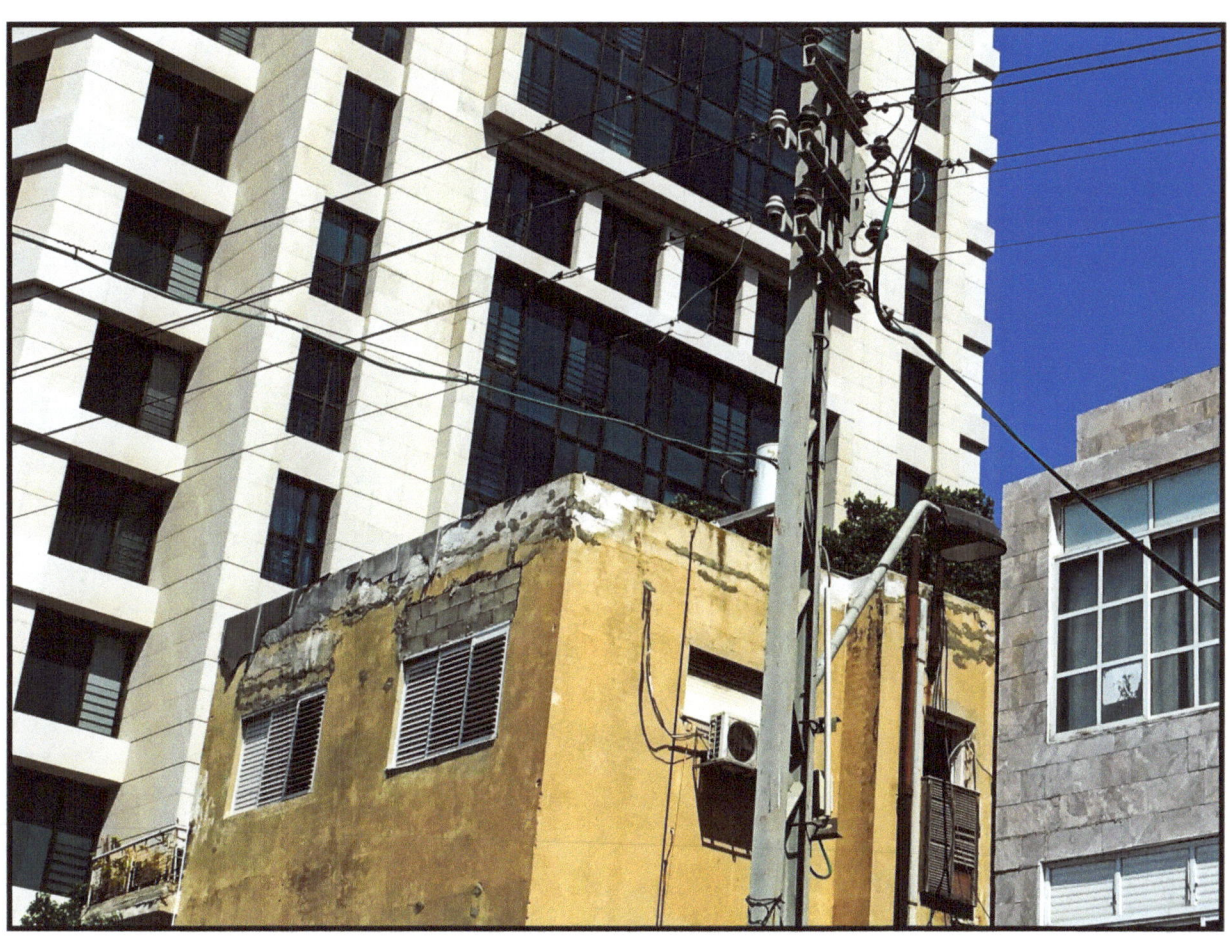

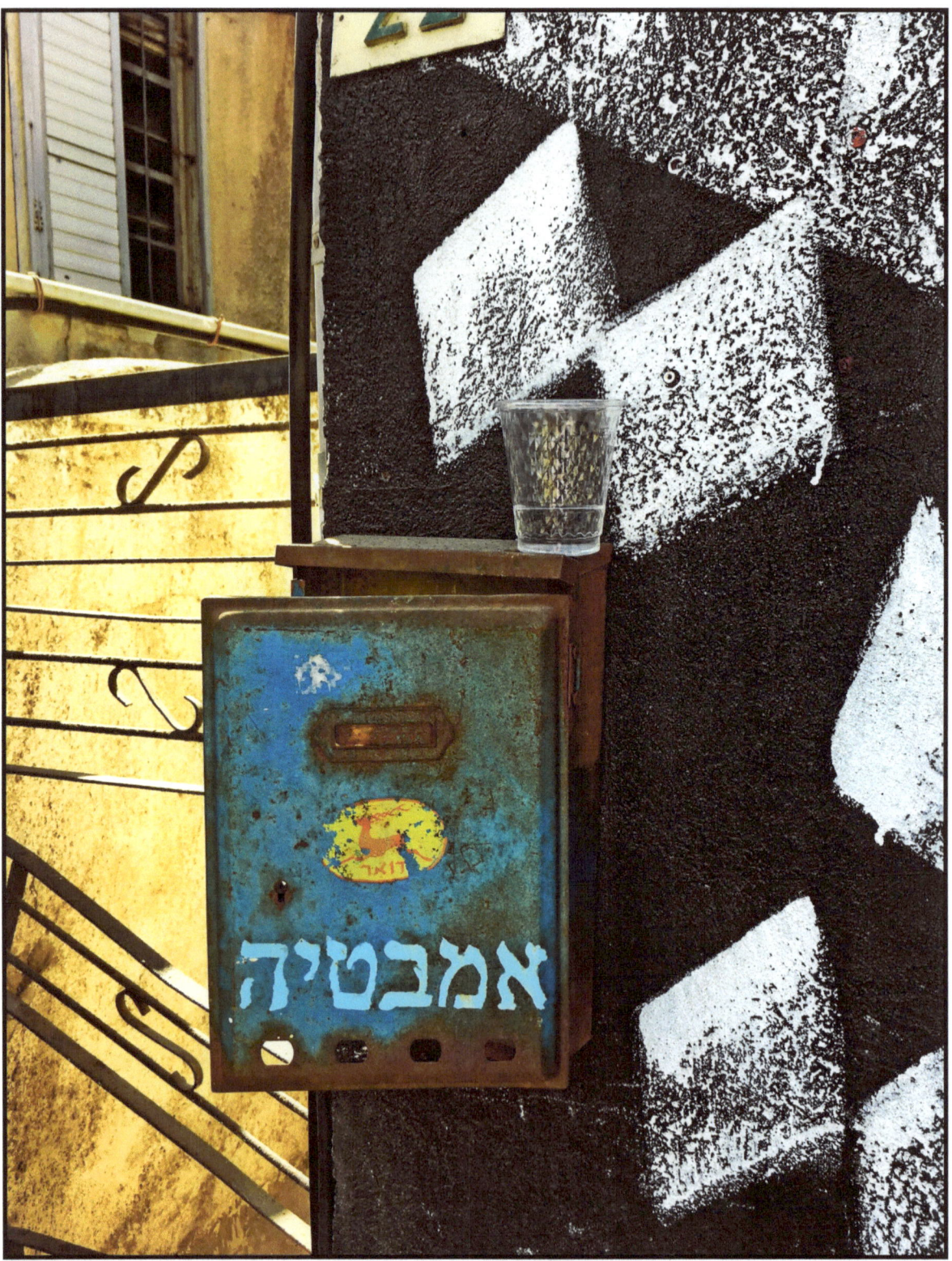

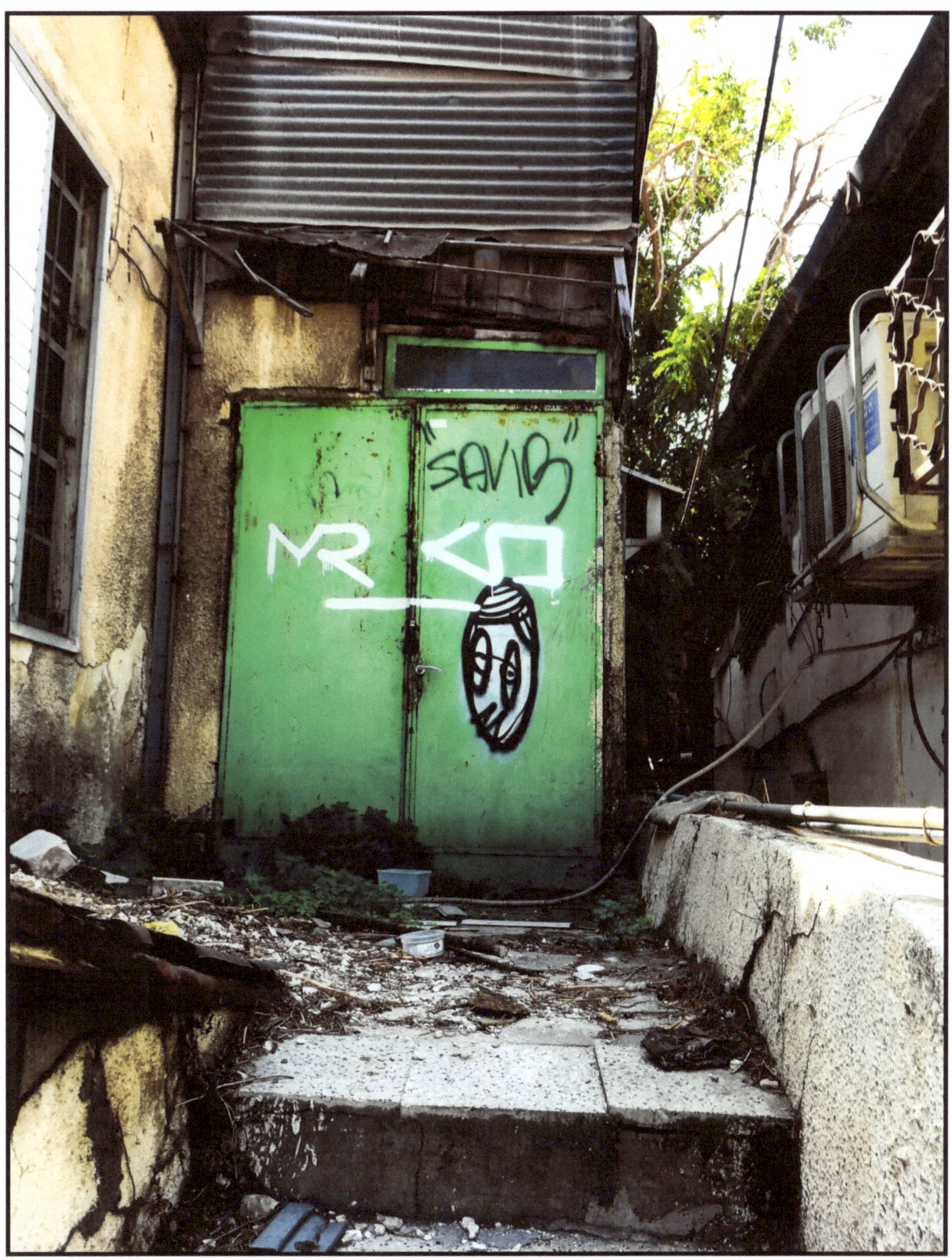

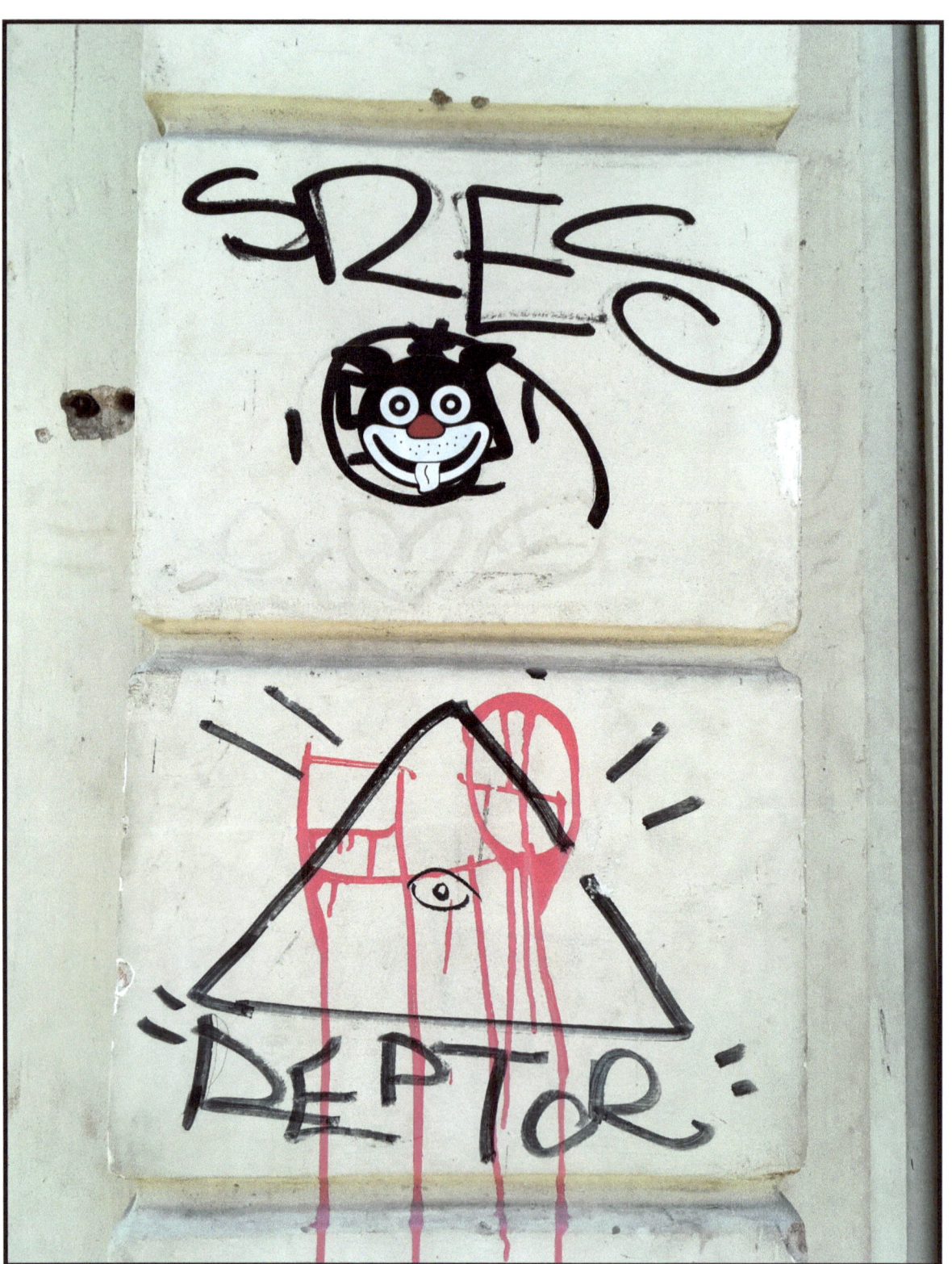

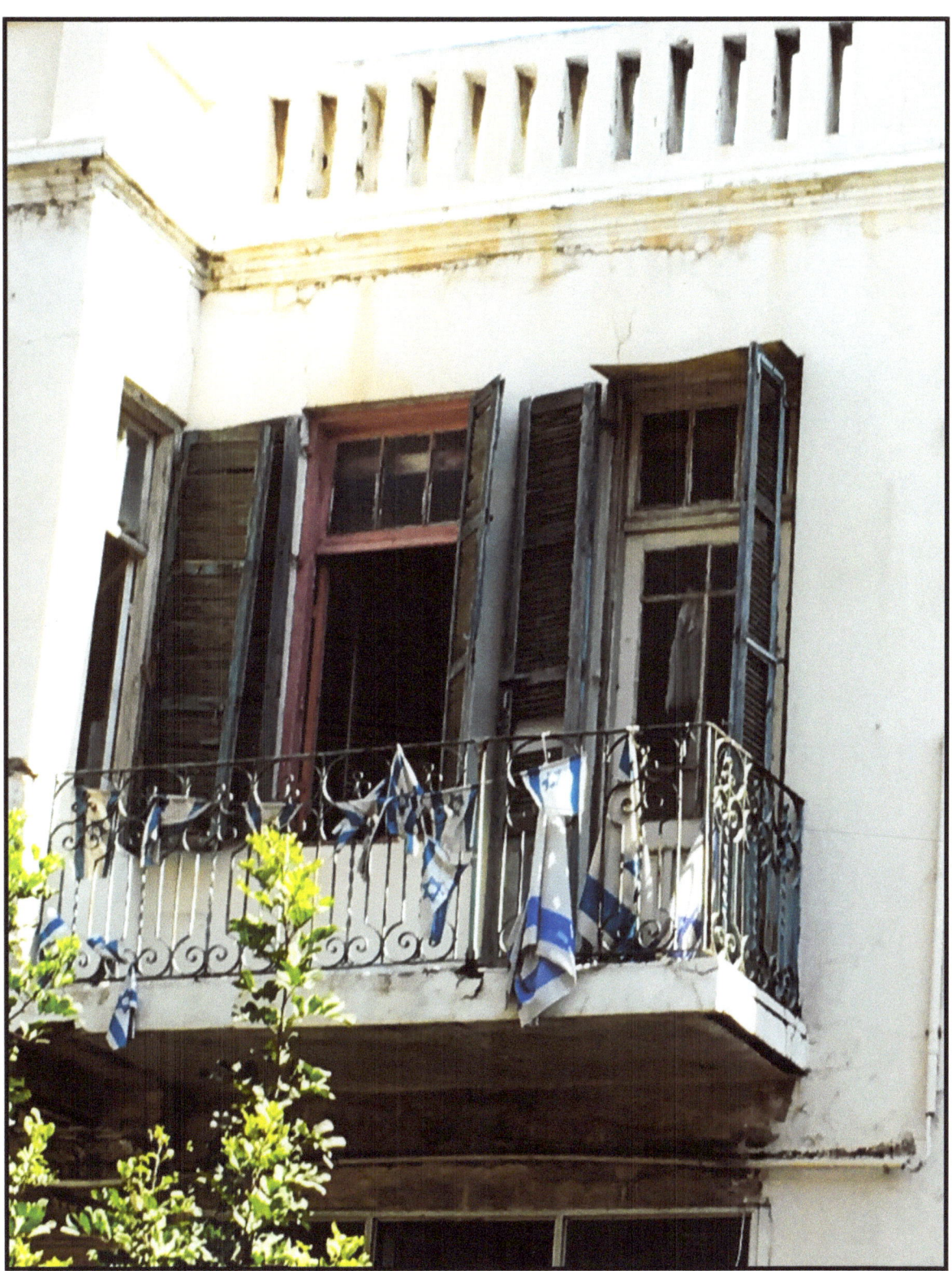

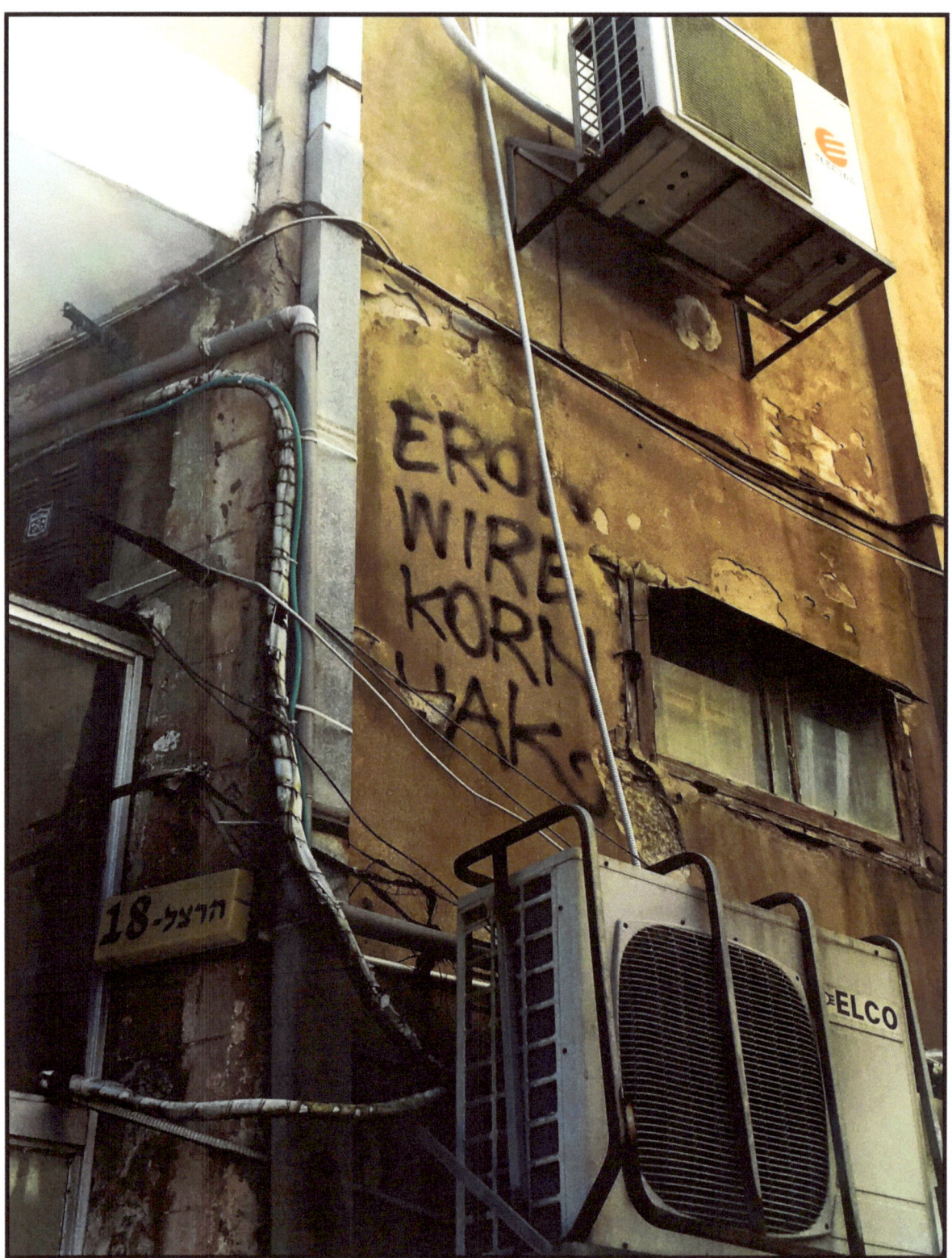

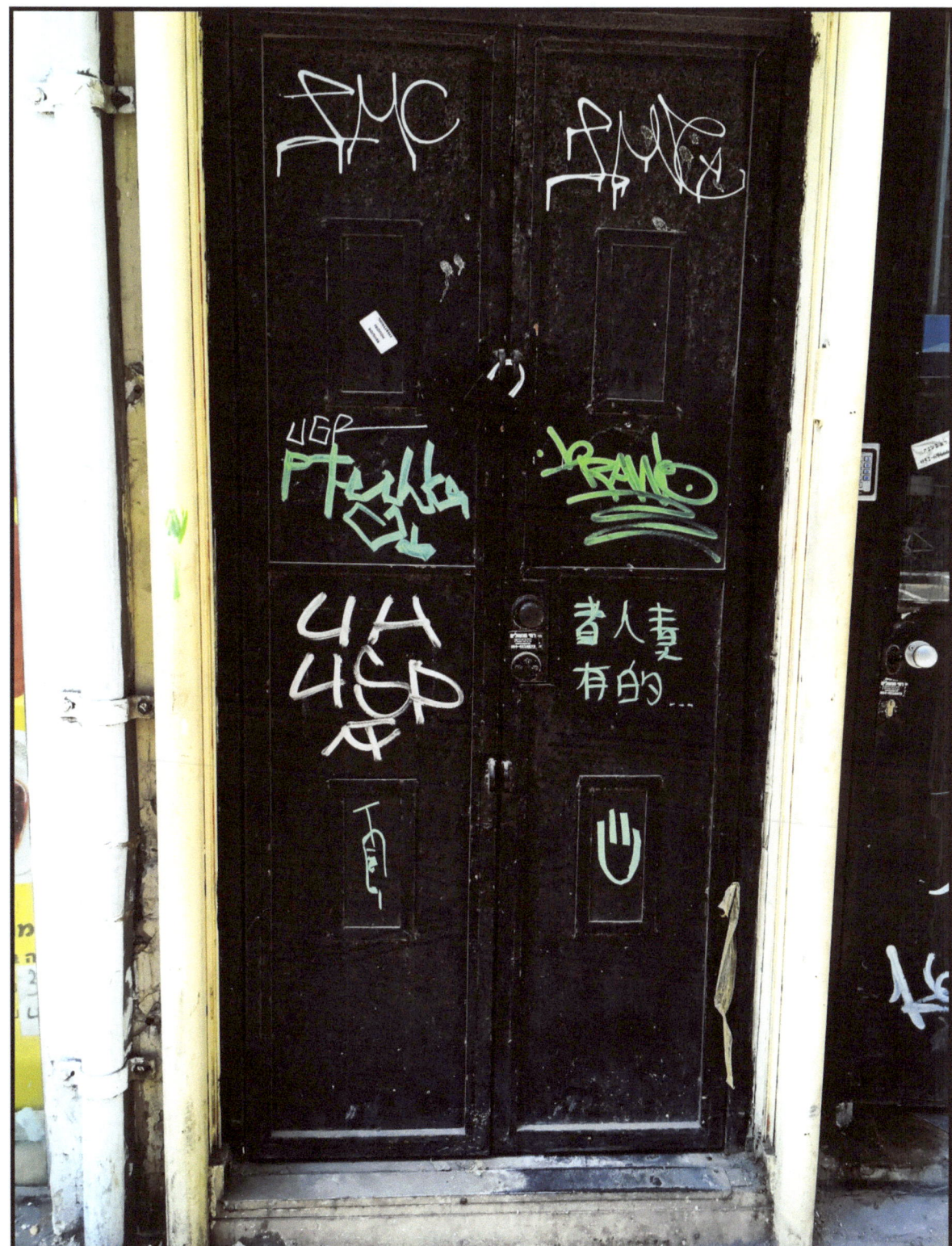

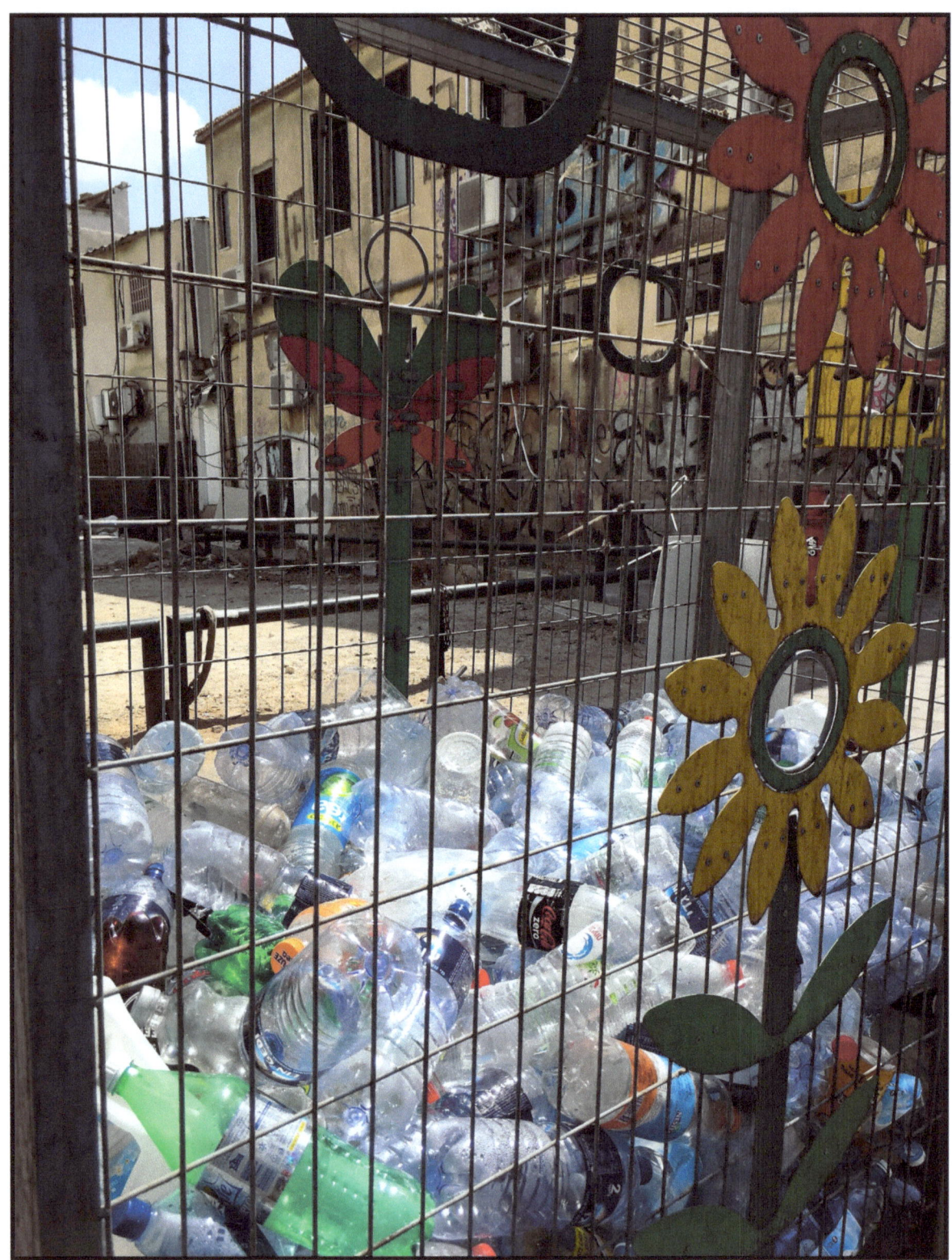

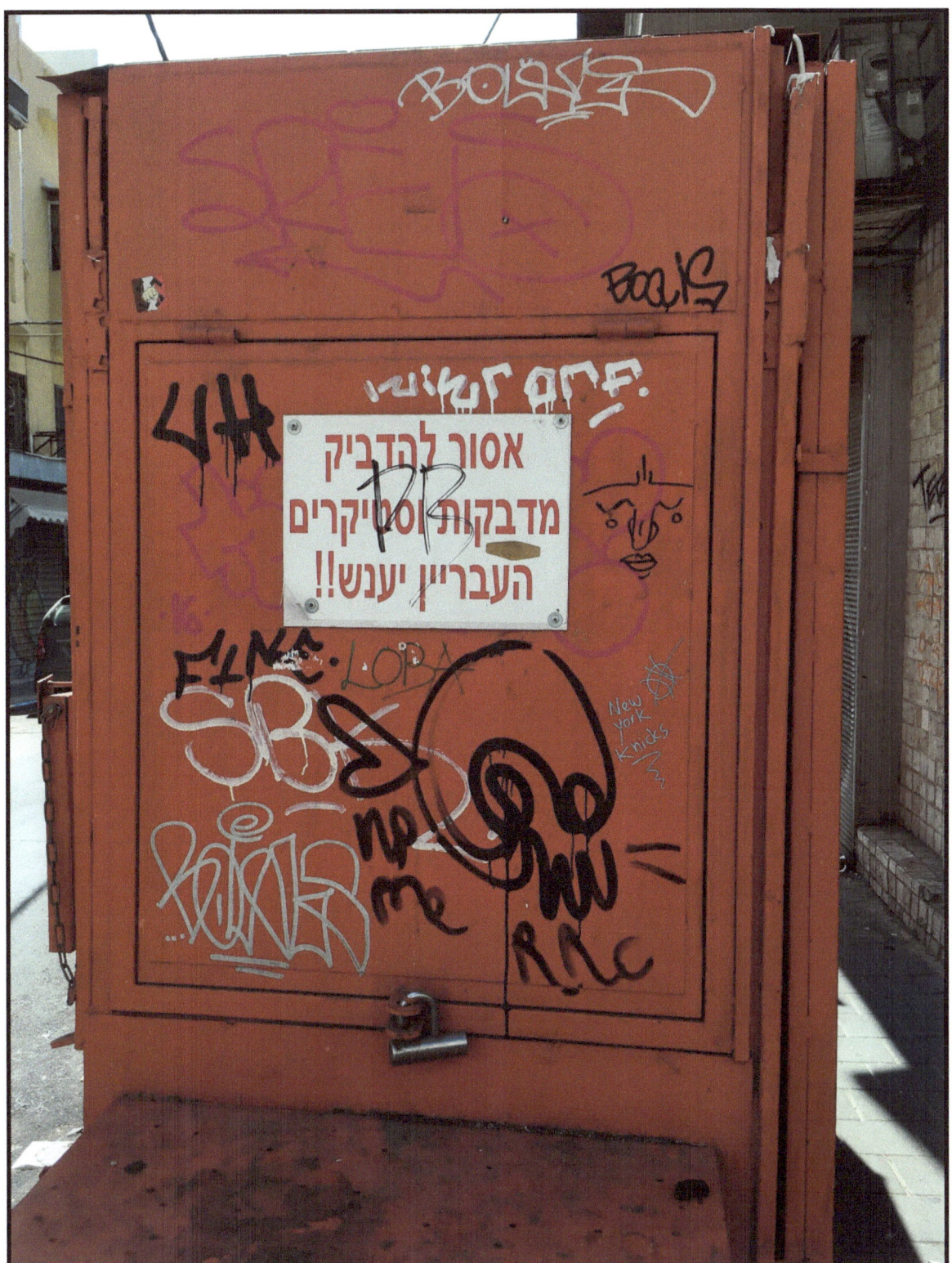

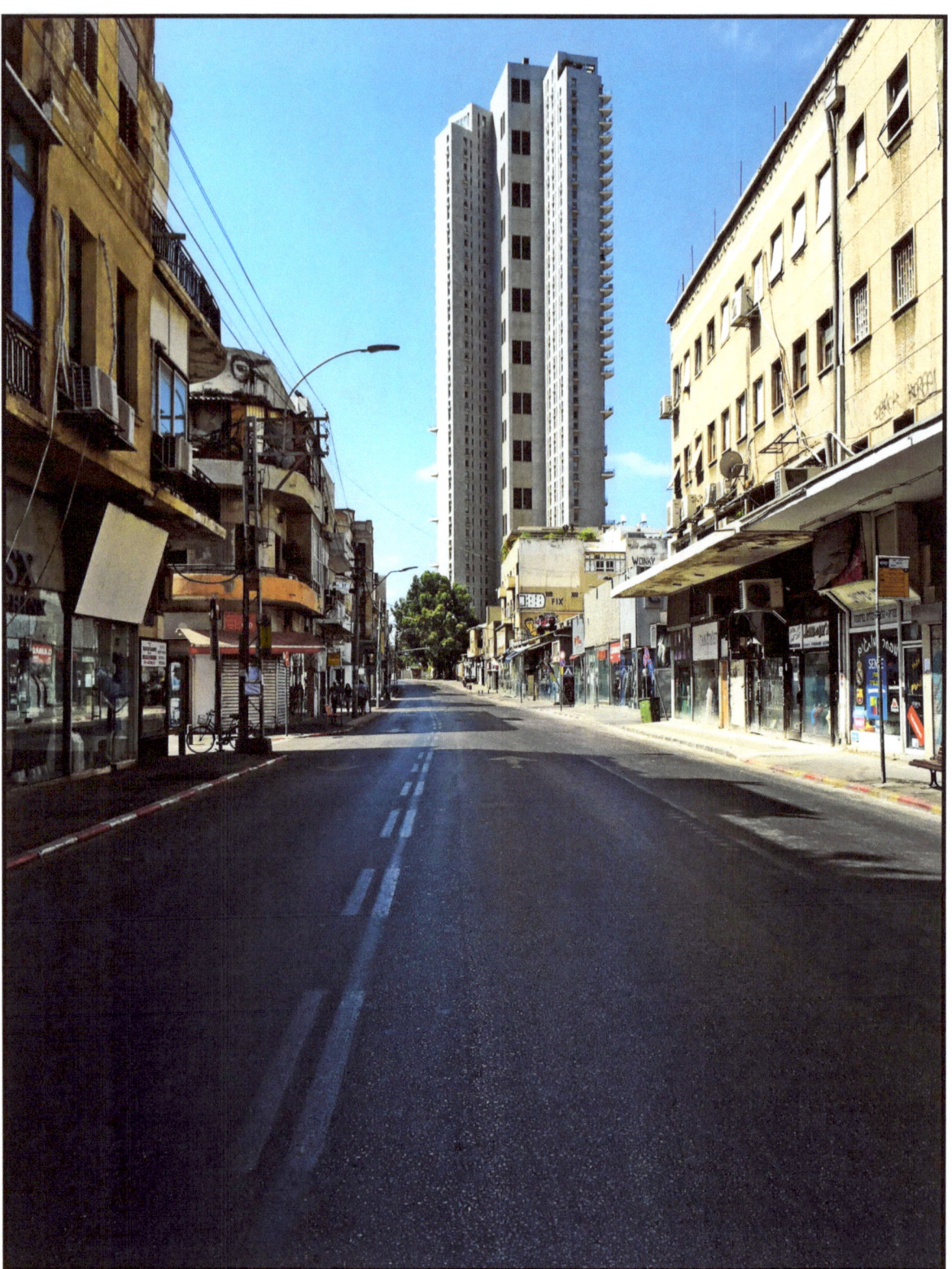

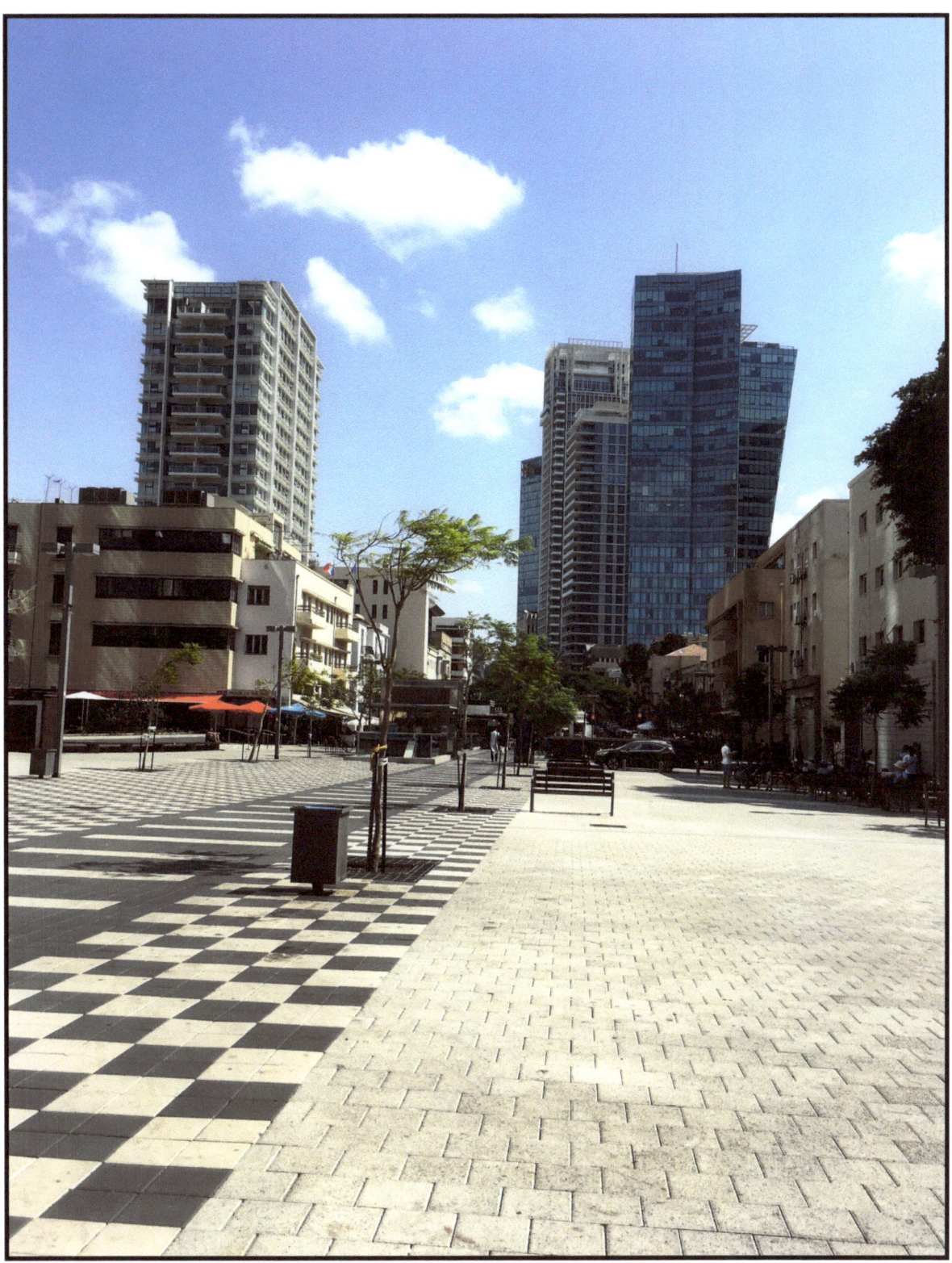

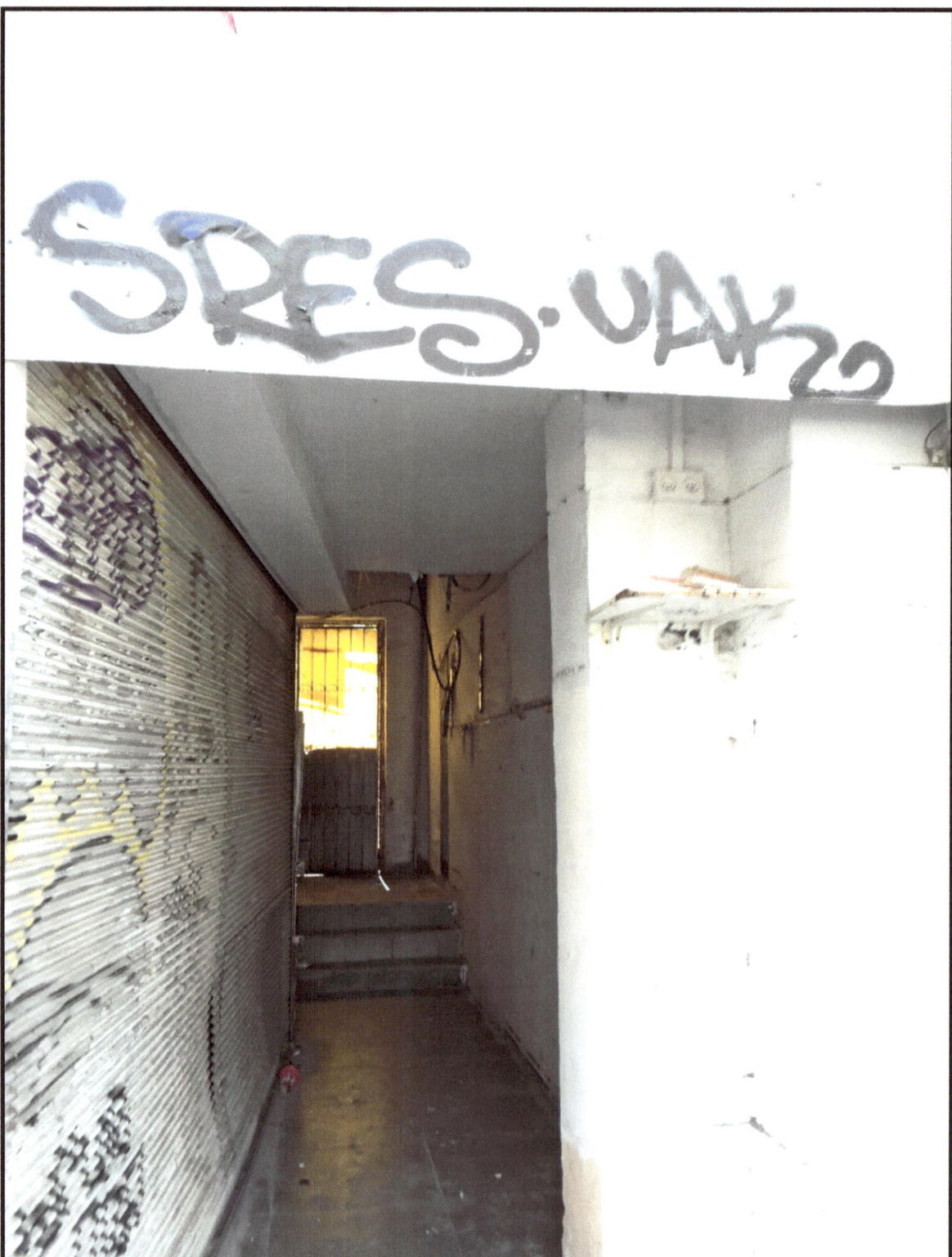

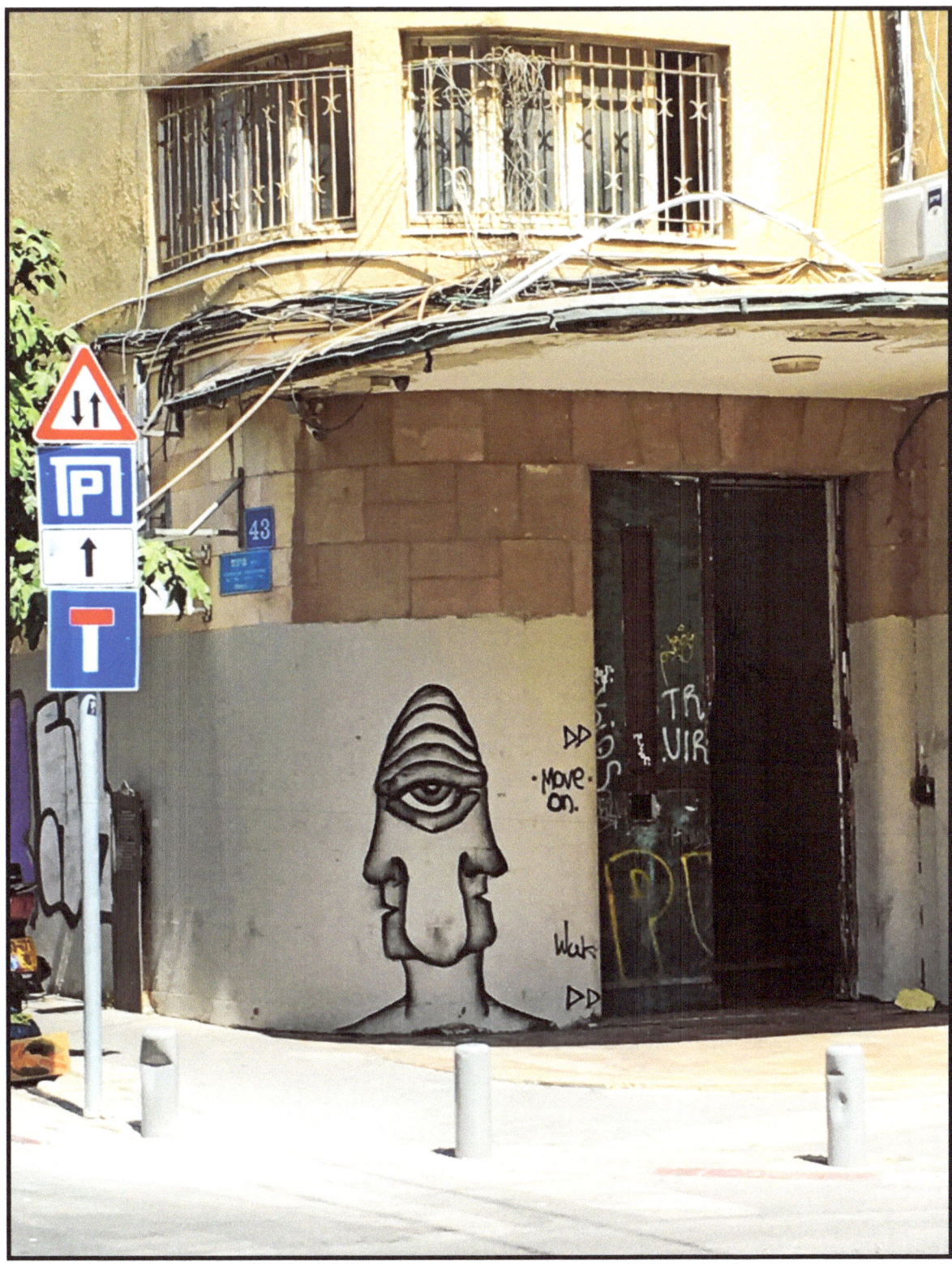

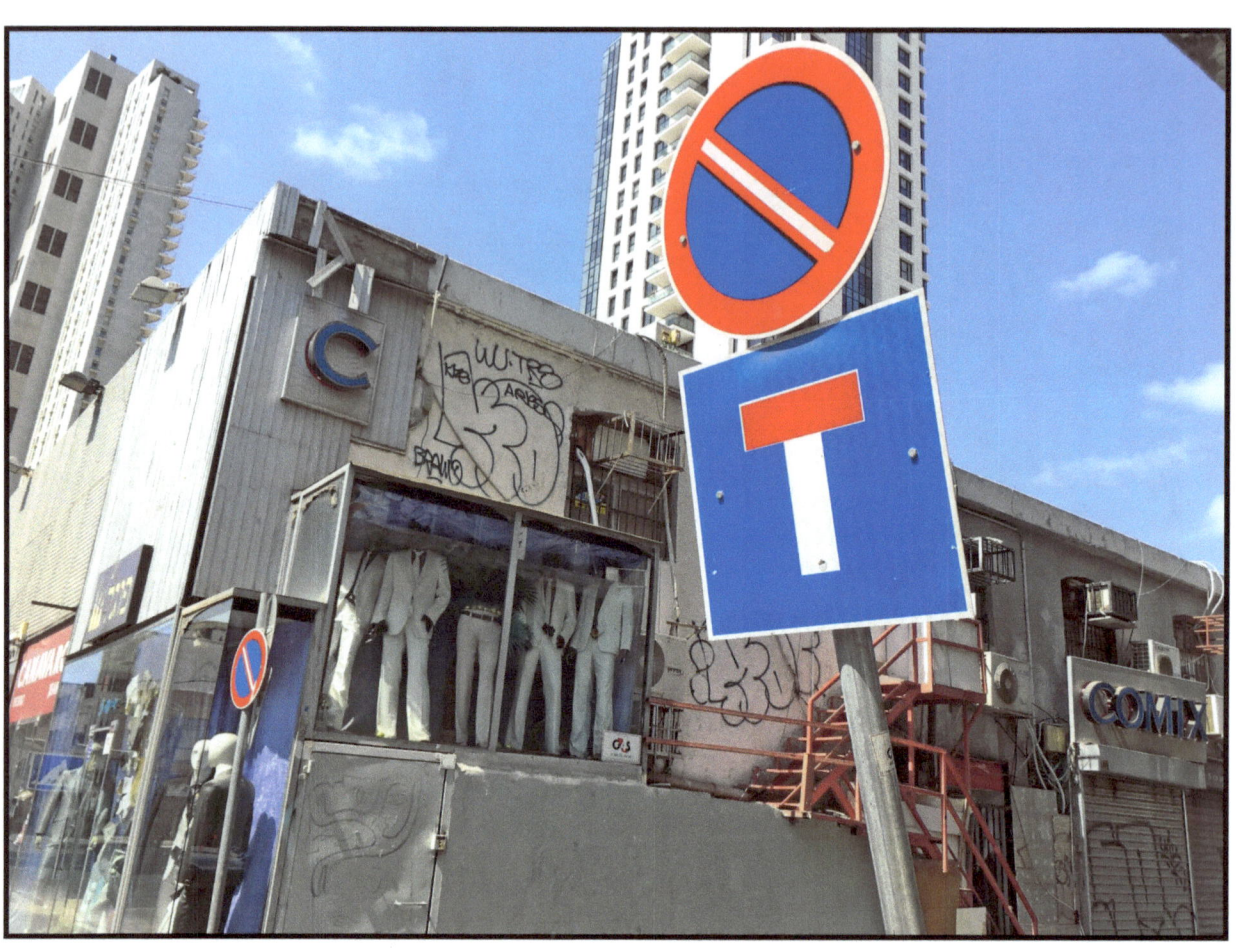

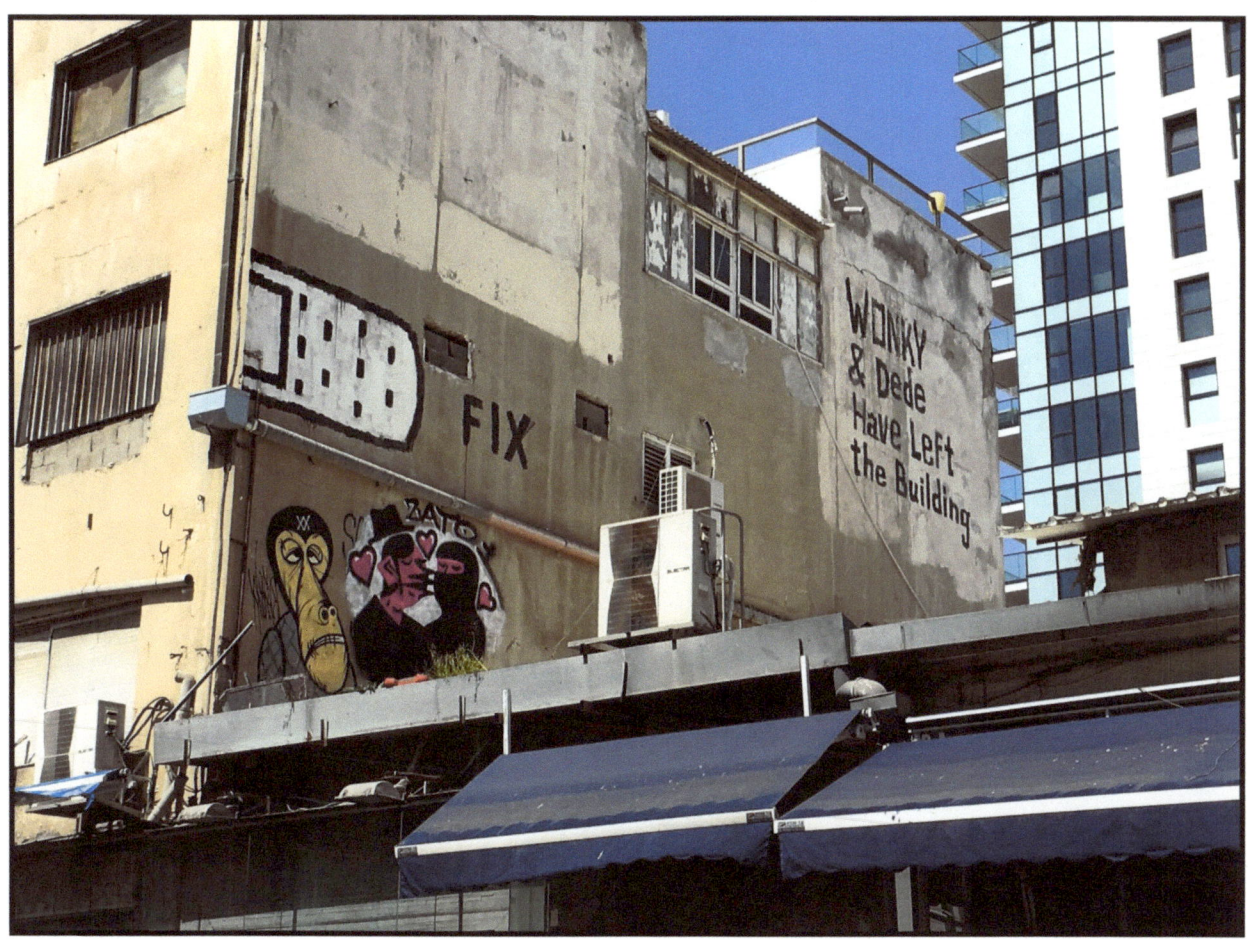

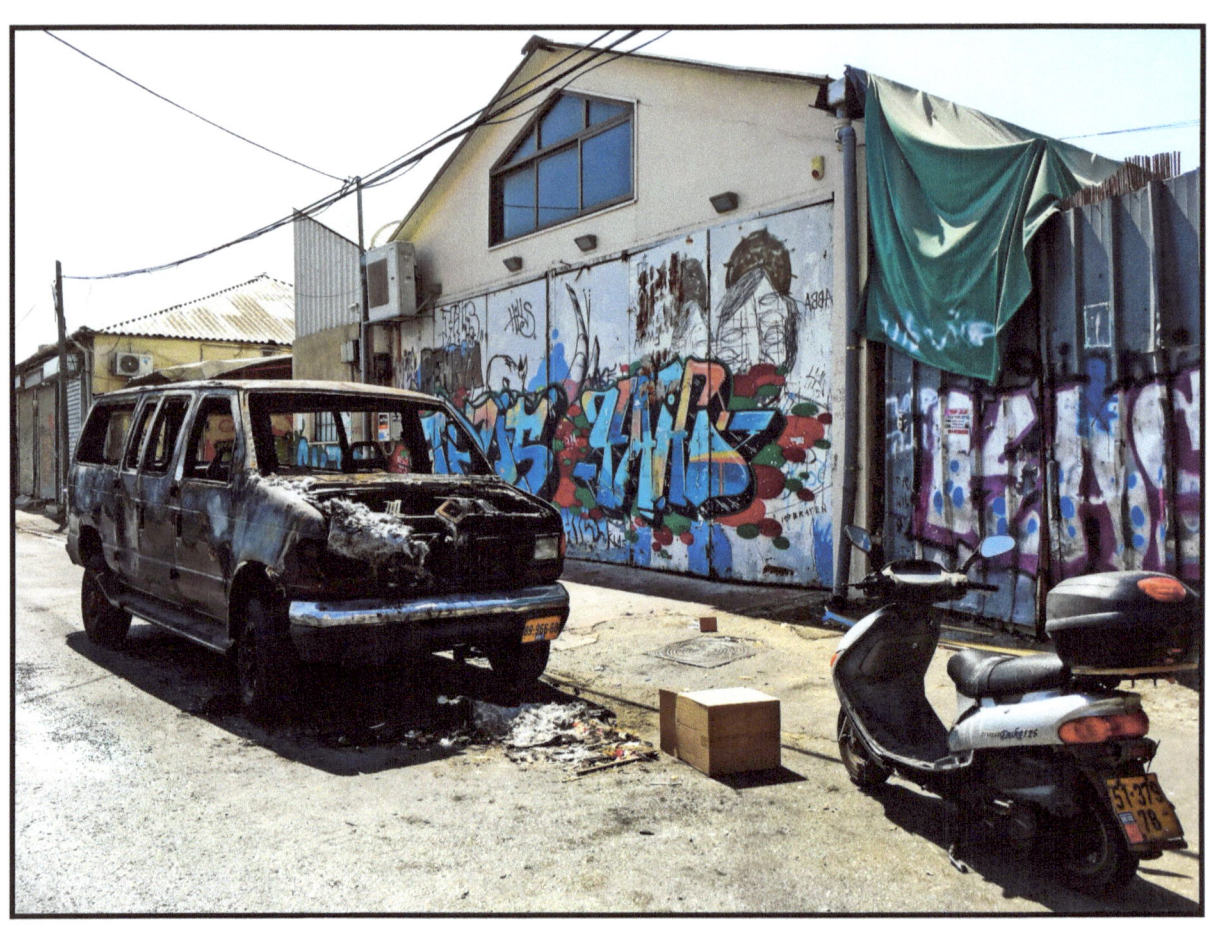

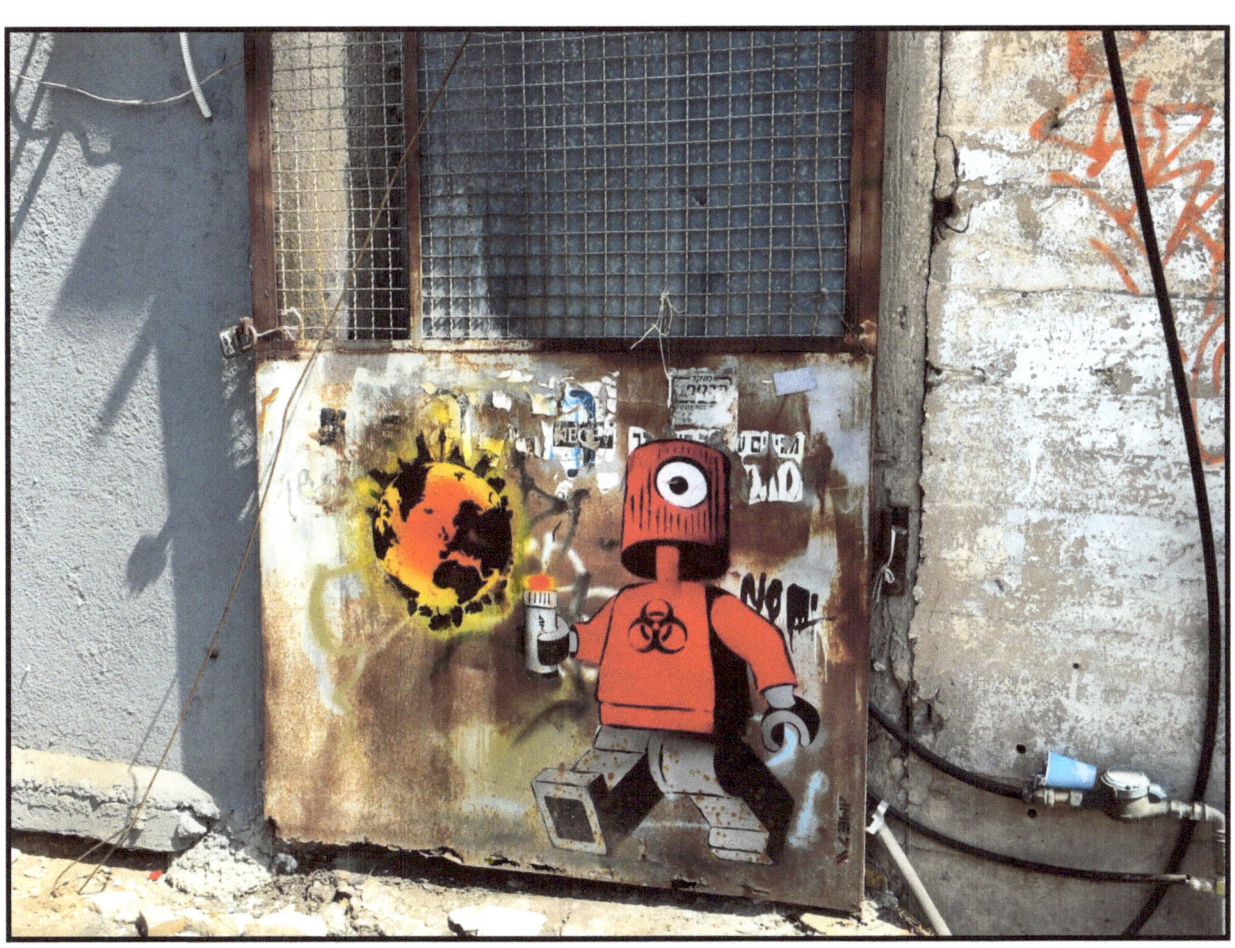

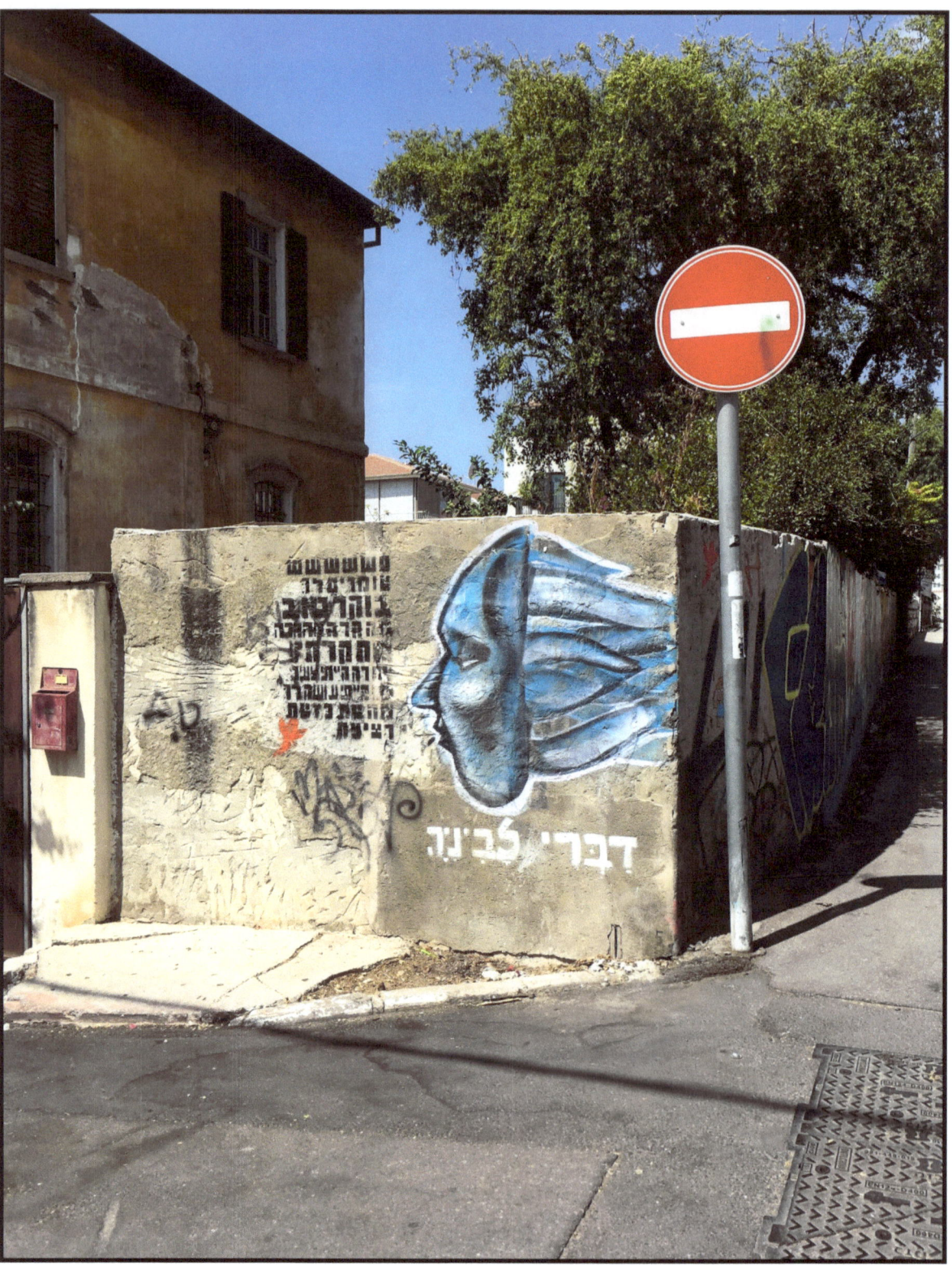

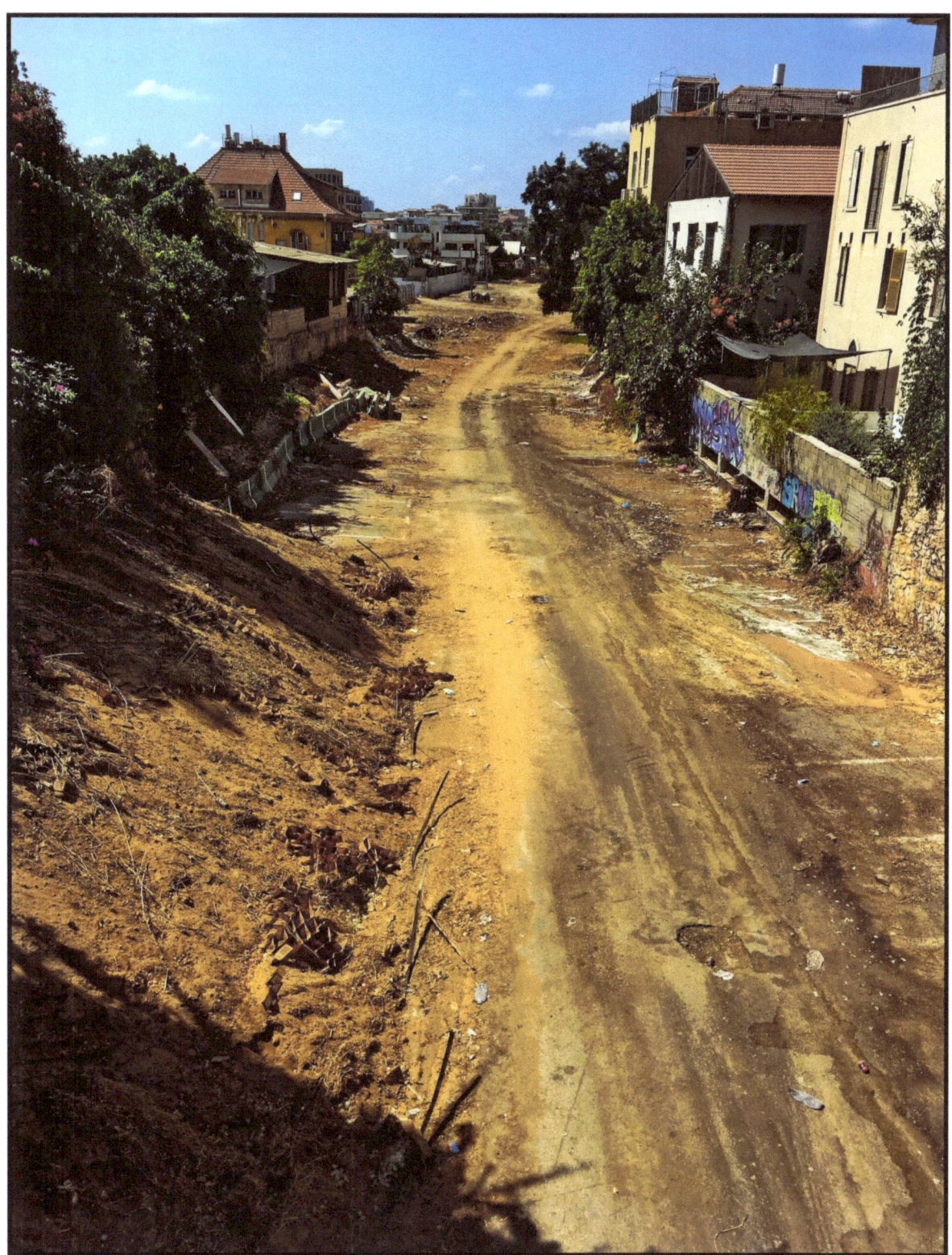

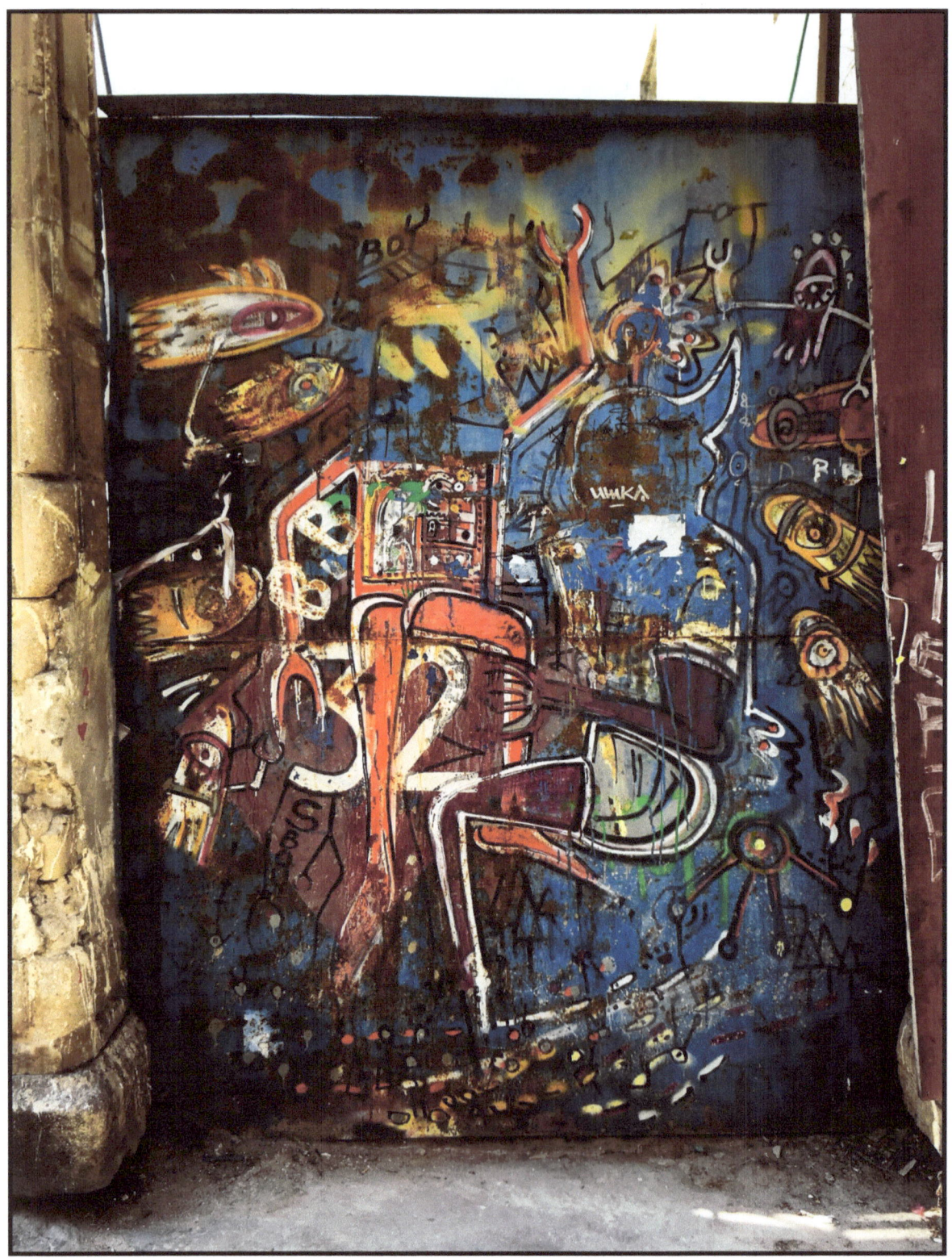

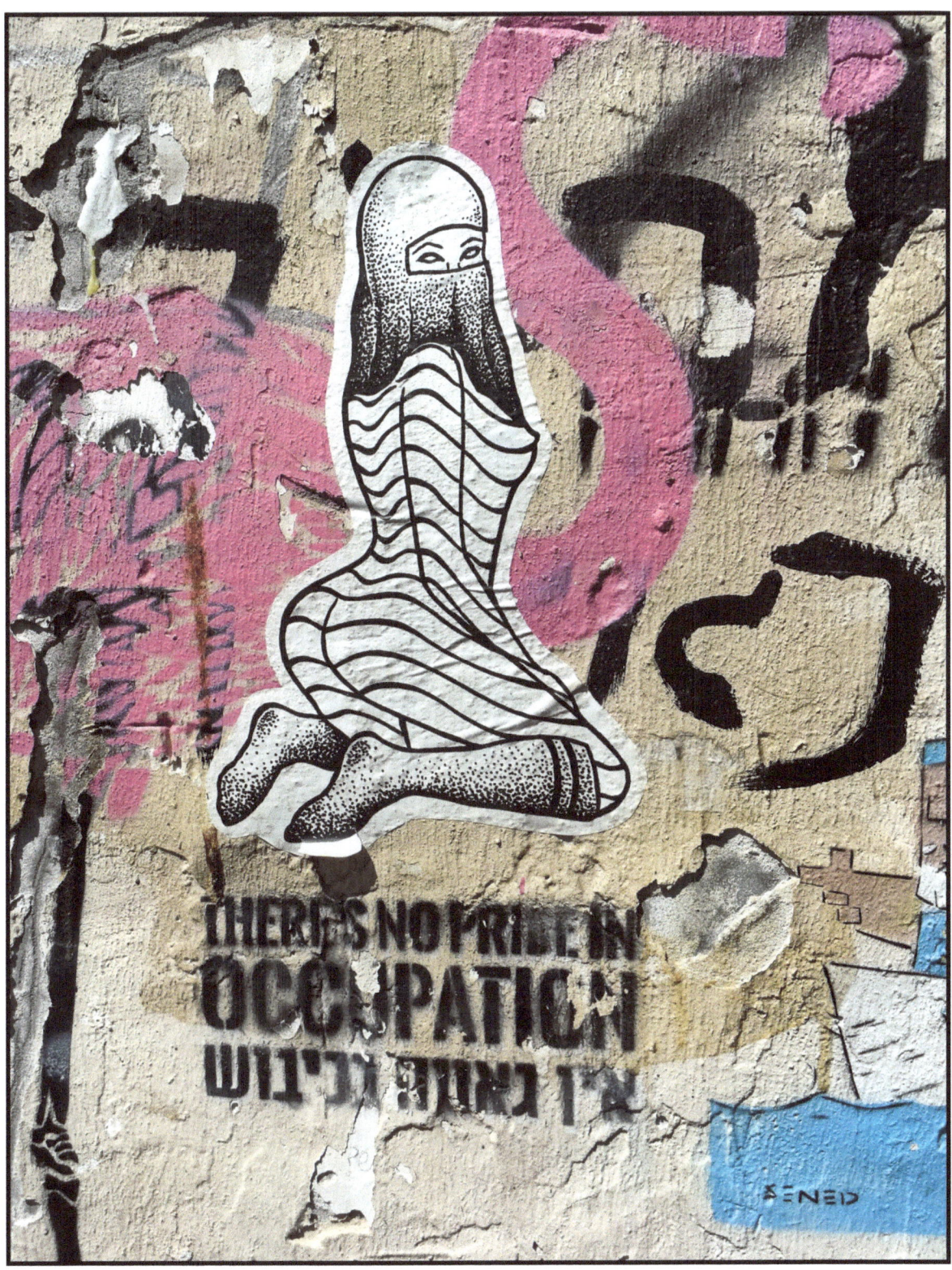

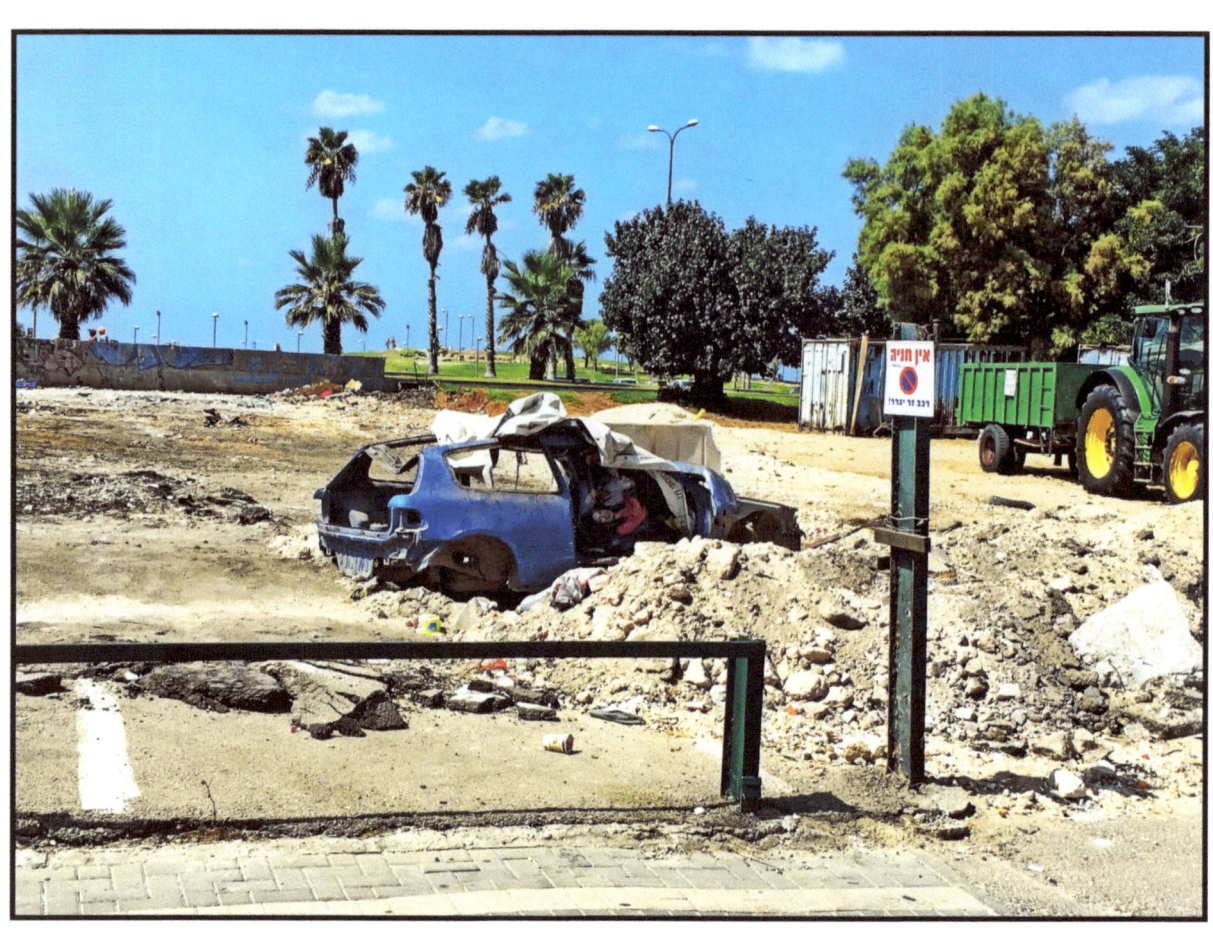

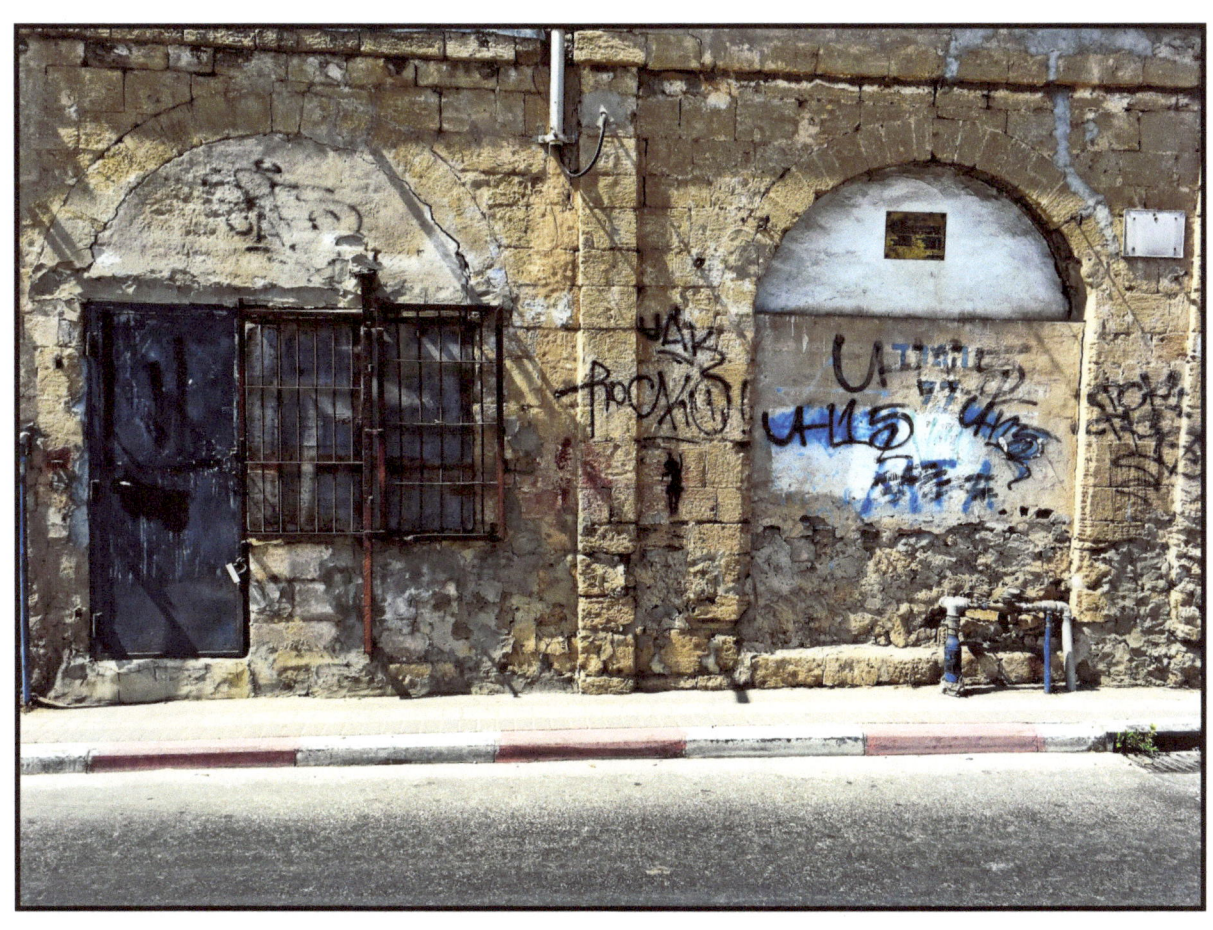

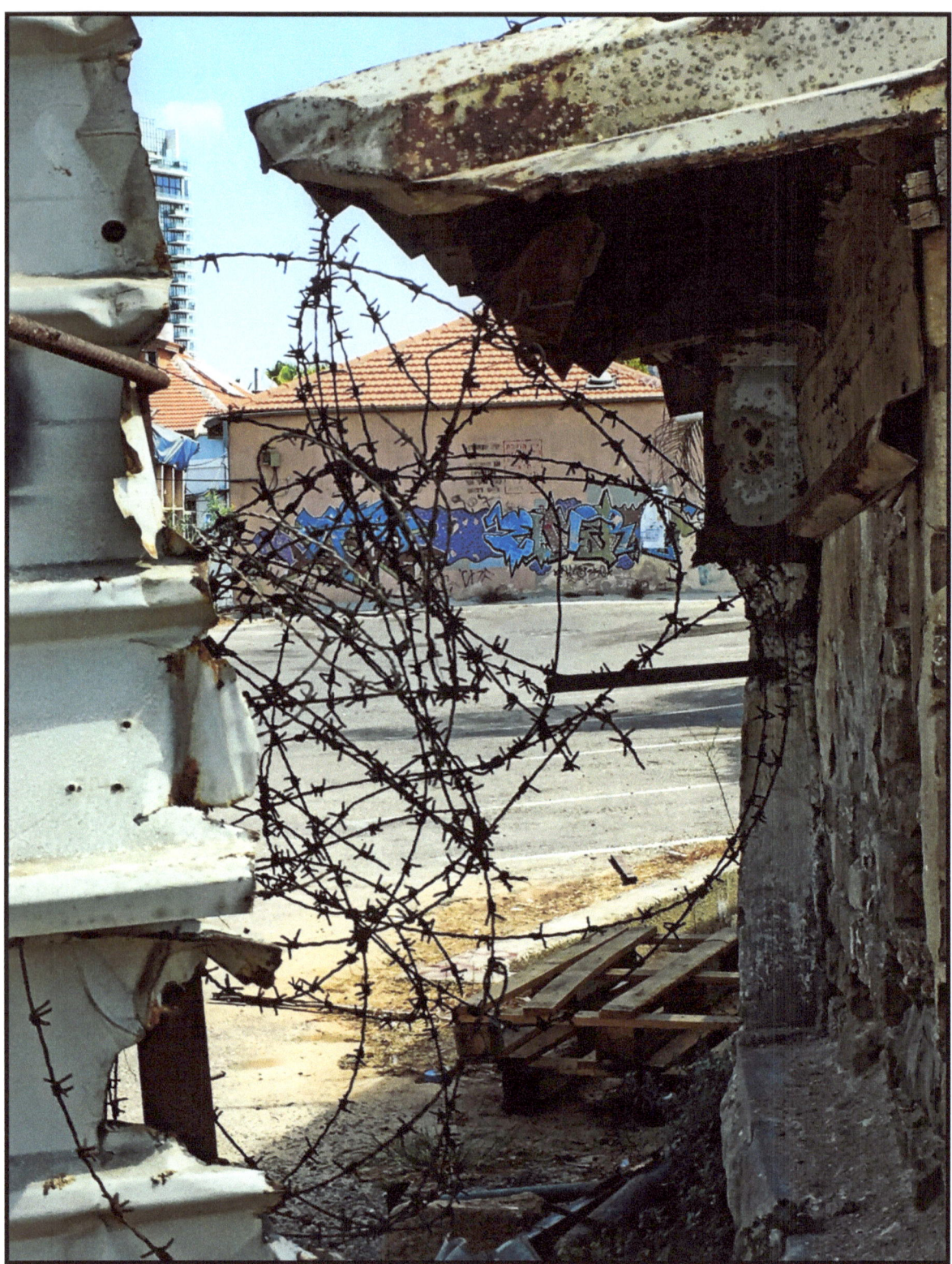

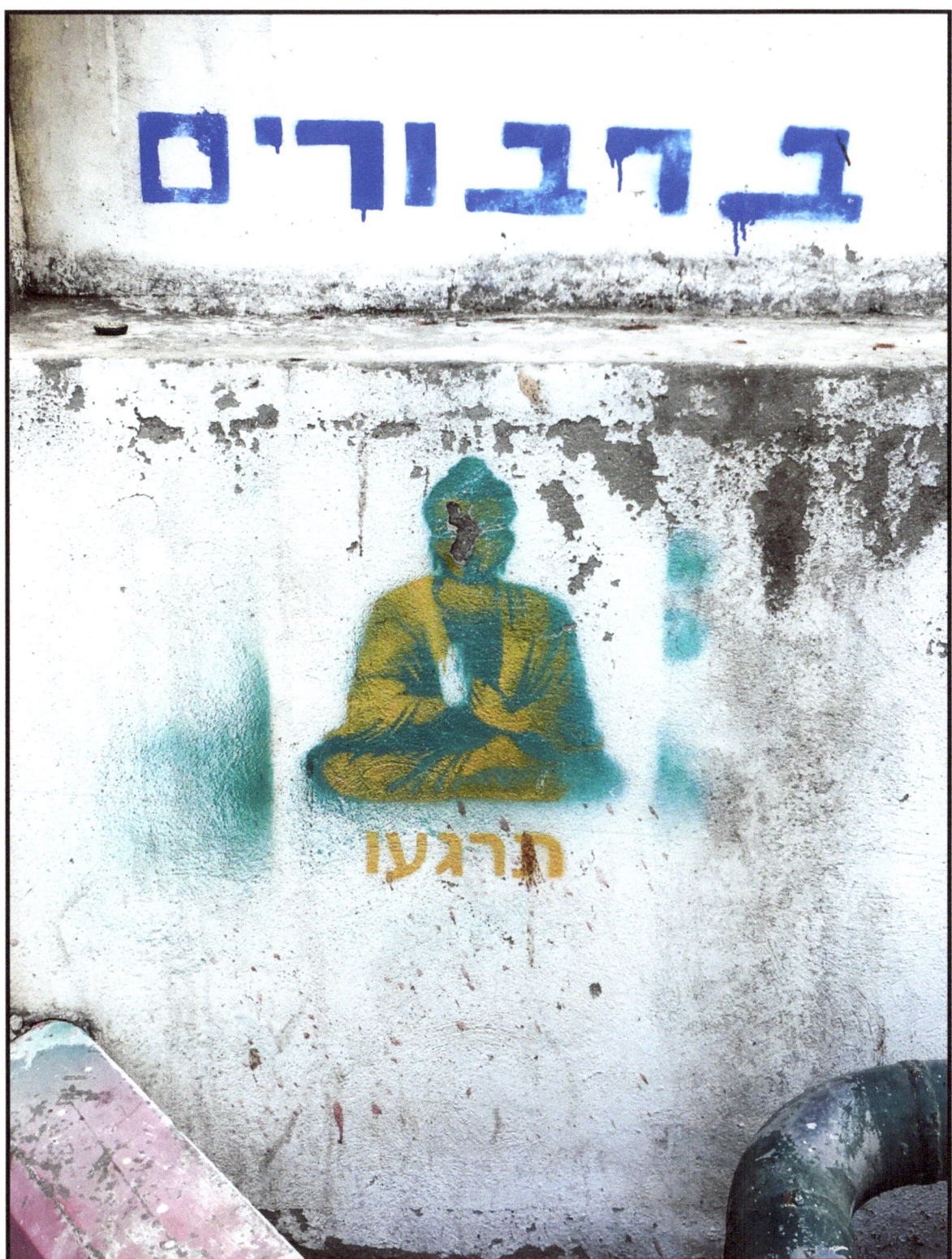

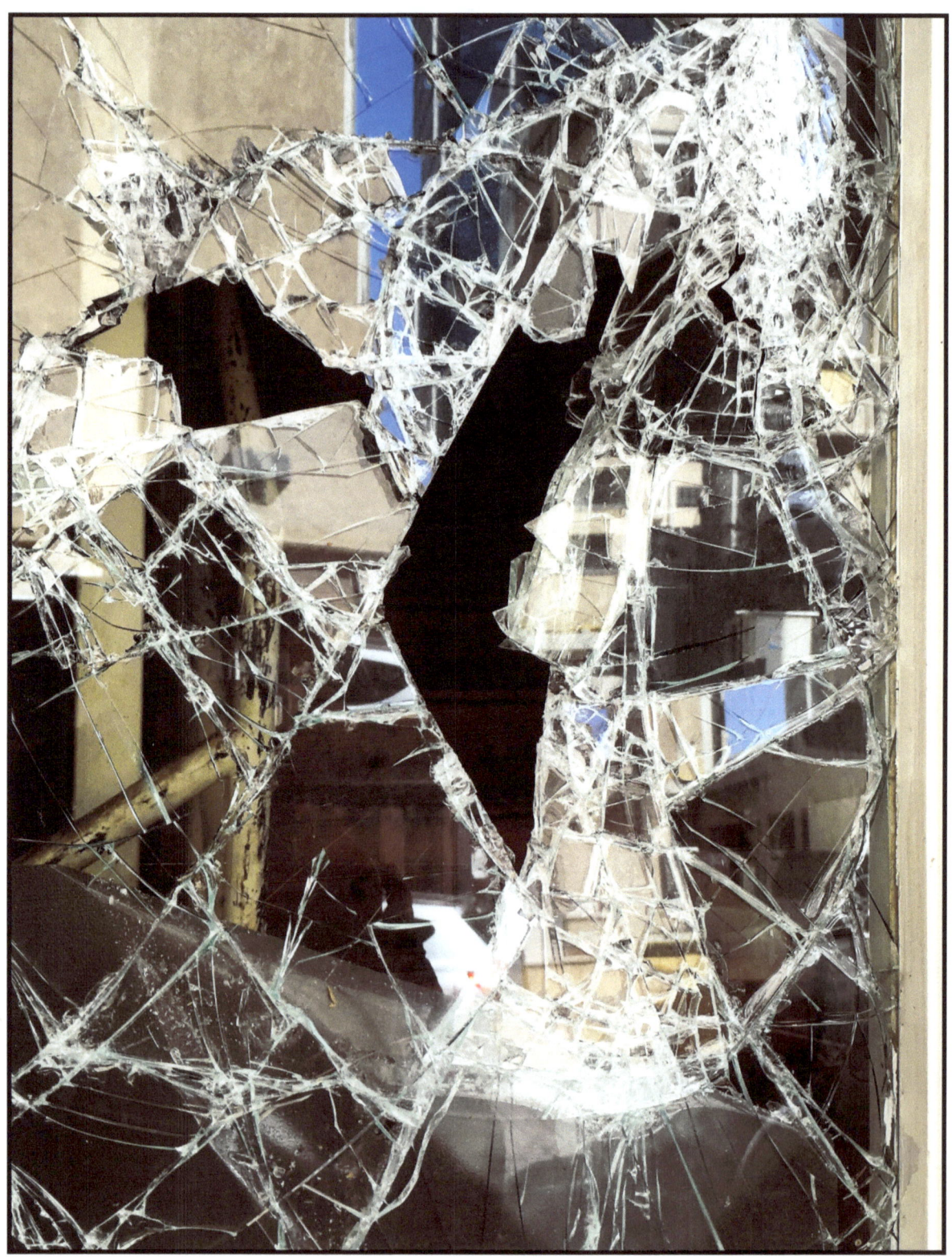

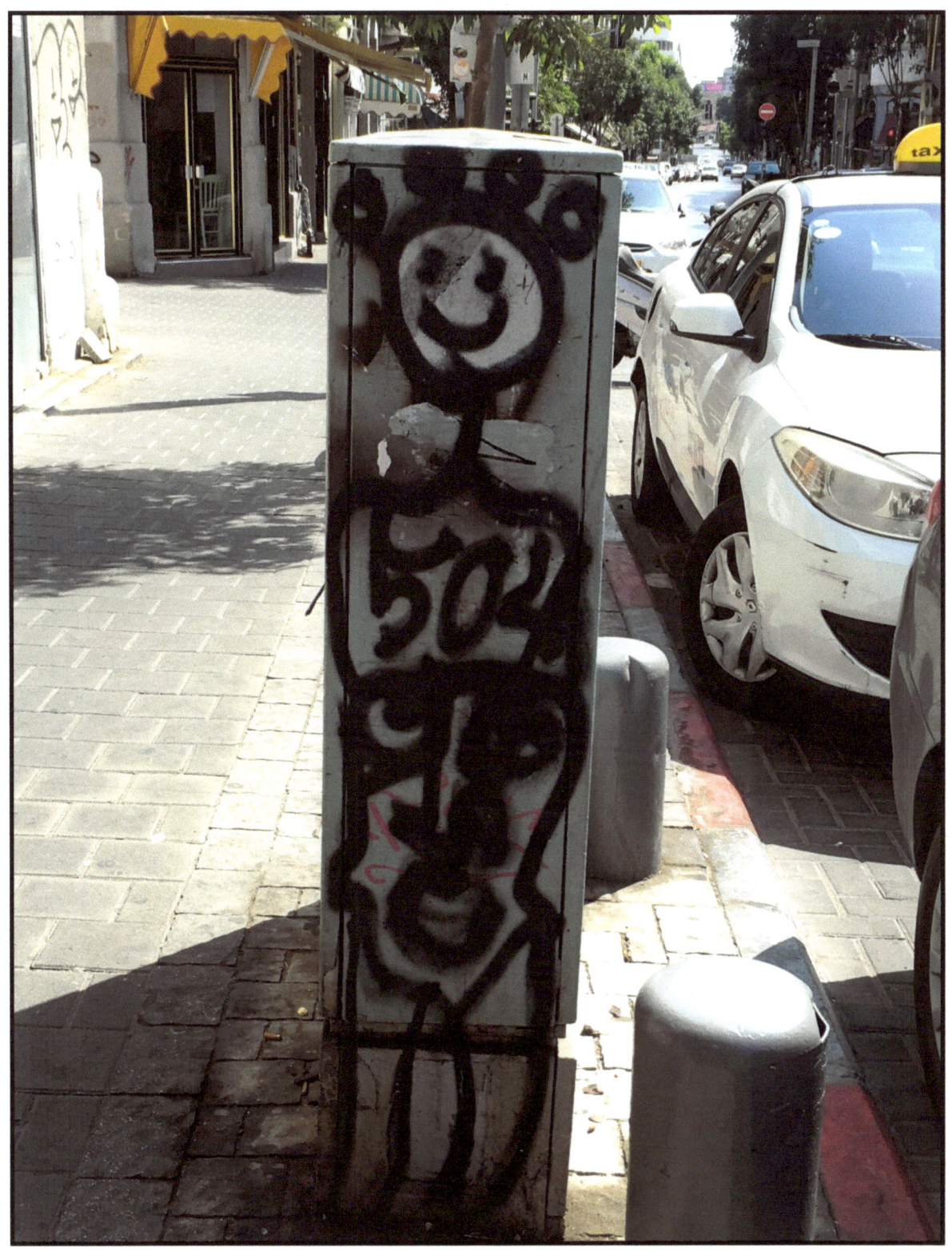

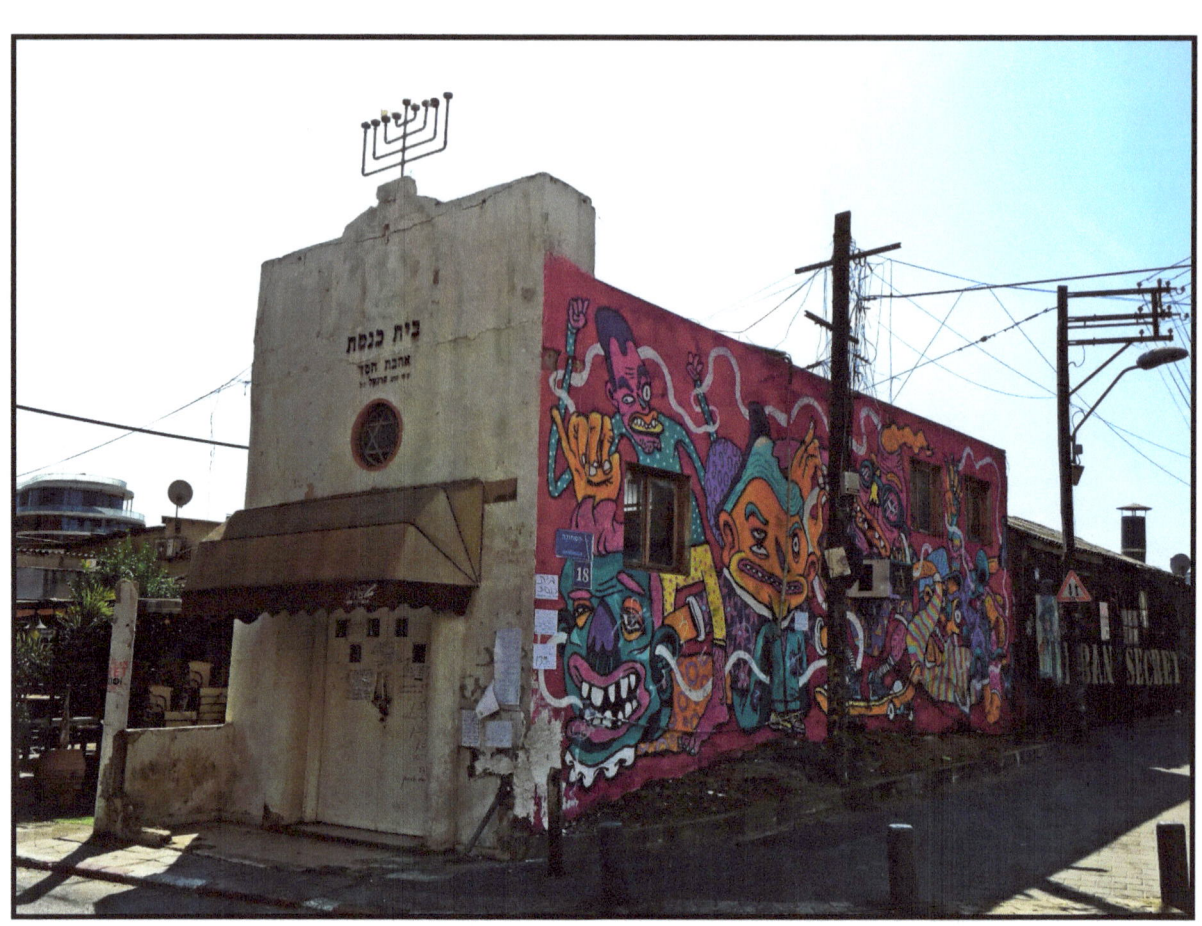

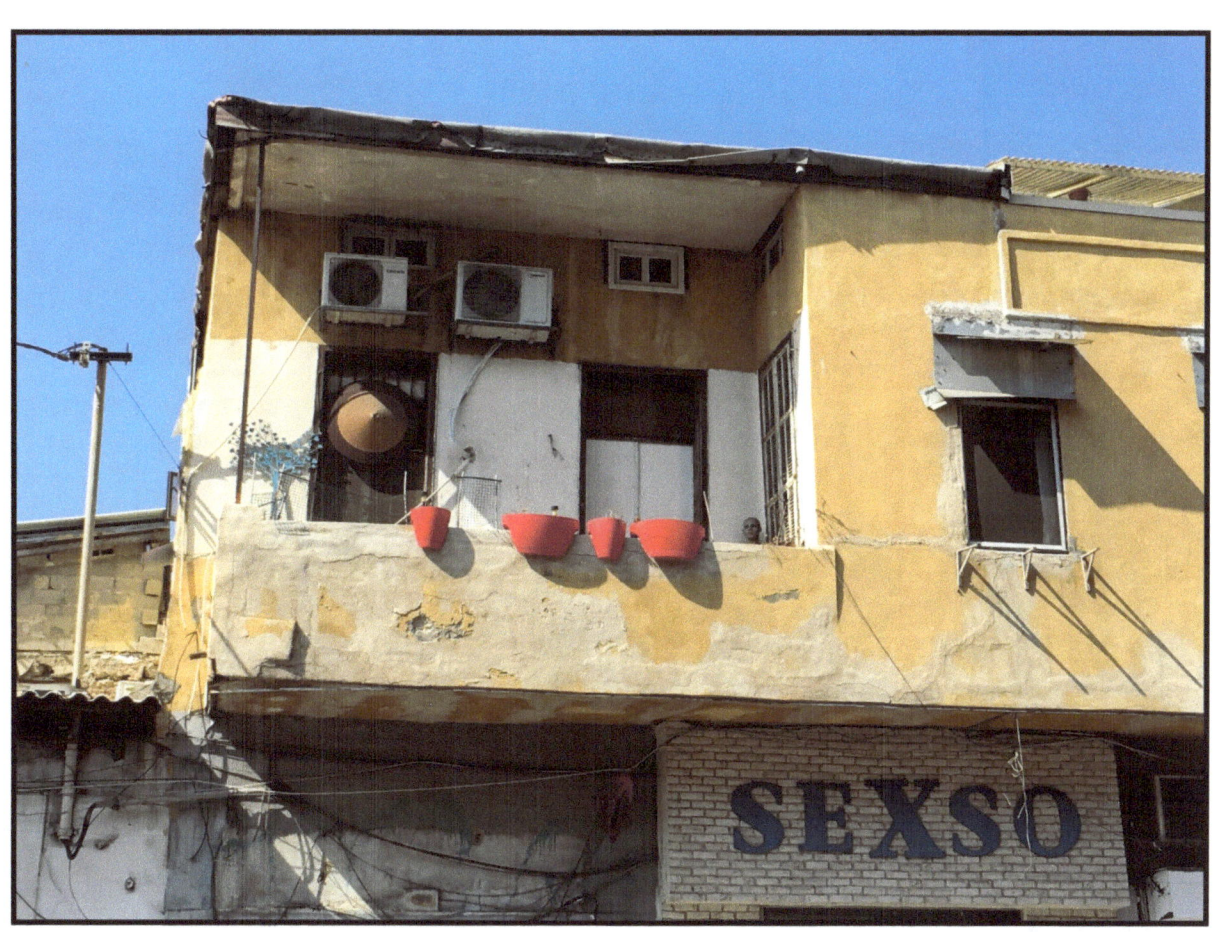

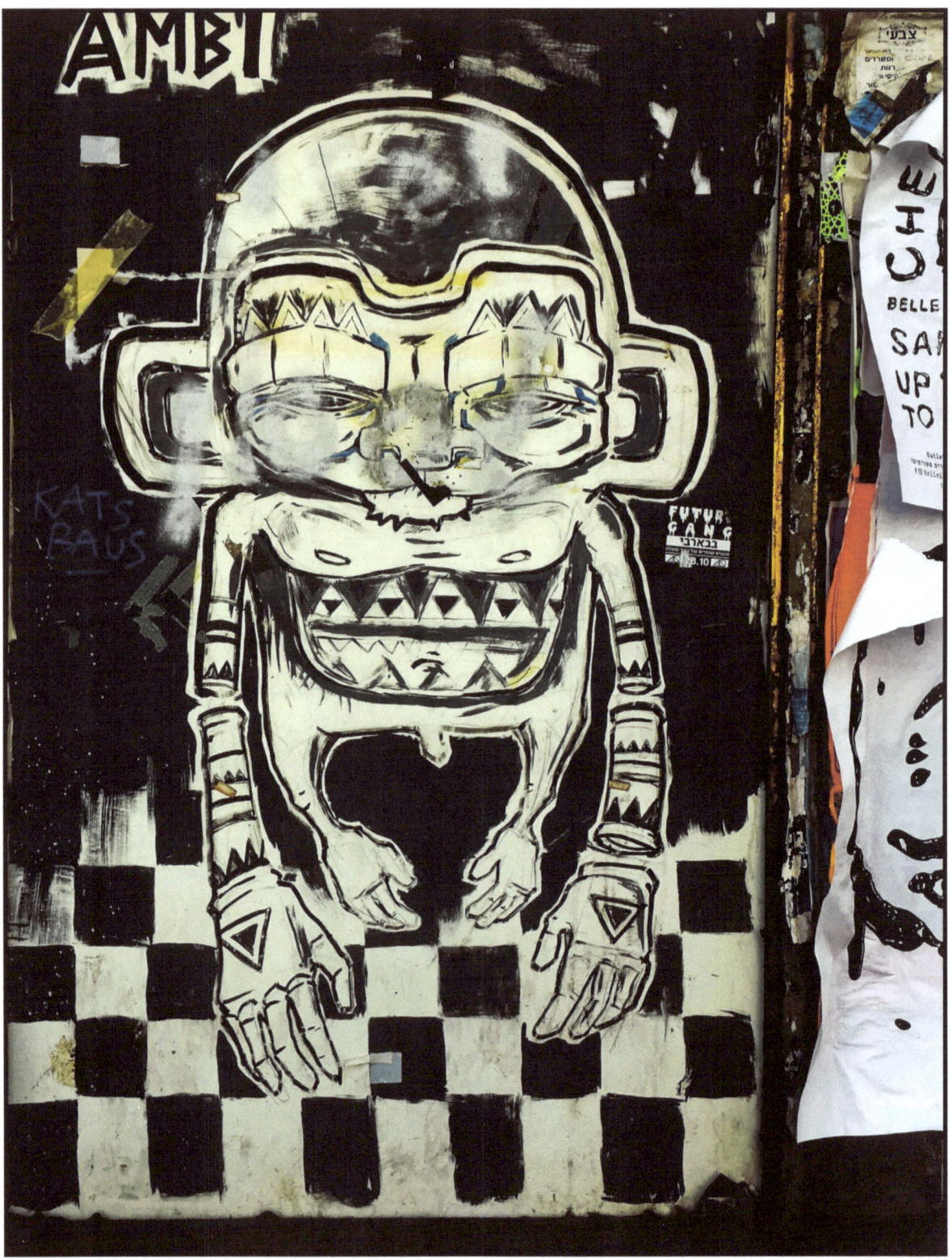

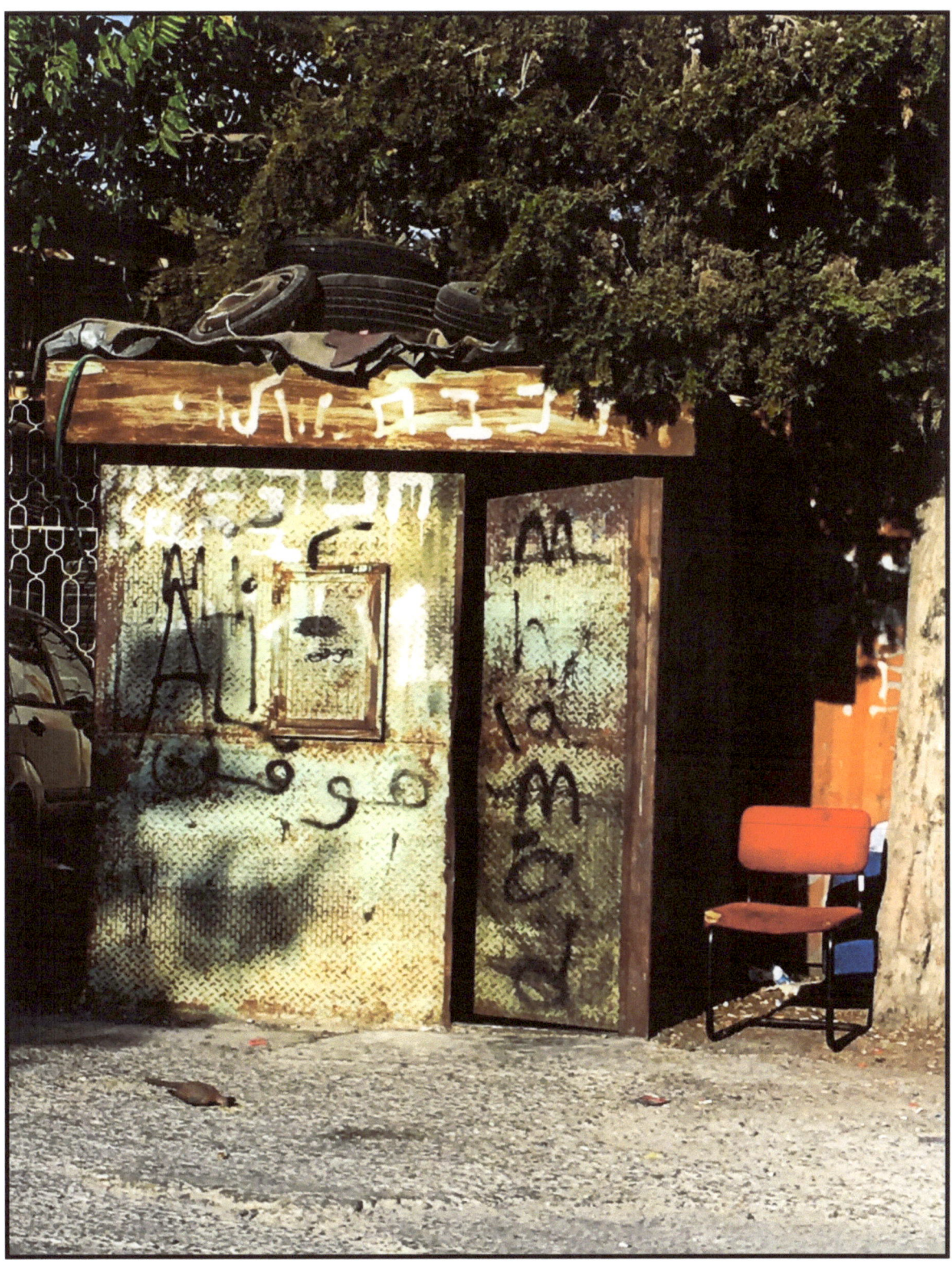

www.ingramcontent.com/pod-product-compliance
Lightning Source LLC
Chambersburg PA
CBHW051145220526
45473CB00003B/667